# The Implementation Challenge

*Edited by*

**D. E. Hussey**

Visiting Professor of
Strategic Management,
Nottingham Business School,
Nottingham Trent University

JOHN WILEY & SONS

CHICHESTER · NEW YORK · BRISBANE. TORONTO · SINGAPORE

*Other Wiley Editorial Offices*

John Wiley & Sons, Inc., 605 Third Avenue,
New York, NY 10158-0012, USA

Jacaranda Wiley Ltd, 33 Park Road, Milton,
Queensland 4064, Australia

John Wiley & Sons (Canada) Ltd, 22 Worcester Road,
Rexdale, Ontario M9W 1L1, Canada

John Wiley & Sons (Asia) Pte Ltd, 2 Clementi Loop # 02-01,
Jin Xing Distripark, Singapore 0512

*Library of Congress Cataloging-in Publication Data*

The Implementation Challenge edited by David Hussey.
    p.    cm
    Includes bibliographical references and index.
    ISBN 0-471-96589-8 (cloth : alk. paper)
    1. Strategic planning.  2. Organizational change—Management.
    3. Corporate culture.  4. Corporate reorganization—Management.
    I.  Hussey, D. E.    (David E.)
    HD30.28.1459   1996
    658.4′012–dc20                                    96—12077
                                                         CIP

*British Library Cataloguing in Publication Data*

A catalogue record for this book is available from the British Library

ISBN 0-471-96589-8

Typeset in 10/12 Times by Dobbie Typesetting Ltd, Tavistock, Devon.
Printed and bound in Great Britain by Biddles Ltd, Guildford and King's Lynn.
This book is printed on acid-free paper responsibly manufactured from sustainable forestation,
for which at least two trees are planted for each one used for paper production.

# CONTENTS

# ORIGINAL PUBLICATION REFERENCE

Unless otherwise indicated the first publication was in the *Journal of Strategic Change*, volume, issue and year shown. New material was written for the book.

# INTRODUCTION

The implementation of strategy remains one of the most difficult areas of management. Success depends both on the selection of an appropriate strategy and converting that strategy into action. If either of these aspects are deficient, the strategy may fail or be less effective than it should be, but often it is difficult after the event to know which aspect went wrong. Although much has been written on change management and transformational leadership, both of which are very relevant to strategy implementation, there have been comparatively few books which have tried to look at implementation as a whole subject, linking the numerous concepts that may be helpful.

This collection of articles begins to provide this linkage, bringing together a number of concepts and approaches, but also recognizing that there are administrative and behavioural aspects to implementation. If no one breaks the big strategy down into actions people can take, or time scales are unrealistic, or the right people are not informed about the strategy, implementation is likely to fail. But it may also fail because it does not fit the culture of the organization, because key managers do not have the motivation to implement, or for a thousand and one behavioural reasons.

Most of the chapters in this book were drawn from the pages of the *Journal of Strategic Change*, and were originally published over the period 1992–1995. The quality of material published in this journal is very high, and I am pleased to have the opportunity of presenting this selection to a wider audience. However, an editor is very lucky if it is possible to make a totally coherent narrative out of published papers, and for this reason there is also some new material which is intended to help integrate the book and touch on other aspects of the subject which should also be given attention.

The aim is to present a readable and useful book, which will give practical aid to those concerned with implementation. In addition to the advice given in various chapters, there are four major case studies which provide practical illustrations of issues and ways to overcome them.

Chapters 1 to 4 provide a framework for thinking about the overall issue of successful implementation. The first chapter sets the scene, and links the 'hard' and 'soft' issues, providing a total view of the challenge. It is followed by a chapter which deals with the evaluation of a business plan.

The whole problem of strategic change is thrown into stark relief in Chapter 3, by Martin and Dowling, which examines the case of Timex in Dundee. Most British readers will know that there is now no Timex in Dundee, and this chapter helps us to understand why, and at the same time illustrates many of the issues that have to be grasped if strategies are to become reality.

Jennings and Beaver in Chapter 4 look at some of the issues which explain failures in small business. This chapter stands slightly on one side of the mainstream of the book, and is included as a reminder that there is much that can go wrong in organizations of all sizes, and that the seeds of failed strategy often lie in the personalities, calibre and motivation of those running the enterprise.

Chapters 5–12 look at issues of managing strategic change. I will always be grateful to Stace and Dunphy for making it so clear that different situations require different approaches to change, and that the universal stricture 'involvement' that is often offered is not appropriate in all circumstances. Fortunately Chapter 5, where their article appears, gives insight into choosing appropriate approaches to each situation. In Chapter 6 Parker and Lorenzini explore culture in some depth, and the issues involved in changing it. Not every strategy requires a culture change, but I would suggest that while the need to fit strategy to culture is widely recognized, erroneous assumptions are often made by the decision-makers about the true culture of the organization.

Vision is a much used work in the literature of strategic management and change, and is a key element of many of the concepts of transformational leadership. Chapters 7 and 8 look at some research into this topic. The contribution of Mainelli is very practical, and is the result of a research study into how organizations convert vision into action. Not surprisingly there is a heavy emphasis on culture, and there are echoes in this chapter of some of the issues discussed earlier in the book. Peyrat offers a different sort of insight, and compares the prevailing approaches to mission statements of a number of countries. This chapter helps to emphasize that country cultures are not all the same, and implicitly reminds multinational companies that there may need to be significantly different approaches to implementation because of this.

Chapters 9 and 10 help us to translate the concepts discussed so far, and take our thinking further, through the medium of some heavyweight case studies. Brege and Brandes offer 20 lessons from the turnaround of ASEA and ABB. Bounds and Hewitt provide a helpful case study of the transformation of Xerox.

There is always a danger that any management subject can be positioned as a series of rules which ignore any underlying philosophical differences. I do not think any of the authors in this book have fallen into this trap, Chapters 11 and 12 are included to help keep us thinking. Farrell provides a chapter on 'Searching for the Spirit of Enterprise', which is based on his best-selling book of the same name. Wee dips into wisdom that is over two thousand years old, and offers perspectives on the change in management process which are drawn from Sun Tzu's *Art of War*.

When considering strategy from the heady heights of the boardroom, it is easy to forget that in the end anything that actually happens in the organization is the result of actions by individuals. In Chapter 13 Lewis and Lawton relate the individual to what they see as the four main functions of the organization.

Communication is critical to successful implementation. In Chapter 14 Caldwell suggests there are four communication styles. Getting the right fit of communication style to an employee involvement and commitment strategy is important for success. Apart from its own contribution this chapter reminds us that there are many things that have to be made to pull in the same direction if we want to implement successfully.

The last three chapters deal with a tool that is much underused in many organizations: the use of specific approaches to management development and training. My own chapter gives a brief overview of what can be done and how to do it. It is followed by a contribution by Tovey who looks at management competencies from a strategic viewpoint. Finally Cannon gives a case study which shows how the principles discussed by Hussey and Tovey have been applied by one major multinational company.

What I hope this book will do is help the reader to meet the challenge of implementation in his or her own situation, and try both to illuminate the possible paths and to mark the pitfalls. The task of implementing a new and complex strategy will never be easy, but there is much here that will help.

*David Hussey*

# 1

# A FRAMEWORK FOR IMPLEMENTATION

### D. E. Hussey

*David Hussey and Associates*

- This chapter stresses that the successful implementation of strategy embraces both the hard and the soft aspects of management.
- It offers an approach to help think through the relationship of strategy to the organizational variables.
- A total approach to successful implementation is provided.

## STRATEGY SUCCESS AND FAILURE

I have long been intrigued by the paradox that in the UK, and probably elsewhere in the world, there have been some three decades where major companies have failed, and whole industries have disappeared. Over the same period, there have been numerous studies showing that organizations which planned their strategy did better than those that did not (see Hussey, 1994, p. 27, for references to this research). Many of the organizations that have suffered what might be termed as strategic failure, which is not necessarily the same as total corporate failure, have had a commitment to strategic planning. In one of my attempts to grapple with this paradox (Hussey, 1984) I wrote:

> The research proves beyond doubt that corporate planning can be beneficial, but does not prove that it will be beneficial in every case. Firstly, if it is applied badly, it is unlikely to succeed. Secondly there are degrees of success and not all companies allow corporate planning to run to its full potential: in the UK many

*The Implementation Challenge*, Edited by D. E. Hussey
© 1996 John Wiley & Sons Ltd

top managers do not set high enough expectations from their planning work and therefore have a satisfaction level which is too low.

Strategic decisions have to be made whether or not the company plans, and these decisions can be good or bad. All managers are prisoners within the boundaries of their own perception, and although corporate planning is supposed to move those boundaries it does not always do so. It is thus possible for a company to achieve better results because of the coordination and motivational impact of its planning processes and yet to be still following the wrong strategic path. This has certainly happened in the UK, and in many companies planning has failed to change these perceptual boundaries, through failings of managers and planners.

By the boundaries of perception I meant the way in which a strategic situation was defined. Centuries ago most people knew beyond doubt that the world was flat. Their strategic decisions wisely took account of this and they tended to avoid sailing their ships too close to the edge in case they fell off. This was a very logical decision. But we now know that the world is not flat, and that making decisions as if it were is not really wise but instead is very stupid. The strategic problem has not changed, but our perception of the problem has.

There is a direct parallel with the way managers often perceive the strategic arena in which they operate. In the past I have had long discussions with managers who refused to accept the increasingly global nature of their industry and the competition: the Japanese entrants to their markets were seen as freak events offering unfair competition and not as evidence that the competitive arena was enlarging.

It may be because of this perception that strategy often follows fashions. In the 1980s financial service companies competed frantically to acquire estate agents: in the 1990s there was a headlong rush to divest these businesses. Airlines round the world saw hotels, car hire, and other services for travellers as the businesses to buy in the late 1970s and 1980s. By 1990 most were preaching the virtues of concentration on the core business, had sold off the peripheral businesses, and talked of segmentation as the way forward.

It is easy to imagine circumstances where a poor strategy may be implemented so well that it hastens the demise of the organization. In other situations a strategy may be impossible to implement, either because it is so bad, or not thought through, or the early feedback on the implementation actions shows that it is just not going to work.

## SOFT AND HARD ASPECTS OF IMPLEMENTATION

Strategic success in the first instance requires an appropriate strategy, but this by itself is not enough. It also requires that the strategy be implemented successfully. For many years many of the planning books seemed to assume that if strategic planning involved line managers, implementation would inevitably follow. There are good arguments for widespread participation in certain circumstances, but only when it fits both the culture of the organization and the strategic situation of the organization. But although participation may improve motivation and increase the buy-in to a strategy, there is much more to implementation than this.

Figure 1.1, which is by no means a complete list, makes the point that there are both behavioural and analytical dimensions to the process of strategic decision-making and the subsequent implementation of strategy. In many cases what appears to be the hard, analytical processes are affected by hidden behavioural or soft considerations. The selection of information for rational analysis would appear to be a totally rational activity. In fact, because a choice has to be made of what information to analyse, it may be overlaid by behavioural issues. The manager's perceptual boundaries will exclude information as irrelevant, when in reality it may be critical. Once an analysis has been completed, it has to be interpreted, and the interpretation, however objective the analysts and managers try to be, will be affected by behavioural considerations. It is not unknown for managers to suppress findings which are at variance with what they would like to do. Steiner (1972, p. 24), had it right when he stated:

> The decision making process in a company is infused with political, social and other considerations. To think that it is a completely rational process, in the sense that any fair-minded person would come to the same conclusions, is to misunderstand not only the decision making process but the human mind.

There are also soft and hard elements which need to fit together if the strategy is to be implemented. These are elements like the culture of the organization, and the way the structure works. If there is a natural fit there may be no problem. This is often the case with an incremental strategy, which effectively requires the organization to do more of the same. Where the strategy requires fundamental change, there may be a clash, in which case either the strategy or the behavioural element has to change. The 1990s have seen a spate of organizations engaged in culture change, to improve the ability of the organization to implement the strategies considered essential for the decade. British Petroleum's widely publicized Project 1990 is one example of change on a massive scale, but there are also examples in the privatized businesses of gas, water and telecommunications, and in what is going on in the National Health Service. In fact it seems now to be almost as fashionable to have a culture change as it was to follow competitors down the same strategic path. But I am being cynical.

This fit issue, or put more simply aligning a number of hard and soft issues, that make up the organization, with its strategy, is something that I will return to later, with two models that can make practical use of the concepts discussed above.

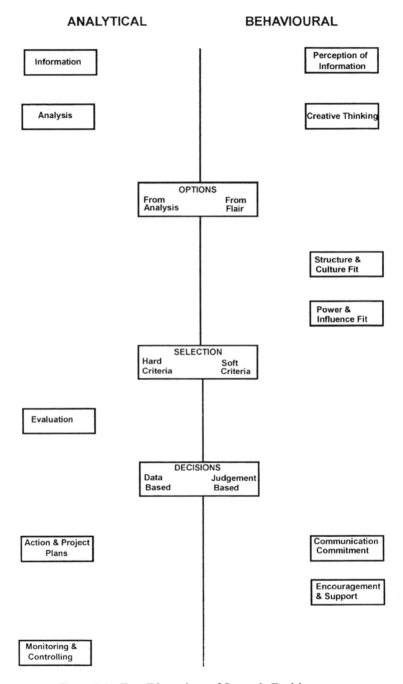

**Figure 1.1**   Two Dimensions of Strategic Decisions

## PRACTICAL IMPLEMENTATION PROBLEMS

Figure 1.2 looks at implementation problems through the research findings of Alexander (1991). The summary descriptions are mine, as is the notation which describes whether it is a hard or soft issue (Alexander did not make this distinction). The research was undertaken amongst both public and private sector organizations, and shows the top ranking in each case of the problems identified. It is worth mentioning that the lowest ranked problem was listed by just over half of the respondents, and the top ranked problems were listed by around three-quarters. There may well be other major problems, and in some cases the things identified may be symptoms rather than causes. My annotation of hard and soft causes also makes an assumption that the managers are genuinely trying to implement the plans. The second problem on the list would most likely be a hard issue of analysis or system, in that the implementation plan had not been properly thought through. Where managers are against the strategy, it might have been a behavioural issue of deliberate sabotage, so that the strategy fails. My annotation should be taken as indicative, and not as the automatic answer to the problems in all circumstances.

The problems identified show that there is much which could have been avoided, and illustrate our tendency to make assumptions to save thinking through a problem. It is an easy assumption, commonly made, that the people in the organization have the skills and knowledge to do what is necessary to implement the strategy. Careful thought about the implications of the strategy in relation to the capabilities would have enabled the organizations to check the assumption, and made solving this problem an integral part of the implementation process.

There are some contradictions in the list, which result from respondents describing the problems as they saw them, which may not have been as they really were. For example, the arising of major unexpected problems, the coordination of implementation activities, and the definition of implementation tasks could well be linked issues. This does not detract from the usefulness of the research in helping us to reach a better solution, and it also emphasizes that we are trying to solve issues that real managers have found to be critical, and are not merely repeating elegant academic solutions to problems that no one knows they have, or consultants' models designed to stimulate consultancy business.

I like to use two approaches to try to ensure that the key aspects of implementation are taken care of. They overlap slightly, although the emphasis of each approach is different: the first helps the organization to think through the implications of a change of strategy; the second gives a six-step approach to implementation.

## Problems

| PROBLEM | ORDER OF IMPORTANCE | | NATURE |
|---|---|---|---|
| | PVTE Firms | Public Orgs | Hard/Soft |
| Implementation took longer than expected | 1 | 1 | H or S |
| Major unexpected problems arose during implementation | 2 | 3 | H |
| Inadequate coordination of implementation activities | 3 | 6 | S |
| Other activities distracted attention | 4 | 4 | H |
| Inadequate capabilities of employees | 5 | – | S |
| Inadequate training at lower levels | 6 | – | S |
| Uncontrollable external factors | 7 | 2 | H |
| Inadequate leadership and direction at departmental level | 8 | 9 | S |
| Implementation tasks not fully defined | 9 | – | H |
| Inadequate information systems to monitor | 10 | 8 | H |
| Employee resistance – incongruent goals | – | 5 | S |
| Lack of teamwork by key people | – | 9 | S |
| Overall goals not understood by employees | – | 7 | S |

**Figure 1.2**   Strategy Implementation. Derived from Alexander, 1991)

**Strategy and the Organizational Variables**

The foundation of my thinking in the first approach was Leavitt (1964). He suggested that organizations were multivariate systems, and all variables interacted on all other variables. He saw the organization as consisting of the variables of task (the things that have to be done), structure, technology (machines and programmes), and people.

Perhaps the most famous development after Leavitt's diamond (named for the way he drew his model) is the Mckinsey 7S model. This stresses the interlinking of all the variables, and shows six around the edge of the model (strategy, structure, systems, style, staff and skills), and the seventh in the centre (shared values). The model has been published in various places, including Peters and Waterman (1982, p. 10).

There is little point in tracing through the other variations on this theme which have been published. The model I use shows the strategic change as the driver of the organization, and results as the desired benefit flowing out of the organization. Eight variables are given for the organization, and the idea is that these should be examined each time there is a change in strategy, since the results, or implementation of the strategy, will be less likely to occur if the machine of the organization is not appropriate for the fuel of the strategy. The key variables of three of Leavitt's originals, tasks, people, and structure, and five others, decision processes, culture, information systems, control systems and reward systems. Each of these can potentially affect all other variables. I suggest this model as the first step to ensuring that a strategy can be implemented. If strategy is out of step with the organization variables, it has a good chance of failing: if all the variables are in harmony, the chances of success are improved.

- STRATEGY   The strategic vision and the strategies must be clearly defined, at least to the point that is possible. Failure to think through the strategy may make it impossible to implement, except by chance. There may be a need to stage the steps in the implementation process, in that it is rarely possible to define every aspect of a strategy too far ahead, and in even the best planned strategy there has to be room for an element of evolution. A strategy to grow by acquisition, for example, may have to be developed in stages because the final shape of the strategy will depend on which organization it becomes possible to acquire. This does not invalidate the steps presented here, but does emphasize the need to revisit them at each critical stage of the implementation process. In addition to being clear about the vision and strategies in terms of products, markets and finance, there is a need to think through the implications on each of the organizational variables. What, if anything, has to change so that implementation can become possible? Is it the variable, or does this seem impossible, in which case we must rethink the strategy?

- TASKS   What new key tasks will have to be fulfilled by the organization as a result of the strategies? What task will have to be approached in a different way? What existing tasks have to be reinforced, undertaken faster, undertaken in a more cost effective way? All this can be summarized in a simple sentence: what will the organization have to be able do in order to implement the strategies?
- PEOPLE   Once we know the tasks we can think about the people. This may just be a question of numbers and locations, but is more likely to throw up questions of skills and competencies, morale and motivation. To do what we have to do, will we need more or fewer people? Are any new skills and competencies, which we know we will need, obtainable? What changes are needed to the way people work, or the manner in which they are employed? The problems of lack of training found in the Alexander survey might have been resolved had more attention been given to the tasks and people variables, and an action plan to deal with the issues developed as an integral part of the implementation process.
- STRUCTURE   People are grouped in various ways in the structure of the organization. It is easy to overlook the fact that the existing structure may have been established to deal with quite a different set of strategic tasks to those the organization now faces. Does the current structure facilitate or hinder the implementation of the strategy? Problems may be the number of layers, the way key strategic tasks are spread across the organization, or dispersion of responsibilities may mean that no one is clear who should be doing what in the implementation process. If the structure prevents implementation of the strategy, then either this should change, or it should be recognized that the strategy will not work for this particular organization.
- DECISION PROCESSES   How are decisions taken, where are they taken, and where does the power lie? In recent years we have seen many attempts to empower lower levels of the organization to take decisions closer to the customer, in order to be more responsive to customers. It is easy to see how this dimension impacts on the people variable: if our strategies require us to be faster on our feet, are our people competent to support the change? People trained throughout their careers in a bureaucracy may be unable to make the change to empowered decision-making. If the key power in the organization is wielded by one function, without being balanced by considerations from the other functions, there will be some types of strategy which will never work unless changes are made. Think for a moment of all the difficulties in the NHS, which are partly about changes in how decisions are made, and where the power and influence lie.
- CULTURE   Culture change has become big business, as organizations review not only their strategies, but the flexibility with which they will have to meet the future challenges. Decision processes are one of the determinants of culture, and we could take this idea further by suggesting that a key

determinant of culture is the way people are managed down the line by their superiors. There may be a need for a flexible, empowered organization, but if the managers do not manage in a way that supports this, the culture will act against the strategy. Culture is affected by each of the other organizational variables, and of course by things not in this listing, such as the history of the organization, and its current patterns of success or failure.

- INFORMATION SYSTEMS Information is power, and the way information is shared in the organization will have a powerful effect on, amongst other things, the culture. The information system must ensure that the right information gets to the right people on a timely basis. I have many times seen a new structure made harder to work because information was provided according to the responsibilities of the old structure. A major strategic change may stand the information system on its head; either the strategy or the system will have to change.
- CONTROL SYSTEMS The issue here is where control is exercised, and how it is exercised. Control systems must relate to the key elements of the strategy. Control also is a strong determinant of culture: it is clear that a control system which tries to apportion blame will lead to a different culture from one which seeks to find the cause of the error to stop it happening again. But this is a two-way link, in that a culture that is competitive will predispose the organization to different control systems than would be the case if the culture were supportive. The key question is not what is right or wrong, but what control system will be most appropriate for the strategies we have to implement.
- REWARD SYSTEMS Reward systems may be critical for success, because they drive behaviour. By reward, I mean money plus recognition, plus career development. A simple example may be the best: a sales force whose income is based on a commission which encourages volume sales will not respond to pressure to reduce volume by concentrating on high margin products. When there is a clash between what management says it wants and how it rewards behaviour, it is the rewards which will normally drive what really happens.

I have presented these ideas mainly as a way of thinking about the impact of strategy of the organization. However, it is possible to turn it on its head and look at the implications of any change in any one of the variables on any of the others. It may also help explain why announcements from the top about the new cultural values of the organization are often greeted with cynicism by all levels of employee. The value statement, often incorporated in a vision definition, only has meaning when all variables reinforce it. When everyone knows that the real drivers in the organization force people in the opposite direction to that stated, it is not surprising if the statements are treated as a top management joke.

**The EASIER Way to Implement Strategic Change**

It is not easy, it is just that I have found it easier to think of the steps this way. EASIER stands for *E*nvision, *A*ctivate, *S*upport, *I*nstall, *E*nsure and *R*ecognize. The first three words deal mainly with the soft aspects of management: the last three cover the hard side, the systems and administrative tasks. Successful implementation depends on getting all six stages right.

However, I should stress that the ingredients presented here should be varied according to the nature of the strategy. An incremental strategy, building on what the organization has done successfully for years, may require less attention to the softer aspects than would a strategy which required a major upheaval of all the organizational variables. Similarly how each element of the model might be applied is also situational, and would be different, for example, when there is a general agreement with the changes than when they are so opposed that consensus could never be reached. Many of these nuances are explored in other contributions to this book. Here I want only to present the framework.

Although the mnemonic is my own, the ideas behind it are drawn from recent research and writings on transformational leadership (for example, Tichy and Devanna, 1990; Nader and Tushman, 1989; Dinkelspiel and Bailey, 1991; Soderberg, 1993; Nicholls, 1993).

- ENVISIONING    This is the process of developing a coherent view of the future in order to form an overarching objective for the organization. The vision may cover such things as size, scope of activities, economic strengths, the relationships with customers, and the internal culture, including the values of the organization. It may be the best in certain fields: the best innovator; the most effective producer, the best employer. The vision does not necessarily have to be of a future that is radically different to the past, but becomes a much more important part of the implementation process when it is inspired by a realization that a change is necessary.

  Defining the vision clearly is an important element in the implementation process. The leader who cannot articulate the vision in a way that has meaning to others, will find it harder to ensure that everyone pulls in the same direction.

  Vision is an appropriate first step for implementation at various levels in the organization, and will be as critical for the leader of a business unit, or the head of a section. Effectively it will provide a reason for the various strategies. The content of the vision would be different at different levels. For example, downsizing of an operation may be accompanied by a vision which is concerned more with a future cost position and internal culture than a view of products and markets. The vision of the manager of a business unit will be constrained by what the overall organization is trying to do.

An inappropriate vision can frustrate the implementation of the strategies. A key leadership task is to think through the vision to ensure that it is both desirable and sound.

- ACTIVATING  Envisioning is a difficult process, because the borderline between empty platitudes and meaningful descriptions is very narrow. Activating is even harder. It is the task of ensuring that others in the organization understand, support and eventually share the vision. The vision cannot be understood unless it is communicated, and it cannot be communicated unless it is defined in a coherent way. Initially the task is to develop a shared vision amongst the key players in the task of implementation, but in many organizations there are benefits in reaching deep into the organization.

A widespread commitment to the vision makes it easier to see the relevance of the strategies, and underlines the importance of coordinated efforts. Even then implementation causes people to lose their jobs, this is more likely to be acceptable to them and to their surviving colleagues when they support the underlying vision that has led to this situation.

- SUPPORTING  Good leadership is not just about giving orders and instructions. It is much more about inspiring them to achieve more than they otherwise might have believed possible, and providing the necessary moral and practical support to enable this to happen. The envisioning and activating steps in implementation are about sharing and sustaining inspiration. The supporting step is about helping others to play a key part in the implementation process.

To achieve this the leader has to have a strong empathy with the people he or she is trying to inspire, and the imagination to see things from their point of view. There needs to be an understanding of both their present capabilities and their potential. Whilst giving support to help a subordinate reach a tough new goal, the leader has to be able to recognize the problems the person faces, without ever implying that there is the slightest doubt that the person will succeed.

There is a parallel with the principles of situational leadership, with the response to each person being adjusted to his/her level of capability and degree of motivation.

There is always a danger when the person leading the change lacks integrity or is insincere. A leader who pretends to give encouragement, when it is clear that he or she does not really care and is merely performing a ritual, is likely to be counterproductive. Supporting needs a base of respect, trust and integrity, and fails when these essentials are lacking.

- INSTALLING  This is the weakest of the words chosen in the mnemonic, and in the earliest version I developed in the context of change management I used the word implementation. This would have been misleading in an approach dedicated to the implementation of strategy. What is important is not so much the word, but the ideas that it is meant to convey. It is the process of developing detailed plans to enable the strategy to be implemented and controlled.

The nature and shape of those plans will vary with the complexity of the strategies and their nature. In only rare circumstances will it be a task that should be totally undertaken by the centre, and in most cases the process would benefit by the involvement of the key people who are expected to carry out the actions which will implement the strategy.

The instruments that may be used will also vary, depending not only on the complexity of the strategies, but also on the time scale for implementation; however, the basic reason is constant. It is to:

—Ensure that all the consequences of the change are understood, in so far as they can be foreseen. This includes the impact on the organizational variables discussed earlier.
—Identify all the actions that have to be taken to bring about the change. This usually requires much more attention to detail than would be appropriate for any formal strategic plan or boardroom presentation. It also has to be accepted that in some cases only the initial actions are clear, and that what happens subsequently will depend on the results of these. The more complex the strategy, the more likely will be the need for several phases of this detailed planning stage.
—Allocate responsibility for the various actions that have to be taken.
—Establish the priorities of the various actions, in particular those that will hold up the whole process if not done to time.
—Provide the budgets needed to ensure implementation of the plans.
—Set up the teams and structures needed to implement.
—Allocate the right human resources to the tasks (if necessary recruiting additional people or using consultants).
—Determine any policies that are needed to make the implementation process work.

There is nothing unique or special about any of these individual requirements, nor the instruments such as plans, budgets, critical path analysis, Gantt charts or other tools which have to be developed to ensure that nothing is overlooked and everything is coordinated. These are all the regular instruments of management.

It should be recognized that when the strategies take the organization into new situations, past experience may be little help in this process, and the planning of the many large and small actions needed to ensure success may be much more difficult than expected. The organization should not be too proud to supplement its implementation skills from consultancy or other sources where it lacks experience of what it is about to do.

- ENSURING    Plans, structures for implementation, and policies may be formulated, and on paper the organization may have covered everything. But this is not enough, and consideration must be given to the monitoring and controlling processes that will ensure that:

  —All actions are taken on time, unless there is a conscious, justifiable decision to change the actions.

  —Where actions are changed, there is both good reason for the change and a replanning for the new circumstances.

  —The results of actions are as expected, and if not, corrective action is taken.

  —Plans are still appropriate if the situation has changed.

All organizations have monitoring and controlling processes, but those that currently exist may be inadequate to monitor the new strategies. One of the actions in the implementing phase might therefore have been to establish supplementary controls so that timely information is made available on a regular basis. When considering controls, attention should be given to qualitative as well as quantitative issues. It may, for example, be as important to survey periodically the morale in the organization, as to measure whether a new strategy has brought the expected reduction in unit costs.

Monitoring and control processes also provide a reason for the various players in the implementation game to meet, thus providing another way of reinforcing the commitment to the vision.

- RECOGNIZING    This is giving recognition to those involved in the process. Recognition may be positive or negative, and should be used to reinforce the change, and to ensure that obstacles to progress are removed.

  Although recognition may include financial reward, this may be the smallest part of what is needed. Public recognition (amongst peers and senior managers) of the part played by a particular manager may show that what has been done is appreciated. Promotion of someone who has played a major role may be a consequence of his or her performance in helping to implement the strategies. That small word 'thanks' may have great motivational value when expressed sincerely by a leader who is respected by the person.

  The negative aspects of this may include the transfer of a valuable person who opposes the strategies to a role where it is not possible to damage the process. In some cases it may include the dismissal of a particular person who is frustrating the change or causing the pace to slow. Strategies that cause fundamental change often bring this type of casualty. It would be unrealistic to suggest that there will never be management casualties, however much attention is given to the first three steps in the implementation process.

The approaches described offer a blueprint for successful implementation. They should be used with sense. It has already been stated that the situation will affect how the concepts should be used, and the more fundamental the change, the more effort will be needed to apply all aspects of the approach. Where the changes are incremental, effectively bringing little difference to what the organization does and hardly affecting the organizational variables, some elements of the approach may not be as important as suggested here. Often the danger is that we do not know what we do not know, and it is human nature to assume things about the impact of the strategy without really thinking them through. At the very least the approaches described should be used as a checklist to stimulate thinking, so that an implementation process can be defined. The underlying message must be to give attention to both the hard and the soft aspects of management. Neglect of either may cause failure in implementation.

## REFERENCES

Alexander, L. (1991). Strategy Implementation: Nature of the Problem. In: Hussey, D. E. (ed.), *International Review of Strategic Management*, Volume 2, No. 1. Wiley, Chichester.

Dinkelspiel, J. R. and Bailey, J. (1991). High Performing Organisations: Aligning Culture and Organisation Around Strategy. In: Hussey D. E. (ed.), *International Review of Strategic Management*, Volume 2, No. 1. Wiley, Chichester.

Hussey, D. E. (1984). Strategic Management: Lessons from Success and Failure, *Long Range Planning*, (**17**)1, February.

Hussey, D. E. (1994). *Strategic Management: Theory and Practice*, 3rd edn. Pergamon, Oxford.

Leavitt, H. J. (1964). Applied Organisational Change in Industry: Structural, Technical and Human Approaches. In: Cooper, W. W., Leavitt, H. J. and Shelly, M. W. (eds), *New Perspectives in Organisational Research*. Wiley, New York. (An abridged version appears in Vroom, V. R. and Deci, E. L. (1970). *Management and Motivation*. Penguin, London).

Nader, D. A. and Tushman, M. L. (1989). Leadership for Organisational Change. In: Mormon *et al* (eds), *Large Scale Organisational Change*. Jossey Bass, San Francisco.

Nicholls, J. (1993). Will Humpty Dumpty Win? In: Hussey, D. E. (ed.), *International Review of Strategic Management*, Volume 4. Wiley, Chichester.

Peters, T. J. and Waterman, R. H. (1982). *In Search of Excellence*. Harper and Row, New York.

Steiner, G. A. (1972). *Pitfalls in Comprehensive Long Range Planning*. Planning Executives Institute, Oxford, Ohio.

Soderberg, K. (1993). Leadership-focused Management Development: Are Today's Practices Meeting Tomorrow's Needs? In: Hussey, D. E. (ed.), *International Review of Strategic Management*, Volume 4. Wiley, Chichester.

Tichy, N. M. and Devanna, M. A. (1990). *The Transformational Leader*, reprint of 1986 edition with additional preface. Wiley, New York.

# 2

# EVALUATING A BUSINESS PLAN

D. E. Hussey

*Harbridge Consulting Group Ltd*

In my role as a consultant I am often asked to review business plans and to comment on them. If you prepare a plan yourself, you know the background situation, the analytical approaches applied and the gaps in the information used to formulate strategy, and you have a good grasp of all the elements of the strategy. The position may be very different when you are asked to evaluate a plan that someone else has prepared. This may happen in situations where the context is known, such as commenting on the strategic plan for your own company or of one of its divisions. It may also happen when the context is not known, such as when evaluating the plan of another SBU, or foreign subsidiary, or of another organization in a friendly merger or joint venture situation. Professional organizations, such as banks and accountancy firms, often also frequently face situations when they have to judge plans of other organizations for various purposes and, as I have said, the same need often occurs with management consultants. The problem which this chapter tries to help to solve is how to begin.

There are at least two aspects which need consideration. The first is the quality of strategic thinking that goes into the plan: the second is the quality of the planning document—the plan—as a communication medium and an aid to implementation. Both are important, and the simple matrix in Figure 2.1 can be used as a way of exploring their significance.

It is worth spending a little time thinking about this matrix. The preferred situation is when the strategy is sound and the plan that describes this is clear, concise, yet comprehensive. There can be few attempts at planning that do not strive for this condition. It gives the organization the best chance of both deciding and implementing the right things.

*The Implementation Challenge*, Edited by D. E. Hussey
© 1996 John Wiley & Sons Ltd

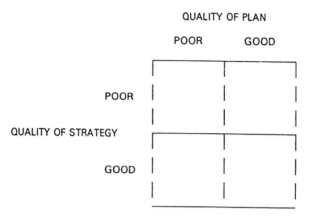

**Figure 2.1**    Relationship of Quality of Plan to Quality of Strategy

When the quality of the strategy is good, but the plan is poor, there is a real danger that it will not be communicated adequately. An SBU, for example, may find that the level of corporate support it expects is not forthcoming because of misunderstandings over the strategy. At any level there may be a failure to implement if there is no clarity about what has to be done.

Perhaps the most dangerous situation is when the plan is good, and therefore convincing, but the underlying strategy is poor. This can result in the wrong things being done with considerable zeal. The quality of the document may be such that the right questions are never asked about the appropriateness of the strategy. The document looks so good and reads so well that everyone believes the strategy is sound.

The poor/poor box in Figure 2.1, which is occupied more commonly than is desirable, leads to a situation where little of the planning effort brings any benefit to the organization. The reasons for this planning failure may be varied. It could be that the rapidity of change in the business environment is too great for traditional approaches to strategic planning to have any impact. It may be that the style of top management makes planning impossible. It may be a lack of competence in those concerned in the planning process.

In this chapter attention will be given to both aspects, but before we start I should like to draw attention to a widely observed tendency which I am sure many readers have themselves noticed about plans.

## THE 'LAWS' OF PLANNING

Years ago I defined two laws of planning, which all written plans seemed to follow. They are as noticeable in project plans supporting requests for capital expenditure as they are in strategic plans:

1.  *In any written plan, everything comes right in the third year*. This does not mean that it will come right, only that the plan says it will. The third year is close enough to appear to have meaning, but far enough away to escape retribution. The underlying psychology is that 3 years is long enough for things to work out.
2.  *The third year never comes*. My second law of planning is that the bounty of the third year is never delivered. Somehow the cornucopia expected 3 years ago when the plan was made is as empty in the third year as it was in the first two.

Of course things can come to pass as the plan suggests. However, knowing that so many plans show two lean years followed by a time of plenty makes me want to probe very deeply into any plans which follow this pattern. This usually means exploring the information on which the plan was based, as well as studying the strategy itself.


## DOES IT HAVE A PURPOSE?


Both of the aspects of the plan which were identified earlier should have a purpose. The most important is the strategic aspect. What objectives is the strategy trying to achieve, and is the expected outcome consistent with the aim? This does not mean that the strategy is sound or the plan good, but it indicates whether the writer believes it to be appropriate. If there are no stated objectives, and the expected results are not stated, the plan will be in a vacuum.

The purpose of the written document should also be understood. Clearly it is to describe the strategy that will achieve the objectives. Behind this is another layer of subtlety: for whom is the plan being written? The written document may well take a different form depending on its target readership, and this will affect any critical evaluation of that plan. For example, a business plan written mainly to record the strategy and communicate it within an organization that is well aware of the background situation may need to contain much less information about the market and company situation than a plan, covering the same strategy, written to gain the support of a remote parent company. In the latter case the decision-makers may have a preferred format for plan presentation, but may lack understanding of the local situation. Part of the rationale for the document may be to persuade and convince upwards, whereas in the first case the purpose was to communicate downwards. A business plan written partly with the intention of gaining support from bankers or major external investors may require a different format again. Before evaluating the quality of a plan, it is worth finding out what it is to be used for.

# TESTING A STRATEGY

Strategies may be good or bad, and even a good strategy may fail through poor implementation, or a poor one succeed because of the skill and flair of individual managers. It is useful to test strategies for basic flaws, and the following points are designed to help this process.

## Is the Strategy Identified and Clearly Stated?

It is impossible to assess a strategy until the strategy is known, a point which is self-evident. Yet surprisingly a very high proportion of the written plans I have seen fail this test. I have ploughed through pages of material on many occasions, and found a history lesson on the company, but have had no idea of the strategy the organization was following. When this happens there is no plan.

## Has it Considered Competitors and the Industry Structure?

Competitive positioning is a critical element of strategy. In addition the strategy should be developed with an awareness of competitors, and the moves they are likely to make. The competitive structure of the industry will also affect the possible strategies that might be successful, which implies that the strategy should be considered in the context of the industry structure. If the strategy is to break the rules by changing the power structure of the industry, the method should be clear from the plan. Many of the plans I have examined assume that the desired changes will happen, without there being any reason why they should. Wishful thinking is not the same as a strategy!

## Does it Match the Realities of the Market?

All strategies face the test of market realism. New products will only have a chance of succeeding if they meet a requirement of the buyers. Old products will not suddenly increase their sales unless there is a reason. One of the hardest things is to persuade an organization that has been expanding rapidly on the back of one major consumer durable that there is a saturation point and that product life-cycle theories do in fact apply. Equally hard has been to convince companies to strike a note of realism when taking a successful product into a 'new' country. People will not necessarily flock to buy that product just because the corporate plan says they should.

## Is the Geographical Scope Appropriate?

In some industries the need for global integration is more important than the need for local responsiveness. The 'globality' of the industry must be examined, and strategy tested against this. What appears to be sound on a one-country basis may not be sound when the global nature of the industry is understood— and this is not a static analysis, since global pressures affect more industries each year. In the UK I have often found that managers do not take a world view of their businesses. When I helped in implementing the merger of Vickers and Rolls Royce Motors in 1980, one of the major achievements was helping to bring about an understanding of the global nature of many of the markets. This led to strategies that were quite different from those previously formulated under the assumption of local businesses (see Stopford, 1989, for a description of this process).

### Is it Consistent With Environmental Forces?

The assumptions on which the strategy is based should be stated. No strategy exists in a vacuum, and there are many environmental trends and forces that have an impact on strategy. One test is to examine the extent to which the strategy considers the outside forces.

### Are the Levels of Risk Acceptable?

A strategy may look very elegant, but it may also be a disaster if it is a 'bet the company' move. In testing a strategy it is important to think of the economic risks the company can take. It may also be valuable to consider whether the chief executive responsible for the strategy is willing to accept the personal risks involved. If not, the strategy may be good but is unlikely to be implemented.

### Does it Enhance Shareholder Value?

Some might argue that this test should be number one. I have put it in its present position only because it is not possible to assess the impact on shareholder value until the underlying soundness of the thinking can be gauged. Increasingly, companies are using value-based planning approaches to measure contributions to shareholder value, effectively expressing the outcome of the plans in discounted cash flow terms. There is more to shareholder value than this. A simple example is whether synergy is gained between business units, or whether they are so competitive that they duplicate resources and miss opportunities for joint working or shared resources. Another example is the role of a head office and whether it adds value through how it operates, or merely adds to costs.

### Does it Match Corporate Competence and Resources?

In other words, can it be done? A common fault is for plans to be too ambitious, to ignore existing factors, or to expect things to happen faster than the organization can implement them. A related question is: does the plan identify and build on core competencies?

### Is the Company Structure Appropriate?

Structure and strategy have to be compatible. Even sound strategies can fail if the structure is designed to fulfil a different strategy to the one chosen.

### Does it Match the Company Culture?

This is a difficult question to answer, but is important. If the strategy calls on the company to act in a manner totally alien to its culture, the strategy has a high chance of failing unless the culture is changed. Scandinavian Airlines offers a good example. In the early 1980s it introduced a strategy, one plank of which was customer responsiveness. The culture at the time was bureaucratic, with all decisions referred upwards. To be responsive meant driving many decisions much lower in the organization, and to make this happen meant that the company had also to plan for a major change in company culture.

### Does it have an Appropriate Time Horizon?

The plan should be developed to cover the time period necessary to fulfil it. A strategy that ended with a major investment, with no outcomes shown for that investment, would clearly be deficient. The plan should not be positioned on the salami system, with just a few slices of investment shown, disguising the fact that the real shape is a semi-circular sausage and not a flat circle! There may sometimes be a need to develop the strategy for a longer period than the company's planning process requires. In fact, one of the problems of business units of a larger corporate entity is that often the corporate planning horizon is too long or too short for their situation.

### Does the Plan have Internal Consistency?

The final test question asks whether the plan is logical and hangs together. It may sound a trivial point to those who plan well themselves, and it is not usually the obvious that goes wrong, such as marketing planning to expand volumes without manufacturing being able to produce them. In my experience the two most common problems are quantification and people. The quantified results of a plan should be related to the strategies in the plan, but sometimes they are put together using ratios and growth factors which do not take account of the costs and rewards of the actual actions planned. The second coordination area which seems to defy logic is the changes that have to be made to structure, culture and human resources. This section of the plan often appears to be put together without any consideration of the strategies.

**The Missing Question**

The discerning may feel that this list of points to look out for misses the most important, which is whether the strategy appears sound. This is of course the most critical issue, and one of the most difficult to reduce to a few sentences. Experience in strategic thinking and knowledge of those principles that have been defined are the two most important elements. Yet experience also shows that, because most of the principles are statements of tendency, rather than rigid rules, a strategy that defies the accumulated wisdom of the experts is not necessarily bad. There is also an element of fashion in strategic thinking, which may be another way of saying that strategies have to fit the age in which they are made. In the 1970s portfolio arguments of having cash cows to fund stars, and wildcats that may become future stars, would have figured in the judgements of strategy, whereas today adding shareholder value is seen as of more significance.

However, there are some principles that are worth mentioning, even though they cannot be used slavishly.

1.  Porter (1980) has codified many principles around the relative power positions of the various players in different industry structures. An appropriate strategy for an industry where there is a dominant leader may be totally wrong for a fragmented industry with no entry barriers. There may even be differences between fragmented industries, like the guard and patrol sector of the security industry, which has little opportunity for differentiation and few niches, and an industry like management consulting, which has many opportunities for differentiation and numerous niches. An awareness of the industry principles is an essential starting point for evaluating any strategy.

2.  Buzzell and Gale (1987) drew a number of lessons from some 15 years' experience of operating the PIMS database, which collects cause-and-effect data from its members to allow the derivation of strategic factors. Among other things, these principles show the importance of market share and quality, and the impact of vertical integration. The danger is if anyone tries to interpret these findings blindly. Yes, higher market share is associated with higher profitability but, as the authors point out, using this to justify a strategy to move from the bottom of the share league to the top may be the road to a totally uneconomic course of action.

3.  James (1985) offers some interesting thoughts on mega-strategies, and draws comparisons between business and military principles. The insights here are of particular value when the strategy involves expansion into another country or market, or when considering defence against an incursion by an invader who is trying to do the same thing to you.

4.    Remember that all the evidence is that more acquisitions fail than
      succeed. Kitching (1967, 1973, 1974) provides many principles derived
      from research in Europe and the USA, and shows the types of merger that
      have the highest chance of success. Porter (1987) showed that the success
      chances of mergers and acquisitions had hardly changed since Kitching's
      work. The practical implication of all this is that I look very hard at any
      strategy which depends on acquisition, and want to see the actions that
      are planned to increase the chances of success. In many strategy plans
      acquisition is a form of cop-out, and a statement of intent to acquire
      replaces real thought about the situation.

All this advice is important. But in evaluating strategy we can borrow the
words of the great economist Alfred Marshall (1920).

> It is doubtless true that much of this work has less need of elaborate scientific
> methods, than of a shrewd mother-wit, of a sound sense of proportion, and of a
> large experience of life.

He goes on to add a qualification:

> Natural instinct will select rapidly, and combine justly, considerations which are
> relevant to the issue in hand; but it will select chiefly from those which are
> familiar; it will seldom lead a man far below the surface, or far beyond the limits
> of his personal experience.

Although applied to economics, the words are equally relevant to that branch
of economic activity, the formulation of strategy.                          .

## TESTING A PLAN FOR QUALITY

Plans are written for different purposes, and the particular purpose should be
considered when the plan is evaluated. There is a wide spectrum of styles and
formats that could be applied, and the suggestions below accept that there is no
one right way to write up the plan.

### Concise but Clear

A plan should be as brief as possible, but must communicate the strategy: a
verbose plan may be less clear than a concise one, particularly if it is also
poorly structured. Sometimes, it is useful to impart information that is relevant
to the plan: a good plan would probably separate the information (for
example, market evolution) from the strategy section, but would demonstrate
that the information has been used through the way the strategy is presented.
Experience shows that lengthy narrative information sections that appear in

plans often have nothing to do with the decision process in the plan. What is there should be integrated.

## Use of Diagrams

One of the best ways of relating strategy to complex data is through diagrammatic displays. For example an industry 'map' may show the key data about the competitive structure of the industry on one piece of paper. A portfolio diagram allows the strategic situation of various business units to be compared, again on one piece of paper. Matrix displays of any type may add clarity, compress information and relate the strategy to the information.

## Structure of the Plan

The plan must have a structure, and that structure should aid understanding. Without being dogmatic about order of presentation or content, there should be, as a minimum, sections on the strategic situation, internal strengths and weaknesses, vision and objectives, the chosen strategies, expected results and the action plan. It does not mean that a plan is bad if it lacks these, but it raises a line of questioning.

## Too Many Actions

Corporate strategic plans are fairly broad. Plans at lower levels exchange breadth for depth. In both, a common error is to be over-optimistic about the number of new initiatives that can be implemented in a given period. All strategic actions planned must be considered against the resources of the unit and other claims on time, and should include realistic assessments of the actual time an action will take. A plan should not become a do-it-yourself hangman's kit.

## Implementation

The final test is around implementation. Even a sound strategy can fail if attention is not given to implementation. The plan should address this, by establishing goals (milestones) to measure progress, breaking down the strategy into main action plans, and dealing with the issues which arise from this.

Issues may include involvement of those who will be required to implement, training in new skills needed to implement, communication and appropriate control mechanisms.

## SUMMARY

All of the points in this article can be compressed into a few sentences. The evaluator needs to:

- Understand the strategy.
- Be convinced of its soundness in relation to industry structure, competitors, the market and the environment.
- Be convinced that it fits the competence and resources of the organization.
- Establish that it can be implemented.
- Know the purpose for which the plan is written.

## REFERENCES

Buzzell, R. D. and Gale, B. T. (1987). *The PIMS Principles: Linking Strategy to Performance*. Free Press, New York.

James, B. G. (1985). *Business Wargames*. Penguin Books, London (originally published in 1984 by Abacus Books).

Kitching, J. (1967). Why do Mergers Miscarry? *Harvard Business Review*, November/December.

Kitching, J. (1973). *Acquisitions in Europe: Causes of Corporate Success and Failure*. Business International, Geneva.

Kitching, J. (1974). Winning and Losing with European Acquisitions, *Harvard Business Review*, March/April.

Marshall, A. (1920). *Principles of Economics*, 8th edn. Macmillan, London, 1956.

Porter, M. E. (1980). *Competitive Strategy*. Free Press, New York.

Porter, M. E. (1987). From Competitive Advantage to Corporate Strategy, *Harvard Business Review*, May/June.

Stopford, J. M. (1989). *Vickers Plc A*. London Business School, London.

# 3

# MANAGING CHANGE, HUMAN RESOURCE MANAGEMENT AND TIMEX[1]

**Graeme Martin and Martin Dowling**

*Dundee Business School, University of Abertay*

This chapter:

- sets out the attempts to bring about strategic change at Timex in Dundee over a 50 year association with the city;
- discusses the problems of moving from a mass production, make-for-stock strategy to a subcontracting, make-to-order strategy in the context of the Timex corporation's global strategy and organizational configuration;
- discusses the role of leadership, management style and human resource management in bringing about culture change;
- explains the problems of Timex as a failure of the US and home-based management to think strategically and think culturally.

## INTRODUCTION

In August 1993, the Timex factory in Dundee was closed following a bitter industrial dispute that had lasted 8 months. The closure meant the end of a 47-year association between Dundee and Timex which set up its first manufacturing facility in the city in 1946.

[1]British Academy of Management Annual Conference, Lancaster University, UK, 12–14 September, 1994

*The Implementation Challenge*, Edited by D. E. Hussey
© 1996 John Wiley & Sons Ltd

Factory closure, of course, is nothing new but what makes the Timex case significant is that the closure, and events leading up to it, caused widespread debate in the UK and beyond. One of the main points of issue was the relationship between multinational companies (MNCs) and their subsidiaries and the future shape of employment relations in mature economies such as that of Britain. However, it was the violence on the picket line—the like of which had not been seen in Britain since *The Times* newspaper dispute and miners' strike of the mid-1980s—that attracted massive media publicity and public outrage. Some saw the dispute as signifying the emergence of a post-Thatcher labour militancy; whilst for others the dispute called into question the state and status of Britain's employment laws, particularly in the context of the European Social Charter and the type of employment law operating in other EC countries (Miller and Woolfson, 1994). Closer to home, the dispute and its aftermath have left a legacy of hatred and bitterness between the strikers (who were dismissed soon after their strike began) and those who continued working in the factory or who replaced the strikers. Relations between the striking workers and their trade union also came to be severely strained. Elsewhere, the impact of the dispute and closure on employment levels in Dundee and on the city's capacity to attract and retain inward investment have also caused much debate and speculation.

Clearly then the Timex case raises many social, economic and political controversies that will continue to be debated for some time. However, it is not our intention here to review all the strands of this debate but to explain the failure of the company to manage strategic change from a context-content-process perspective (Pettigrew and Whipp, 1991; Dawson, 1994). Specifically, we focus on the historical context of Timex (Dundee) and its relationship with its US-based parent company (Bartlett and Ghoshal, 1989; Chakravarthy and Perlmutter, 1990; Hendry, 1994); the role of leadership in influencing events (Leavy and Wilson, 1994) and, briefly, the attempt to transform the company's fortunes through a culture change programme and the application of a 'greenfield' site human resource management (HRM) strategy in a unionized environment (Guest, 1989; Sisson, 1993; Anthony, 1994).

The first part of this chapter documents the development of the Dundee plant over the period 1947–1990, its role in the emerging 'global' strategy of the US-based headquarters (Johnson and Scholes, 1993, pp. 10–11; Doz, 1990) and the management of human resources (HRs) in Dundee over the same period. The second part of the chapter focuses on the attempted transformation of the factory in the early 1990s which resulted in the dispute and eventual closure of the plant. In the third part we provide a two-stage analysis of the case: firstly, in terms of the emergence of a global strategy that saw Timex (Dundee) become increasingly 'marginalized'; and, secondly, the attempt to manage the 'marginalized' position over the period 1983–1993. In particular, we focus on the failed culture change and HRs strategies used during that period. At the same time we try to draw out some lessons for the managers and employees of multinational companies and their host country subsidiaries, particularly concerning their internal relationships and the strategies they pursue (Hendry, 1994).

The case material is drawn from two sources. The first are interviews with shop stewards, former managers, local politicians and ex-employees of Timex, quite a few of whom are either friends, acquaintances or managers we have taught during our 15 years' connection with the business school in Dundee. The second source are the many local and national newspaper accounts of the dispute and the analysis of radio and television news programmes of events at Timex.

## TIMEX AND DUNDEE: STRATEGIC CHANGE, DEVELOPMENT AND HRM

The Timex Corporation is a US-based multinational owned by a Norwegian shipping, oil and engineering businessman, Fred Olsen, who took over from his father in the 1960s. In the 1970s the corporation employed 17,000 people throughout the world. Currently it has an estimated annual turnover of $640 million and employs 7,000 people in the US, Europe and the Philippines marketing and assembling watches and, until 1993, electronics components in Dundee, Scotland. Timex appears to have pursued a 'global' strategy, driven by the need to achieve cost advantages through centralized, global-scale operations (Bartlett and Ghoshal, 1989). Just prior to the closure of the Dundee plant, Timex effectively 'wound up' its last manufacturing operation in the US and transferred all remaining watch assembly work to the Philippines where labour costs are much lower. Since 1988, the Timex Corporation appears to have altered its strategy by integrating forwards into retail outlets for watches, initially to assist in its test marketing and pricing but also to take advantage of the larger margins associated with retailing (*Business Week*, 1993). It has also had some recent success with new product development in the form of 'back-lit' watches. Like many of the traditional watch manufacturers, the company was criticized in the 1970s for failing to understand the nature of market trends where watches were moving from being seen as functional objects to becoming fashion accessories, e.g. *Swatches*, and failing to capitalize on the nature of the value chain for wrist watches where the vast bulk of added value is created at the wholesaling and retailing stages (Gilbert and Strebel, 1992).

### The Early Years in Dundee and the Development of an Adverserial Culture

Timex's association with Dundee began in 1946 when it set up the first of its plants in purpose-built accommodation to produce low-priced, value-for-money wrist watches. Its cost-leadership strategy, based on mass production, allowed the company to become a leader in the market segment for more than a decade (Rue and Holland, 1986). At the time demand for watches far outstripped UK production capacity. Such was the demand for watches, diversification into other product lines came relatively late on in the company's history. It was only in the 1960s that the company began to manufacture the Polaroid Swinger camera, a product with a much shorter life cycle.

In such buoyant post-war demand conditions, the Fordist-type mass production approach coupled with innovative product development (the company were the first to introduce self-winding and battery-operated watches) and heavy promotional expenditure led to a gradual expansion of the workforce. The labour force peaked at more than 6,000 during the 1970s, located in three plants throughout the city. The Dundee operation became the largest production facility in Timex's worldwide operations, a fact that a former senior and long-serving manager suggested was extremely important in explaining the attention paid by the US management to the plant's manufacturing strategy and industrial relations. At the same time, the Dundee operation had always been a manufacturing/assembling facility with what a senior ex-HR manager described as a 'cost-centre mentality'. It had little product design tradition or capacity itself, with most product innovation initiated in the US. Timex became the largest single private sector employer in the city of Dundee accounting for about 8% of the total employment and, along with other US-based employers such as NCR, the company provided attractive, secure and well-paid employment in an area dominated by traditional but declining industries such as jute manufacture and shipbuilding.

Dundee was, and still is, characterized by a strong unionized tradition, and Timex found itself from the outset employing a unionized workforce and obliged therefore to recognize and deal with powerful trade unions for most sections of its blue and white collar workforce. In particular the engineering union (today called the Amalgamated Engineering and Electrical Union) became the dominant union force in the plant. Fred Olsen's well-known anti-union reputation gained in his home country, Norway, was never overtly in evidence in Dundee and over the years a traditional pattern of employment management via strong collective bargaining with the unions was established (Purcell and Sisson, 1983). With the Dundee facility operating a successful volume-based strategy based on low costs and high margins it soon became something of a 'cash cow' for the Timex Corporation. This in turn also became a source of union bargaining power which was used to secure economic benefits and job controls at the point of production—concessions which the management seemed willing to give to secure continuity of output.

Over time it seems that the industrial relations (IR) culture began to resemble something of an 'indulgency pattern' (Gouldner, 1954). Both sides came to an accommodation with each other and whether through cooperation or conflict secured their objectives. The engineering union especially was able to secure a strong position over both the *content* and *process* aspects of the employment relationship, particularly in the craft-dominated Milton plant which developed a history of 'militant' shop floor unionism. This adverserial tradition was later to be of great significance in the months leading up to closure.

Despite the conflictual nature of industrial relations and apart from a major redundancy in 1971, Timex enjoyed a positive external image in the city until the early 1980s. It was considered by many of its staff and potential recruits to be an organization which offered a career for those who were willing to take advantage of the substantial investment by the company in training and good employment for an increasing number of females seeking part-time employment. The company was also regarded by a succession of civic dignitaries and local employer groups as the type of firm with which the city 'fathers' wished to be associated—forward-looking and usually an exemplar of progressive US management techniques such as quality management and personnel initiatives.

## The Decline of Mechanical Watchmaking and the Move into Subcontracting Electronics

Timex's fortunes in Dundee began to change in the 1970s, following the decline in demand for mechanical watches in the sector of the market in which the company was dominant. The competition from solid-state watches from the Far East led to Timex setting up new plants, initially in Taiwan and subsequently in the Philippines to produce the cheaper watches using solid-state technology. Timex also opened other plants in France and Portugal to take advantage of the lower labour costs that existed in these countries at the time.

It is from this point in the 1970s that the importance of the Dundee plants in Timex's global operations began to decline. However, the commitment to remain in Dundee was still very evident and, in a change in emphasis of product-market strategy, the Dundee plant entered into the first of a number of subcontracting agreements with electronic companies, initially with the entrepreneur, Clive Sinclair, to assemble the ZX computer range and then the Japanese-designed Nimslo cameras. Such a change was not as fundamental as it first appears. Firstly, the Timex Corporation worldwide had begun a short-lived diversification into electronics manufacture in the early 1980s, producing two computers in the US that subsequently failed to achieve profitability. Secondly, as explained by a former senior manager, the Dundee plant's competences lay in assembly rather than in design and manufacture; to begin to develop a set of new products from scratch neither lay in their capability nor in the time frame available to them to maintain plant utilization. Contract electronics thus seemed a workable solution as it required little development in skills for many of the existing workforce nor a great deal of investment in new plant.

However, these initial subcontracting ventures did not prove to be long-term successes for the Dundee plant. The ZX computer range was taken over by

IBM and production of the Nimslo camera was moved to Japan. Meanwhile the company decided to relocate its remaining mechanical watch assembly to production facilities in France. As a result, employment levels in Dundee began to fall continuously from 1978 when Timex employed 4,200 in the city. In 1983 a major redundancy of 1,900 was declared. Workers undertook a sit-in that had no positive results regarding the transfer of work away from Dundee. The company fought the sit-in and insisted on compulsory redundancies and changes in flexibility for the remaining workforce which they secured in large measure. It appears that, following the industrial action, discussions over the future of the Dundee plants took place between senior management in Dundee, which also involved Olsen and some of the US managers. The problems of the high and relatively fixed cost structure of the Scottish operation were identified as a major problem in competing effectively in the contracting electronics market, but this evidence did not dissuade the management team from attempting to penetrate that market. A former HR manager explained the problems that Timex faced in moving into the electronics market in the following way:

> a strategy based on competence in assembly and manufacturing seemed eminently possible if a labour run-down, new contracts and (changes in) labour practices could be managed. The company achieved the first two but was always going to find it difficult to overcome the union practices and influence and the accommodating style of management–union relationships developed during the high volume/high margin watch manufacturing days of the 1960s and 1970s.
>
> (Contract electronics) was a low-margin industry. Rapid technological change, fluctuation programmes, quality and delivery. This was mainly a non-union industry with a younger workforce, much lower fringe benefits and greater flexibility.

Alternative means of reducing costs were discussed at planning meetings during the early 1980s, including the setting up of new 'greenfield' plants outwith Dundee. However, these were rejected, partly on investment grounds but also because of the commitment shown by the then general manager, Graham Thompson, to Dundee which closely mirrored that of Olsen.

A new general manager, Barry Lawson, was brought in by the US management team. He had greater knowledge of the electronics industry and Timex (Dundee) continued to develop as a contract manufacturer throughout the 1980s, providing manufacturing and ancillary services to original equipment manufacturers (OEMs) such as the major computer companies. When IBM took over the ZX computer range, the company's association with Dundee began with Timex producing the metal frames for the personal computers (PCs). Contracts were also secured from Amstrad to assemble PCs and then printers in 1986, and electronic control units were manufactured for Minolta,

Bang and Olufsen and Creda Cookers. By the late 1980s, then, Timex had secured a place for itself within the contract electronics manufacturing market.

## The Nature of the Contract Electronics Market Environment and its Implications for HRM at Timex

During the late 1980s favourable demand conditions for contract electronic manufacturers (CEMs) existed. Many of the OEMs began to focus on their core competences of seeking new markets and providing them with management solutions. This led to much of the subassembly work being carried out to the CEMs and by 1988 the estimated annual growth rate of the contracts electronics market had reached 45%. Although this declined during the recession, by 1993 demand had increased by 21% over the previous year's level (*Scotland on Sunday*, 1993). In addition to the contracting out policy of the OEMs, EC rules on the content of finished equipment that had to be sourced in the EC also augured well for the prospects of European-based CEMs like Timex.

In 1993, just prior to the factory closure, the *Financial Times* (1993) reported a glowing future for the contract electronics manufacturers which had become the fastest growing sector of the European electronics industry and worth, in global terms, an estimated $22 billion by the mid-1990s. It depicted the industry in terms of strategic alliances between the OEMs and the CEMs that had transformed the image of firms operating in a low-technology 'sweatshop' environment to sophisticated contract manufacturers offering full 'turnkey' services from design and printed circuit board layout through to product distribution. Such images have become *de rigueur* in explaining post-modern manufacturing relationships (Storey, 1994). The major OEMs such as IBM, Motorola, Bosch, AEG, Sony and Matsushita, it was argued, were linking up with CEMs that could provide fast response times, flexibility and high quality as well as low cost manufacture. These demands ensured that the successful CEMs would have to be able to bring new products to market as well as manufacture them to strict standards.

Experience of working in a subcontracting relationship with IBM in particular is best described as combining elements of both a 'market' and 'hierarchical' nature (Williamson, 1975). IBM, which by the early 1990s was supplying 70% or more of Timex's business, took advantage of a highly competitive market environment, intensified by Far Eastern competition to set exacting costs and delivery standards. The Scottish plant of IBM, itself, was under severe pressure to secure the monitor production for the whole of IBM and was aiming at a 25% reduction in inventory at its Greenock plant. Thus subject to limited negotiations, it specified how much it was willing to pay for subassemblies, the cost and source of bought-in parts and strict just-in-time-related delivery schedules.

IBM's electronic control systems replaced personal control in Timex: an electronic data management system was installed in Dundee that allowed IBM's managers in Greenock instant access to production information. Interview data also showed that the Dundee managers had little discretion over either sourcing or scheduling.

Moving into the contracting market had major implications for the Dundee plants' management. IBM, in particular, not only exercised strict control over price but also over conformance to design, quality and production standards and, during the initial stages of the contract, had a permanent group of production staff resident in Dundee. The nature of HRM in Dundee was also to change as a consequence. As one of Timex's former managers explained:

> The company had lived for years in a situation where compromise with the unions was the name of the game because it could pass on the costs. Moving into subcontracting meant that this was no longer possible and the unions didn't like it.

The cost structure of the Dundee plant was estimated to be some 20–30% higher than the main competitors in the contract electronics industry and continued to remain so for much of the period in question. As a result, redundancies continued throughout the 1980s but provoked no industrial action as they were achieved by voluntary means for the most part. By 1985 employment was down to 1,000 and by 1990, reduced to 580.


## CULTURE CHANGE, COST REDUCTION AND HRM: 1990–1993

In 1990, the US management team initiated a major change programme at Timex under the logo of a *Fresh Start*. A former consultant who worked with both the US and UK management teams described the situation as one where the US management team wished to break with all past industrial relations traditions and bring about a change in organizational culture more conducive to the competitive circumstances of the industry. The programme resulted in more voluntary redundancies together with changes in working practices. Those who remained received £2000 for accepting the new agreement and in addition an employee share ownership scheme was introduced and a worker director elected to the board of Timex UK. A saving scheme and a profit-sharing scheme were also proposed. Meanwhile two of Timex's three factories in the city had been closed and demolished by 1991. Production was now concentrated in one part of its original factory and by 1992 less than 500 workers remained. The former senior HR manager saw the US management team in particular as extremely committed to make the *Fresh Start* effective.

> They had a belief, as Americans do, in their ability to make things work . . .

However, it appears that the local management team were much less convinced of the new HRM approach. The response of the unions was:

> . . . to say thanks very much, accept the money up front, and to go about their business as they had done for many years. The Americans couldn't really understand why the unions in particular didn't see it their way. . . whereas some of the local managers couldn't believe why they (the Americans) were so naive.

Thus, both 'hard' and 'soft' variants of HRM practice can be detected (Storey, 1992) as can attempts to move away from a traditional 'personnel and IR' approach to a more sophisticated HRM approach (Guest, 1987). However, the success of these changes was never marked given the scepticism of the local managers and a union presence that ensured the continued existence of an overtly adversarial relationship between the two sides.

By 1993, although it had seen massive reductions in its workforce, Timex had become one of the 'big six' CEMs in the UK. The company had invested heavily in new manufacturing plant and many managers were confident of future success. However, the cost of restructuring and the change programme had contributed to the accumulated losses of 10 million since 1987, which was to prove a deciding factor in subsequent events.

### The Strike and Closure in 1993

The final phase began in June 1991 when the company recruited Peter Hall to manage the Dundee plant and to turn the factory around given its dismal financial record in recent years. Many seemed to agree that it was make or break time for the Dundee factory. Speaking on BBC radio, Timex's employee director commented after the closure,

> When Peter Hall was hired to take over as the manager in Dundee it was made clear to the local trade union officials and to everyone in the plant that Peter Hall was the last throw of the dice.

His initial actions seemed to be approved by the management team. As one senior manager put it:

> Hall came in with lots of good ideas on how to run a company of this size . . . he seemed to know what he was doing and saved us quite a bit of money in the short term by replacing an expensive mainframe computer system with networked PCs and by cutting out a lot of unnecessary overtime.

He was also renowned for his highly personal style of management.

> To a woman at Timex, Mr Hall at first seemed rather charming, with his blow dried hair, quick eyes and pep talks in the canteen. On Valentine's Day last year, he handed out sweeties to the women . . . (*Independent on Sunday*, 1993.)

To his trade union counterparts, however, he appeared very different:

> He came in with a very aggressive style in discussions. The man had no industrial relations background and had very fixed views. Management should dictate and any concessions made by the union were immediately seen as weaknesses by Hall. This was a great misreading of the signals. (Senior shop steward.)

The trigger for the dispute that eventually led to the closure began late in 1992 when major problems arose over the IBM delivery schedule that resulted in a need for a severe production cutback in the first half of 1993. Hall developed a plan for cutting costs in the Dundee plant in conjunction with his management team and also with advice from two US-based vice-presidents of Timex. It was this plan and in particular the approach to HRM that it implied which was at the centre of the dispute and later closure of the Timex factory.

Time and space preclude the detailed discussion of the dispute as it emerged during 1992–1993 and these are described elsewhere (Dowling and Martin, 1994). Briefly, the 'storyline' is as follows. The management side sought a four-point lay-off and wage reduction scheme that the workers, after initially rejecting and striking, agreed to accept 'under protest'. Peter Hall argued that this grudging commitment was not good enough if the company was to be competitive in the future and sacked 340 workers. They were replaced in a few days with new, non-union employees who were 'bussed' in from outlying districts, a tactic that provoked extreme anger from the sacked employees and their union officials. Mass picketing resulted that became a nightly feature on local and national television channels and went on for nearly 4 months. Management's handling of the dispute and their use of the law led to questions asked in Parliament and an appearance by Peter Hall in front of a parliamentary select committee. Later secret meetings were held and a peace plan was proposed by the management involving a 27% cut in benefits. The national union officials put this to the workers who overwhelmingly rejected it. Shortly after Peter Hall suddenly resigned and in a 'shock' decision the US management announced the plant would be closed within 6 months. Despite numerous appeals the US management team would not reconsider their decision.

### The lead up to and aftermath of closure

Prior to the decision to close, and whilst the plant was literally besieged in late May of 1993, Fred Olsen, the owner of Timex, visited Dundee and indicated his personal wish that the plant remain open. Many believe that it was his personal intervention in 1983, following the demise of mechanical watch production, that saved the Dundee factory. Speaking on local BBC radio Olsen declared:

> You must understand that we have kept this place going. And you might say we had no reason to because after the mechanical watch went out and we went to electronic watches the whole artistry of making watches changed. Some of you remember we had the Sinclair computers, we had the 3D camera, we did everything we could to put something in to keep it going because we had a history of being here since 1946 and we failed in many of them. Now we seem to have built up a niche making these boards for other people. But it takes a lot of effort.

In the middle of June 1993 it seemed that a breakthrough had come with the sudden announcement of Peter Hall's resignation 'for private reasons'. More talks were planned but by now Timex was interested only in offering the strikers a financial inducement in order to facilitate an orderly rundown of the plant. This was rejected by the union and on 15 June 1993 Timex announced it was to close its operations in Dundee before the end of the year (which was earlier than planned). Two months later on 19 August 1993, the factory closed. Announcing the decision, Mohammed Saleh, Timex vice-president for human resources, said:

> Well I feel personally very bad, I feel sad . . . on a personal level I've been involved with Dundee for 20 years. I've been with this company that long. I wanted it to remain open. I did everything—I'm not the only one who wants it to remain open. We did everything we could and from a personal standpoint I'm very unhappy about it, I'm sad about it but I really feel I and my colleagues did everything we could. I pleaded personally sometimes with the union to consider the situation and tried every creative ways (sic) to find a solution, every creative way, just as much as we tried creative ways when we introduced the Fresh Start. But in spite of all this effort I'm afraid we couldn't make it a go. (BBC local radio.)

The union announced the dispute would continue and the strikers continued with their attempt at a consumer boycott of Timex products. Applications for unfair dismissal to an industrial tribunal had been lodged by all the sacked workers and these would be carried through with, it was said. However, by mid-October 1993, Timex offered all strikers a cash settlement if the boycott and industrial tribunal applications were withdrawn and the strike fund (some £180,000) disposed of in a way not likely to harm Timex. This was agreed by the strikers and the dispute declared officially over.

Inevitably claim and counter-claim were soon being exchanged as an attempt was made to try to explain the reasons for closure. Some blamed the intransigence of the unions or the management or both and maintained that a settlement could have been negotiated given goodwill from all sides. Managerial tactics over the way that the issue was handled from the outset came in for severe criticism in some areas of the mass media. The personalities and styles of Peter Hall and John Kydd Jnr (the union convenor at the plant) were said to clash so much that the dispute was almost inevitable from the start. Perspectives differ and inevitably explanations will too. However, two quotes are illustrative. Asked why he thought closure had occurred, Mohammed Saleh replied:

> I would say certainly this dispute aggravated it. I think the fact that the sub-contract manufacturing is a competitive thing and I think the fact that the cost base in Dundee is very high which you could say created that dispute in a way or in a big way. So it is in the competitive nature of the business and the individual dispute contributed to the closure. (BBC radio news.)

In answering the same question, Bill Spiers, assistant general secretary of the Scottish Trades Union Congress argued:

> It does look at some stage the company thought that they could get by with the, as they call it, replacement labour, I would call it a scab workforce, that they thought they could get by with it, they weren't serious about negotiating and by the time they realized that the workforce they'd recruited didn't have the skills to maintain the quality of service that you have to maintain in the electronics industry these days it was really too late. . . . I think really the responsibility does lie with management. It was the same people they were dealing with that they'd always dealt with before and there was no reason why they couldn't have come to an agreement that could have got them through what we hope is a short-term downturn in the electronics market. What the company seem to have done is when they brought in Mr Hall from the south is to have misjudged the situation and I think it's a classic example of bad management misjudgement that has led to tears all round. (BBC local radio.)

## ACCOUNTING FOR THE FAILURE OF STRATEGIC CHANGE AND ITS LESSONS FOR HRM

The Timex dispute can be seen as part of an attempted organizational transition that, from the point of view of the many workers and managers involved, the local community, national trade union officials and many outside commentators, went horribly wrong. Many months after the closure, former friends and colleagues who ended up on different sides of the picketline still show visible hatred for one another in the streets of Dundee. As is the case in all disputes, how one explains the causes depends to a large extent on where one stands. Perhaps fuelled by the press and the desire of people to attribute causes to individuals rather than situations, the links between circumstances and outcomes have become highly personalized—in this case, a search for 'villains'. From the point of view of the sacked workers the blame is usually attributed to an intransigent management, led by one of the *cause célèbres* of the dispute, Peter Hall. Managers, on the other hand, may blame the intransigence of local union lay officials, who either failed to grasp the 'facts of life' or were willing to sacrifice jobs in the interests of maintaining union principles and influence. Such explanations have tended to focus on the immediate events surrounding the conflict, rarely transcending beyond poor communications, personality clashes and self-interest. The result has been a failure to take into account, except in a cursory fashion, the wider context that relates the present to the past or to situate the conflict in the emergent and interrelated nature of business decisions and HR practices.

In a somewhat similar fashion, many of the popular explanations of successful and unsuccessful organizational change have usually emphasized the role played by managers or transformational leaders in taking action or failing to take action that has a deliberate and immediate impact on their organizations. Examples include success stories such as the well-documented (in the UK context) cases of Nissan and British Airways and the 'excellent' companies in the US (Wickens, 1987; Young, 1989; Kanter, 1984, 1989; Pascale, 1994). These accounts are characterized by what Wilson (1992) sees as 'planned' models of organizational transition, the features of which are their acontextual and ahistorical approach to analysis and their reliance on relatively simplistic prescriptions concerning the content and process of change. More sophisticated attempts to analyse both successful and less successful organizational change fall into the 'emergent' perspective that emphasizes the importance of understanding context, content and process (Wilson, 1992). Good examples of this more recent and more scholarly tradition can be found in the works of Pettigrew and Whipp (1991), Pettigrew et al (1992) and Leavy and Wilson (1994).

From the perspective of strategic change and HRM, the failure of Timex can be analysed in two stages. The first of these concerns the 'content' of the 'incrementalist' strategy that Timex management adopted as a response to the decline of watch manufacturing in Dundee. The focus here concerns the relationship between the emergence of a strategy, corporate and plant culture and HRM and the lack of consensus over the organizational 'career' of the Timex plant throughout the 1980s and early 1990s. Incrementalism here is not used in the logical sense described by Quinn (1980), as that would probably overstate the planned and rational aspects of the strategy and underplay the emergent and reactive character of what happened at Timex (Mintzberg, 1994). Indeed, it is part of the argument of this chapter that 'reactor' strategy-structure configuration more closely matches the situation as it emerged (Miles and Snow, 1978). Events at Timex over the 1980s depict an organization that responded inappropriately to environmental challenges, performed poorly and as a result was unable to commit itself aggressively to a specific strategy for the future.

The second stage focuses on the failure to manage the 'process' of culture change, most notably in the area of HRM, once the company and the Dundee plant in particular had become locked into the incrementalist or 'first-order' change strategy (Bate, 1994). The latter of these two levels of analysis has been the focus of much of the comment and interest in the Timex dispute because of the media interest. However, it is with the former that some of the most important lessons might be learned.

## 'Incrementalism', Culture and Strategic Leadership

We have suggested that the foregoing description of Timex's (Dundee's) attempts to manage strategic change from the 1970s onwards was, at best, incrementalist and, at worst, reactive (Johnson, 1988; Miles and Snow, 1978). A combination of contextual factors, both internal and external, resulted in a perceived need to change and the form that change should take—at least in the eyes of management. International competition and technological developments in both watch manufacturing and electronics coupled with the cost advantages of manufacturing in the Far East and southern Europe provided the external context. The salient features of the internal context were the organizational characteristics accompanying Timex's global strategy—a high degree of centralized decision making and knowledge retention at the centre with subsidiaries largely implementing parent company strategies (Bartlett and Ghoshal, 1989). This resulted in a strong manufacturing culture and lack of a design and business development capability at the Dundee plant. Thus the move into subcontracting in the contract electronics market, inevitably accompanied by a cost reduction strategy, was conceived as the only way forward for the Dundee 'problem'. However, as explained by an ex-senior manager, success in the electronics industry required a move from 'cost centre to profit centre mentality' that proved too difficult to bridge. In particular the lack of focus on external assessment of the business environment was seen as a major reason for subsequent failure (Pettigrew and Whipp, 1991).

In explaining how this came about it is fruitful to consider some of the politics of change, the role of strategic leadership and the notion of organizational careers in helping explain this development (Bate, 1994; Dawson, 1994; Leavy and Wilson, 1994). It is clear that senior Timex management in the US and, to a lesser degree, the Dundee management team shared a definition of the relationship between context and strategy. Key aspects of the context—the international trading environment and the need to diversify relatedly by building on their manufacturing capabilities—were collectively selected, anticipated and felt to be important in shaping strategy. There is also evidence that the influence of the context was internalized by Dundee management which, in turn, was manifested in the value it placed on manufacturing and the need to stick with what the company was good at. Both groups of managers came to see that the only way forward was to enter the contract electronics market and pursue market share through a series of redundancies and efficiency exercises. The alternative, more radical second-order strategy of new product development was never seriously considered, partly it seems because of the failure of Timex to succeed in the US with such a strategy and also because of the absence of a solid design, development and marketing tradition in Dundee. As late as 1987 when the US management met with senior officials of Tayside region to discuss the problems in Dundee, the stated intention of the US and UK management teams was to concentrate on subcontracting and once they had a 'firm core business' only then would they look at new product development. Thus it appears that Timex headquarters in the US were reluctant to commit the necessary resources to fund a new product development strategy given (a) their global strategy of integrating forwards into retailing and the rationalization of their worldwide manufacturing capacity, and (b) the history of plant losses, past IR problems and the operational and HRM consequences of pursuing 'radical surgery'.

By 1987, electronics was no longer part of Timex's core business on an international scale according to one ex-senior manager. In this context it is likely that the Dundee plant came to be seen by some of the US-based managers as a 'side-show' which, in turn, was likely to contain strong elements of a self-fulfilling prophecy. Such an interpretive view of the relationship between strategy formulation and implementation is central to the notion of organizational or cultural careers (Bate, 1994; Leavy and Wilson, 1994). This concept emphasizes the subjective and voluntarist ways in which organizational strategies are patterned over time in contrast to the determinist life cycle perspective that implies an inevitability and linearity about strategic change. Thus, it is evident that the US management team increasingly came to see the Dundee plant as 'deadwood', terminology associated with some of the cruder career theory literature and a definition of the situation that many of the Scottish managers came to accept. For example, it has often been put to the authors that the Dundee plant should have been closed in the early 1980s when watch manufacturing ceased in the plant. This, according to one ex-personnel officer, would have been akin to performing an act of euthanasia for a terminally ill patient, a metaphor probably shared by some of the US-based managers whose views came to dominate at the end. As a result of such shared definitions of the 'career' history of the Scottish plant, the funding relationship between the US headquarters and the Dundee plant and the patterns of action that subsequently emerged served to produce a situation that many predicted.

The fact of the Dundee plant's continued existence throughout the 1980s would appear to owe a great deal to Olsen's vision of electronics as a key feature in Timex's strategic development and a 'sentimental' attachment to maintaining a presence in Dundee. These 'visionary' and sentimental ideas were evident in many of his speeches and, according to the ex-vice president of Timex in Dundee, one of the most important reasons of Timex's continued presence in Dundee. Olsen's desires and belief in the eventual success of electronics and Timex (Dundee) seemed to predominate over the wishes of some of the more 'hard-nosed' US-based management team. When Timex first established themselves in Dundee, Olsen's father had reportedly given a commitment to maintaining a presence in the city, a position that Fred Olsen, the son, continued to hold until 1993. As already explained, this commitment to Dundee was also fervently supported by the Dundee-based vice-president, Graham Thompson.

The role of strategic leaders and their sentiments in shaping strategy is well documented and are amongst the key influencing factors in the strategic predispositions of MNCs (Chakravarthy and Perlmutter, 1990). Strategic predispositions refer to factors such as the length of association of the MNC with the host country subsidiaries and the leadership style and values of the CEO. Chakravarthy and Perlmutter (1990, p. 77) describe four such predispositions, two of which are relevant here:

> Ethnocentrism—where all strategic decisions are guided by the values and interests of the parent. Such a firm is predominantly concerned with its viability world-wide and legitimacy only in its home country.
> Polycentrism—where strategic decisions are tailored to suit the cultures of various countries in which the MNC competes. A polycentric multinational is primarily concerned with legitimacy in every country that it operates in, even if that means some loss of profits.

Thus although the relationship between the Timex corporation and its Dundee subsidiary was ethnocentric in nature it is evident that the strategic predisposition of at least some of the headquarters management team—Olsen in particular and also Saleh, the US-based HR director—is better described as polycentric. This line of argument has two implications.

The first is that the closure of the Dundee plant became the local culmination of a gradually emerging position, shaped by the interests, politics and sentiments of different management and union groupings within Timex, rather than any deliberate strategy to close the plant down (Mintzberg, 1992). From the perspective of the Timex headquarters management, the 'hard' decision to close the plant in 1983 was avoided, partly for reasons of 'legitimacy' and sentimentality in and towards the host country and partly as a consequence in the beliefs held by Olsen of the importance of electonics to Timex's international future. The sequence of events in the dispute, however, suggests the Timex headquarters management team were given an opportunity and justification to realize an important aspect of their global, rationalization strategy that had been emerging for 10 years. The stumbling blocks to achieving the 'rational' decision would appear to have been Olsen and some of his US and UK managers who had maintained an association with Dundee over a long period of time. However, the local management teams, the unions and the workforce were both forced to manage and chose to manage the incrementalist strategy in such a way that effectively took the 'hard' decision for Olsen and his colleagues. Such an interpretation is evidenced by Olsen's comments during a television interview after the dispute when he stated he now regretted having kept the plant open so long. When asked why he did, his reply was 'for old time's sake'. The second implication concerns the lessons for host country managements and their workforces. As Doz (1990) and Goss et al (1993) point out the usual response to crises is to follow an incrementalist strategy that extrapolates from the past. Associated with this are programmes of rationalization, cost reduction and the application of current management techniques—in this case, union derecognition—that appear to offer a panacea to organizational problems. Although with the benefit of hindsight, it is reasonable to suggest that the local management, in conjunction with its workforce, could have been more adventurous in the 1980s in attempting a more radical 'transformation' through the development of a new product strategy for the Dundee plant. Kotter and Heskett (1992), Goss et al (1993) and Bate (1994) argue that such radical or second-order changes require managers and employees to 'unlearn the lessons of past successes', free themselves from their cultural constraints and 'manage from the future' instead of 'managing from the past'.

The role for strategic leaders (in this case, at local level) is critical in setting out a vision of the future and how a company should be organized and function (Brandes and Brege, 1993). These prescriptions, though frequently criticized for their simplistic solutions and lack of grounding in context and history, have gained some impressive support from the evidence on successful turnaround strategies. In the local context, the comparisons and contrasts with another major US-based MNC in a plant in Dundee, NCR (now part of AT and T), are instructive here. As with Timex and its watch production in the early 1980s, the NCR plant in Dundee was facing the rundown of its historically important product, the electromechanical cash register. Both companies had a very similar history in Dundee, drawing from the same labour force and operating with the same unions. However, NCR secured from their US parent group the right to develop one of the first automated telling machines (the ATM), after much political in-fighting. As a consequence of this and a far-sighted HRM strategy based upon job security and heavy investment in training and development, it has subsequently gone on to become a world leader in the design and manufacture of the ATMs, now controlling from its Scottish headquarters some of the US plants that were once its masters or competitors for internal funding.

## Strategic Change and HRM

The second stage of analysis focuses on the failure to manage the largely 'incrementalist' strategy. Based on the evidence presented so far, our belief is that the move into subcontracting was a reactive measure in part undertaken for sentimental and the highly individualistic beliefs in the power of electronic developments rather than rational business reasons. Without the necessary injection of investment to develop new product capability and the business skills to support an independent operating company strategy, it is unlikely that the 'fire-fighting' culture, volatile demand cycles and highly competitive nature of electronics subcontracting, especially when set against the high cost structure of the Dundee plant, were ever going to generate sufficient internal funding, the management skills or time to realize a move away from subcontracting. In short, Timex in Dundee during the early 1980s created an organizational history, combining a particular asset configuration and administrative heritage that would severely contain future options (Bartlett and Ghoshal, 1989). Nevertheless, given the commitment of Olsen and his management colleagues to keeping the Dundee plant operating, albeit at a much lower level of activity, some questions have to be asked about the strategies and tactics pursued by the local management, unions and work-force(s) in taking advantage of the situation.

The literature on 'successful' strategic change and HRM (e.g. Beer et al, 1985; Schure and Jackson, 1987; Pettigrew and Whipp, 1991) points to a managerial failure to apply a coherent and integrated approach to the implementation of its chosen business strategy, both in relation to the traditions and characteristics of its workforce and the HRM policies eventually pursued in the 1990s. The situation at Timex closely mirrored what Sisson (1994, p. 41) argues is the reality of employment relations in Britain rather than the rhetoric of the transformation to human resource management:

> Rather it appears to be taking the form of substitution of individualism for collectivism, a reduction in standards and an assertion of managerial freedom from constraints.

It is clear that from the workforce's point of view both the content and intended process of management's strategy meant a stand had to be taken and resistance shown to the developments to which Sisson refers. Many of the workers and their union representatives had been at Timex for upwards of 20 years and had witnessed the transition from a male, craft-dominated skills base and strong union culture to a largely female, semiskilled and less aggressive and less powerful union stance. Gradually, a new accommodation with manage-ment had been evolved over the 1980s and 1990s. The end of the pre-1980s 'indulgency pattern' was recognized and the dilution of the power base of the union was recorded through the various changes in employment practice secured by management during the 1980s as the reality of the needs of a contracting strategy emerged. Management's success in bringing about a more compliant workforce was abruptly halted with the 1992/1993 proposals from

Hall which the union clearly felt went too far particularly when after a 4-month strike the price of a settlement came to be on terms worse than those which had initially provoked the dispute.

Given these positions and perspectives it is not surprising that the methods of conflict resolution adopted proved to be spectacularly ineffective. Amid acrimonious claim and counter-claim each side accused the other of failing to engage in 'honest negotiation'—in other words an acceptance of the premise of 'our side', which clearly neither side was prepared to do. Hence the reversion by the management side to a 'coercive' approach and the recruitment of a substitute workforce and the attempt by the union to seize the 'moral highground' and to force management to adopt a 'more reasonable' stance.

Another explanation rests in the often misplaced faith of managers in cultural change which results from the problems often inherent in such programmes. Bate (1994) and Legge (1994) outline four ways in which organizations in the past have attempted to introduce cultural change in organizations: (i) 'empiricist-rational' strategies where managers attempt to teach workers the 'facts of life' and where workers are expected to accept these in self-interested terms; (ii) 'normative re-education', where managers work on group norms and culture to engender behavioural and attitudinal change; (iii) 'power strategies' where managers attempt to bring about behavioural change through threats and sanctions; and (iv) conciliative strategies where managers look for win–win outcomes and stress collaboration. In turn, these strategies usually translate into different types of change programmes: re-education, replacement of old and selection of new workers, reorganization of structures, appraisal and reward systems, and productivity bargaining.

Timex in Dundee pursued all four strategies and their associated programmes throughout the 1980s and 1990s—from the 'empiricist-rational' approaches connected with the redundancies of the early 1980s, through 'normative re-education' and productivity bargaining associated with *Fresh Start*, to the 'power-coercive' methods during the last months of the factory's existence. Clearly, none of these succeeded in bringing about positive fundamental change which may, in turn, be explained by the paradoxical nature of culture change management (Anthony, 1993; Legge, 1994). Firstly, as is often the case in culture change programmes, the attempt to secure a new set of values, in this case through *Fresh Start*, is often met by a cynical and resigned behavioural compliance (Hopfl, 1993). Paradoxically, this surface acceptance is frequently treated by management as evidence of success and leads to a desire by managers to push such programmes further and faster with ever diminishing effects. Secondly, as Smircich (1983) argues, organizations 'are cultures' rather than to be treated as 'having cultures' (i.e. something additional to the organization and thus subject to easy manipulation). From this perspective, to expect successful cultural change to result from insights by either 'insiders' (in this case, managers) who are part of that culture (and trapped in their own 'psychic prison') or 'outsiders' (in this case, Peter Hall and some of the US management team) who are unable to sensitize themselves to the deeply held values is to fail to understand the very nature of culture. Thirdly, a related but additional problem with culture change programmes is that they are usually associated with attempts to impose the instrumental values of a small group of leaders on cultures which are sometimes more widely shared and morally based. The responses of the remaining Timex workers and some of their local union officials, which was to see the factory closed down and to regard that as a limited form of success rather than to accept the changes imposed by management, is dramatic evidence of this aspect of culture change.

Thus it can be argued that the failure of Timex was, in part at least, a failure by Peter Hall and the US management team to understand the fundamental nature of organizational cultural change, which rests upon gaining insights into the historical development, the context and the deeply held values, beliefs and ambitions of all participants. Strong evidence of this lack of understanding is cited by one senior ex-manager who had been close to the American team. He pointed to the incredulity of the US managers concerning the oppositional stance taken to the end by the workers and their representatives. Hall and the US management team remained convinced of the virtues of their own position throughout and, at the same time, gradually became more and more convinced that they could never do deals with the 'irrational' Timex workers (nor national union officials who could not get the workers to see 'sense'). This was the 'straw that broke the camel's back' and likely reason why Olsen and the US management team took the 'snap' decision to close the plant.

## CONCLUSIONS

We have attempted to document the history of the Timex Corporation in Dundee over a 50-year period and answer questions as to why it failed to bring about strategic change. Our analysis is rooted in the global strategy and accompanying organizational configuration pursued by Timex world-wide. The Dundee plant did not appear to fit with the rationalization programme or the corporation's move into downstream activities; nor does it seem that the US headquarters were sufficiently able to will the means as well as the ends of a move to a more multinational strategy, based on the existence of independent operating companies that were able to take advantage of local market circumstances. Instead, the signs point to a reactive posture largely adopted for sentimental and legitimacy reasons. In one sense the failure to manage this position during the 1980s and 1990s is irrelevant since future options were bound to be constrained. The lessons that can be drawn from this case seem to accord with the recent work of Bartlett et al (1990) and Hendry (1994) in arguing that the growth of international firms is dependent on them being able to adopt more fluid organizational structures and 'leveraging core competencies' into national markets. The HRM implications of this are the need for firms to pay more attention to the training and development of managers for international assignments, an increasingly diverse and dispersed management cadre and a broader effort to internationalize the organization at large (Hendry, 1994).

Turning to the failure of the management team to take advantage of Olsen's commitment to keep a presence in Dundee, one is left with the inescapable conclusion that the failure to 'read the situation' by both the US management team and Peter Hall (i.e. the factory culture and likely opposition to a unitary HRM strategy) shows a remarkable lack of understanding of the nature of organizational culture and the impact of HRM techniques in securing cultural changes. The lessons here for managers operating in multinational environments are that the successful transformation towards truly transnational organizations is heavily dependent on the ability of managers to understand and work within the host country cultures and learn from each other. As Mead (1994, p. xvi) argues:

> Today's managers cannot afford to ignore the evidence of difference. Cultural differences are real and how they are expressed can vitally affect the workplace. . . . Mistakes in understanding the other person's culture can be expensive and even life threatening.

## REFERENCES

Anthony, P. (1993). *Managing Culture*, Open University Press.

Bartlett, C. A., Doz, Y. and Hedlund, G. (eds) (1990). *Managing the Global Firm*, Routledge.

Bartlett, C. A. and Ghoshal, S. (1989). *Managing Across Borders: The Transnational Solution*, Hutchinson.

Bate, P. (1954). *Strategies for Cultural Change*, Butterworth-Heinemann; Oxford.

Beer, M. et al (1985). *Human Resource Management: A General Manager's Perspective*, Free Press.

Brandes, O. and Brege, S. (1993). Strategic turnaround and top management involvement: the case of ASEA and ABBE. In: Chakravarthy, B., Lorange, P., Roos, J. and Van de Ven, A., *Implementing Strategic Processes: Change, Learning and Co-operation*, Blackwell.

*Business Week* (1993). 12 July.

Chakravarthy, B. S. and Perlumutter, H. V. (1990). Strategic planning for a global business. In: Vernon-Wortzel, and Wortzel, L. *Global Strategic Management: The Essentials* (2nd ed.) Wiley.

Dawson, P. (1994). *Organizational Change: A Processual Approach*, Paul Chapman Publishing.

Dowling, M. J. and Martin, G. (1994). When the tough get going what price HRM? Lessons from Timex. Paper presented to the Fifth International Conference on Strategic HRM, St Gallen, Switzerland, March.

Doz, Y. L. (1990). Managing manufacturing rationalization. In: Vernon-Wortzel and L. H. Wortzel, *Global Strategic Management: The Essentials* (2nd ed.) Wiley.

*Financial Times* (1993). 16 March.

Gilbert, X. and Strebel, P. (1992). Developing competitive advantage. In: H. Mintzberg and J. B. Quinn (eds), *The Strategy Process*, Prentice Hall.

Gospel, H. (1983). Management strategies and structures: an introduction. In: H. Gospel and C. Littler (eds), *Managerial Strategies and Industrial Relations*, Heinemann.

Goss, T., Pascale, R. and Athos, A. (1993). The reinvention of the roller coaster: risking the present for a powerful future, *Harvard Business Review*, November–December.

Gouldner, A. (1954). *Patterns of Industrial Bureaucracy*, Free Press.

Guest, D. (1987). Human resource management and industrial relations, *Journal of Management Studies*, **24**.

Guest, D. (1989). Human resource management: its implications for industrial relations and trade unions. In: J. Storey (ed.), *New Perspectives in Human Resource Management*, Routledge.

Harrison, A. (1994). Just-in-time manufacturing. In: J. Storey (ed.), *New Wave Manufacturing Strategies*, Paul Chapman Publishing.

Hendry, C. (1994). *Human Resource Strategies for International Growth*, Routledge.

*Independent on Sunday* (1993). 28 March.

Johnson, G. (1987). *Strategic Change and the Management Process*, Blackwell.

Johnson, G. and Scholes, K. (1993). *Exploring Corporate Strategy: Text and Cases* (3rd ed.) Prentice Hall.

Kanter, R. M. (1983). *The Change Masters*, Simon and Schuster.

Kanter, R. M. (1990). *When Giants Learn to Dance: Mastering the Challenges of Strategy, Management and Careers in the 1990s*, Unwin Hyman.

Kotter, J. P. and Heskett, J. (1992). *Corporate Culture and Performance*, Free Press.

Leavy, B. and Wilson, D. (1994). *Strategy and Leadership*, Routledge.

Legge, K. (1994). Managing culture: fact or fiction. In: K. Sisson (ed.), *Personnel Management* (2nd ed.) Blackwell.

Mead, R. (1994). *International Management: Cross Cultural Dimensions*, Blackwell.

Miles, R. E. and Snow, C. C. (1978). *Organizational Strategy, Structure and Process*, McGraw-Hill.

Miller, K and Woolfson, C. (1994). Timex: industrial relations and the use of the Law, *Industrial Law Journal* (in press).

Mintzberg, H. (1992). Crafting strategy. In: H. Mintzberg and J. B. Quinn (eds), *The Strategy Process*, Prentice Hall.

Mintzberg, H. (1994). *The Rise and Fall of Strategic Planning*, Prentice Hall.

Pettigrew, A., Ferlie, E. and McKie, L. (1992). *Shaping Strategic Change*, Sage.

Pettigrew, A. and Whipp, R. (1991). *Managing Change for Competitive Success*, Blackwell.

Purcell, J. and Sisson, K. (1983). Strategies and practice in the management of industrial relations. In: G. Bain (ed.), *Industrial Relations in Britain*, Blackwell.

Quinn, J. B. (1980). *Strategies for Change—Logical Incrementalism*, Irwin.

Rue, L. W. and Holland, P. G. (1986). *Strategic Management*, McGraw Hill, New York.

Schuler, R. and Jackson, S. (1987). Linking competitive strategies with human resource management practices, *Academy of Management Executive*, **1**, August.

*Scotland on Sunday* (1993). 30 May.

Sisson, K. (1993). In search of HRM, *British Journal of Industrial Relations*, **31**, (2), June.

Sisson, K. (ed.) (1994). *Personnel Management* (2nd ed.) Blackwell.

Storey, J. (1992). *Developments in the Management of Human Resources*, Blackwell.

Storey, J. (ed.) (1994). *New Wave Manufacturing Strategies*, Paul Chapman Publishing.

Wickens, P. (1987). *The Road to Nissan: Flexibility, Quality and Teamwork*, Macmillan.

Williamson, O. (1975). *Markets and Hierarchies*, Free Press.

Wilson, D. A. (1992). *A Strategy of Change*, Routledge.

Young, D. (1989). British Airways: putting the customer first. Ashridge Management Centre, July.

# 4

# THE MANAGERIAL DIMENSION OF SMALL BUSINESS FAILURE

**Peter L. Jennings**

*Sheffield Business School*

**Graham Beaver**

*Nottingham Business School*

- The majority of existing studies of small business failure tend to focus upon either the symptoms arising from problems within the firm or upon the reasons cited for failure. Comparatively little analysis of the root cause has been undertaken.
- Failure and success are usually defined in rational terms which ignore stakeholder aspirations.
- Many owner-managers pursue personal objectives which inhibit the probability of success if measured using these rational criteria.
- The root cause of small business failure is almost invariably a lack of management attention to strategic issues.
- Notwithstanding the fact that common skills and abilities are required, the management process in small firms is unique and cannot be considered to be the same as professional management in larger firms practised on a reduced scale.
- The multiplicity of roles expected of the owner-manager often causes dissonance which enhances the probability of poor decision-making and inappropriate action.

*The Implementation Challenge*, Edited by D. E. Hussey
© 1996 John Wiley & Sons Ltd

- Successful small firms practise strategic management either consciously and visibly or unconsciously and invisibly.

## INTRODUCTION

The 1971 Bolton report explicitly highlighted the

fervently guarded sense of independence

which is seen to be a prime motivator for many small business owner-managers. Contrary to popular belief, and a great deal of economic theory, money and the pursuit of a personal financial fortune are *not* as significant as the desire for personal involvement, responsibility and the independent quality and style of life which many small business owner-managers strive to achieve. Consequently, the attainment of these objectives becomes one of the principal criteria for success, as defined by the entrepreneur/owner-manager. However, the pursuit of independence brings with it the power to influence events and the other stakeholders, surrounding and within the small business, who may be seeking to satisfy alternative aspirations. Whilst there can be little doubt that the power, capability and influence of the entrepreneur, which according to Chell et al (1991)

the rarely gifted individual exhibits

is of vital importance in determining the creation and development of the organization, the relentless drive for personal achievement may inhibit growth potential and, ultimately, may threaten the very survival of the small firm.

Researchers, such as Foley and Green (1989) who have studied small business failure and success, have attempted to provide a taxonomy of causal factors which are said to be the root cause. However, the majority of studies simply identify *symptoms* and fail to highlight *causes* when providing explanations within the context of 'rational management theory'. Equally, many surviving small businesses are seen, in terms of rational theory, to operate at sub-optimal levels of performance. The actual root cause of failure may be seen to lie with the apparently non-rational behaviour and decision-making of the entrepreneur and/or owner-manager who does not obey the 'rules' of classical management theory.

## MANAGEMENT IN THE SMALL FIRM

The management process in the small firm is unique. It bears little or no resemblance to management processes found in larger organizations, which have been the subject of substantial academic research resulting in numerous models, prescriptions and constructs (Jennings and Beaver, 1993; Beaver and Jennings, 1995).

In the larger organization, management is seen primarily as a *predictive* process concerned with the clarification of long-term objectives, the formulation of appropriate policies to meet such objectives and the feedback of information to indicate successful or unsuccessful achievement of predetermined goals (cf. Faulkner and Johnson, 1992). In contrast, management in the smaller firm is primarily an *adaptive* process concerned with manipulating a limited amount of resources, usually in order to gain the maximum immediate and short-term advantage. In the small firm efforts are concentrated not on predicting but on controlling the operating environment, adapting as quickly as possible to the changing demands of that environment and devising suitable tactics for mitigating the consequences of any changes which occur.

In the smaller enterprise, the management process is characterized by the highly personalized preferences, prejudices and attitudes of the firm's entrepreneur, owner and/or owner-manager. The nature of managerial activity expands or contracts with the characteristics of the person fulfilling the role(s). Such expansion or contraction is partly conditioned by the adaptive needs of the context in which the business operates, and is partly dependent upon the personality and needs of the owner, manager or entrepreneur. Consequently, the management process in the smaller enterprise cannot be viewed in isolation from the skills demanded of the three key roles (entrepreneur, owner and owner-manager) mentioned earlier. However, in the smallest firms all these roles may be enacted by one individual. It is only following a period of business development, leading to a certain quantity of growth and expansion, that each role may become enacted by separate individuals. Thus, *the small firm management process* cannot *be separated from the personality set and experience of the key role player or players.*

Another characteristic, of the small firm management process, is the closeness of the key role players to the operating personnel and activities being undertaken. This provides the key role players with extraordinary opportunity to influence these operatives and activities directly. However, relationships are often informal, with no precise definition of rights and obligations, duties and responsibilities. Appointments and promotions are often made on the basis of birth or personal friendship rather than on the basis of ability, education and/ or technical qualifications. Organization structures, in so far as they exist, are likely to develop around the interests and abilities of the key role players. Such organization structures are likely to be organic and loosely structured rather than mechanistic and highly formalized. Thus, *the management process in the small firm is seldom a readily visible process. It often has an abstract rather than concrete form.*

However, the key role players *must* fulfil a number of basic managerial functions, duties and roles if the organization is to survive and prosper. Logically, it follows that the lack of attention to these fundamental managerial activities and tasks will, at best, lead to sub-optimal performance and may even threaten the survival of the firm. These essential managerial activities have been defined and refined throughout a long history of management research.

Applying these principles specifically to the small firm management process discussed earlier, suggests that the key skills and abilities shown in Figure 4.1 need to be utilized.

The complexity of the small business situation dictates that all of these skills must be present in establishing and operating a successful organization, irrespective of the precise definition of success which is applied to a particular case. Specific operating circumstances will demand a unique blend of these skills whilst inherent dynamism will demand fluidity. Thus, the lone small business practitioner may be asked to enact any one of seven roles at any one time. These seven roles are:

1.   entrepreneur;
2.   owner;
3.   manager;
4.   entrepreneur-owner;
5.   entrepreneur-manager;

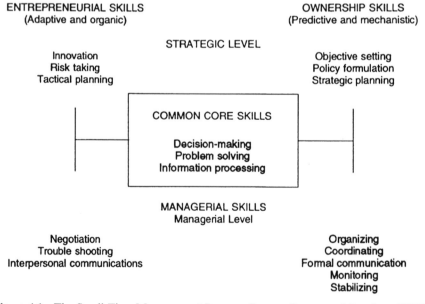

**Figure 4.1**   The Small Firm Management Process. Source: Beaver and Jennings (1995)

6.   owner-manager;
7.   entrepreneur-owner-manager.

In any given small business management situation these seven roles can be considered to be seven different stakeholders, each demanding the possession and application of specific skills and abilities. As Mitroff (1983) points out:

...different stakeholders do not generally share the same definition of an organisation's 'problems', and hence, do not in general share the same 'solutions'.

Each stakeholder approaches the organization's problems from a unique perspective and demands a unique solution. Traditional concepts of decision-making would emphasize the need to achieve consensus and agreement between alternative stakeholders in order to lead to effective outcomes. However, Mitroff (1983) goes on to argue that in fact individual human psyche or personality contains a

plurality of selves

—alternative and sometimes conflicting perceptions of self—which constitute stakeholders thus influencing behaviour. The small business practitioner is, therefore, subject to a number of competing and conflicting influences which may cause dissonance leading to erratic, unpredictable and unacceptable behaviour which is in complete contrast with the rational, professional and acceptable management behaviour portrayed by Mintzberg and others. Frequently, as Osborne (1991) points out, the power which accompanies majority ownership cannot be challenged by other stakeholders in the smaller enterprise situation and therefore the ability of the key role player(s) to cope with absolute power *and* leadership responsibility has a significant impact upon the survival and growth potential of the enterprise.

## ENTREPRENEURS AND SMALL FIRM OWNER-MANAGERS

Small business research frequently fails to distinguish explicitly between entrepreneurial behaviour and the behaviour of small business owner-managers. The fundamental questions, which have yet to be answered satisfactorily, are whether small firm owner-managers *are* entrepreneurs and whether there are specific characteristics which separate entrepreneurs from small business owner-managers. Furthermore, whilst very small businesses are likely to exhibit a congruence of ownership and management and, therefore, potentially entrepreneurship and owner-management, as the small firm grows there comes a point at which the owner *must* delegate management responsibilities to others if the organization is to survive and prosper. Ultimately, the seven roles (identified earlier) may be enacted by seven radically different individuals who, naturally, interpret the world in terms of their own mind set and cultural paradigm leading to differing interpretations of problems and solutions in their business situation. Therefore, a separation of ownership and management does occur in businesses which are still regarded as small firms and raises questions of the relationship between the three key roles in small business—the entrepreneur, the owner and the manager.

For example, Carland et al (1984) focus upon the essential factor of growth in distinguishing the small business venture from the entrepreneurial venture, and the 'small business owner' from the 'entrepreneur'. The *small business venture* is seen as any business that is independently owned and operated, not dominant in its field, and does not engage in any new marketing or innovative practices. An *entrepreneurial venture* is one that engages in at least one of Schumpeter's (1934) four categories of behaviour; that is, the principal goals of an entrepreneurial venture are profitability and growth and the business is characterized by innovative strategic practices. A *small business owner* is an individual who establishes and manages a business for the principal purpose of furthering personal goals. The business must be the primary source of income and will consume the majority of one's time and resources. The owner perceives the business as an extension of his or her personality, intricately bound with family needs and desires. An *entrepreneur* is an individual who establishes and manages a business for the principal purpose of profit and growth. The entrepreneur is characterized principally by innovative behaviour and will employ strategic management practices in the business.

An alternative but complementary view is provided by Stanworth and Curran (1976) who distinguish three types of small business activist:

- the *artisan* who seeks intrinsic satisfaction from business activity;
- the *manager* who seeks recognition for managerial excellence in business;
- the *'classic entrepreneur'* who seeks to maximize profits.

Dunkleberg and Cooper (1982) differentiate on the basis of motivation and distinguish between the growth-orientated, the independence-orientated and the craftsman-orientated small business owner.

Birley (1989) comments upon the motivation to become an entrepreneur. Several factors denote a challenging of accepted routine, e.g. the 'eureka syndrome', the 'if only syndrome', the 'misfit syndrome' and the 'moonlighter syndrome'. The accepted routine may involve employment in a large, medium or small organization or, indeed, activity as a small business owner-manager. Birley, therefore, shows that entrepreneurial behaviour can be distinguished from small business owner-manager behaviour by dissatisfaction with the current environment triggering specific actions to modify accepted practices.

The creation of a small business, therefore, does *not* require entrepreneurial activity as an essential prerequisite. The artisan who drifts into small business ownership, perhaps on the basis of the 'unfriendly push' syndrome or the 'no alternative' syndrome, may have absolutely no intention or desire to maximize profits and growth through risk taking strategic management. Equally, entrepreneurial behaviour is *not* limited to the creation of new, small businesses. A manager in an established business, irrespective of size, may, at times, engage in innovative strategic behaviour designed to challenge established routines and to maximize profits and growth. Therefore, *the longer term outcome, in terms of success or failure of a specific small firm, may be strongly influenced by the personalities, expectations and abilities of the founders and their fundamental motivation in establishing the enterprise.*

## DEFINING SUCCESS AND FAILURE

Existing studies commonly define success in narrow, accountancy terms using criteria based upon financial analyses and ratios such as sales growth, profitability, cash flow and productivity. More crudely still, quantitative measures such as job creation are frequently regarded as primary evidence of success especially by the small business support infrastructure. Further traditional analyses assert that the assessment of success for small business ventures, solely embraces explanations, reasons and motivations of why people start their ventures, what problems business ownership overcomes and generates for the owner(s) and specifically what the firm owner(s) actually wish to achieve for themselves (cf. Chaganti and Chaganti, 1983; Hornaday and Wheatley, 1986; Storey et al 1987; Thorpe, 1989; Kelmar, 1990).

Equally, the analysis of small business failure is founded upon similar, narrow criteria and always regards failure as *not* occurring until the business has ceased trading whether voluntarily or through enforced receivership and liquidation (Foley and Green, 1989; Jennings and Beaver, 1993).

However, the attribution of success and/or failure to small firms is complex, dynamic and problematic. This chapter departs from the narrow considerations of traditional analyses but does *not* reject the individual criteria suggested. There is, instead, a need to think imaginatively about the construction and application of success or failure criteria recognizing the pluralistic nature of business by adopting a stakeholder perspective. *The ways in which success and/or failure will be defined and measured are then dependent upon the stakeholder's orientation towards the enterprise and can be expected to change over time.* Furthermore, the relative positions of stakeholders will invariably reflect a wide variety of objectives and aspirations, with respect to the enterprise, some of which will undoubtedly be mutually exclusive. Therefore, the small firm cannot possibly fulfil all criteria of success and may indeed be simultaneously judged to be a success *and* a failure by differing stakeholder groupings.

Given the very nature of small business, it would seem appropriate to regard the entrepreneur or owner-manager as the primary stakeholder and to begin by considering how he/she might define success and failure. Clearly, many of the criteria used will reflect the underlying motives and reasons which predispose people to enter self-employment. These will be influenced by characteristics such as gender (Jennings and Cohen, 1993; Marlow and Strange, 1993), ethnicity (Ward, 1991), social marginality (Curran and Stanworth, 1973) and so on. For example, Carter and Cannon (1992), in their study of female entrepreneurs, sought to recognize the centrality of gender in defining success and, rather than imposing externally defined criteria, canvassed the views and opinions of a sample of women owner-managers. Their research revealed eight principal common criteria:

1.   independence;
2.   customer service;
3.   personal satisfaction;
4.   employment for the owner;
5.   quality of working life;
6.   growth potential;
7.   employment of staff;
8.   finance/income.

Paradoxically, it would appear that these factors are not, in fact, gender specific and other studies of mixed or male samples reveal very similar measures (cf. Foley and Green, 1989; Stanworth and Gray, 1991; Wood and Woodruff, 1993).

Some of the criteria cited reflect the centrality of the entrepreneur and the recognition of his/her responsibility in facilitating the satisfaction of other stakeholders' aspirations. For example, financial measures such as cash flow assume responsibility for loan repayments to financial institutions, payments to suppliers, wages for employees and other working capital needs. Profitability assumes responsibility for venture capital returns and investor support, as well as one of the justifications for venture development.

The reasons why other stakeholders would wish to see the new venture succeed are equally personalized and this results in narrow, particular criteria for judging performance. *No one single set of criteria are, per se, any more or any less valid and important than any other set.* Each is equally appropriate, in the right circumstances. Examples of some of the typical stakeholder groupings and their likely success requirements are illustrated in Figure 4.2. (Please note: this is *not* intended to be a comprehensive listing.)

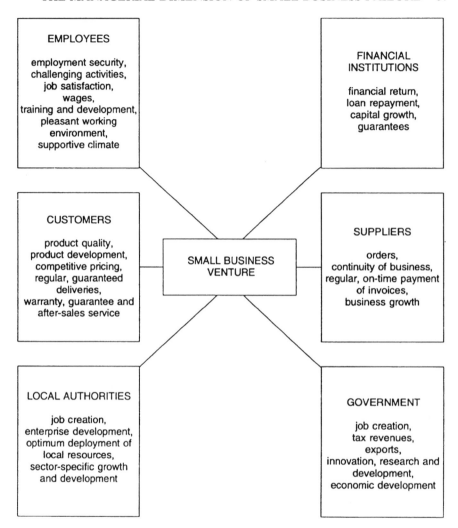

**Figure 4.2**    The Stakeholder Web of the Small Firm. Source: Beaver and Jennings (1995)

An additional complicating consideration is that the relative weighting and importance of these measures will change over time as the business progresses from start up through periods of transition and growth to maturity as an established, hopefully successful, corporate entity.

The forementioned discussion illustrates that there is no single criterion, label or definition of success or failure. Accordingly, a revised definition of small business success is:

*the sustained satisfaction of principal stakeholder aspirations.*

Logically, a revised definition of small business failure would be:

*the inability to satisfy principal stakeholder aspirations.*

It is immediately apparent that success is no longer regarded as synonymous with optimal performance as this represents an extremely elusive concept. Similarly, failure can no longer be regarded in terms of the traditional, inflexible paradigm of the cessation of trading. Rather, success can be viewed as the attainment of certain predefined objectives which satisfy stakeholder aspirations and which may culminate in performance which falls substantially below the optimal level attainable (Beaver, 1984; Foley and Green, 1989). Equally, failure implies that stakeholder aspirations have not been and are unlikely to be satisfied even though the business may be perfectly capable of continuing to trade, albeit at a sub-optimal level and may even enjoy a period of growth and business development.

## SMALL BUSINESS SUCCESS

Being able to define success, no matter how personalized or how generalized, is not the same as being able to explain it. The fundamental question remains, therefore, why do some small businesses succeed whilst others fail? The quantity of research and publications which addresses this issue confirms that there are no easy answers and no consensus of agreement. A detailed review of the existing literature is beyond the scope of this. However, an analysis of the major points may be summarized as shown in Figure 4.3.

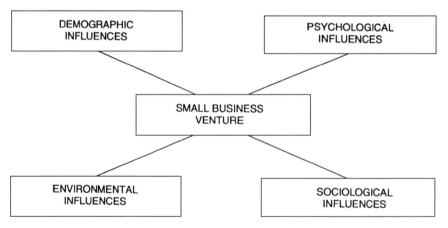

**Figure 4.3**   Influences Upon Success Potential. Source: Beaver and Jennings (1995)

The sociological influences paradigm focuses upon explaining success in terms of gender, age, social class, marital status, education, ethnicity and so on (cf. Schumpeter, 1934; Birley and Norburn, 1986; Ward, 1991; Cohen, 1994; Rosa et al, 1994). As may be expected, there does not seem to be a given combination of these factors which leads to success. Men and women of all backgrounds create and manage both successful and unsuccessful businesses.

The psychological influences paradigm centres mainly upon personality traits and has several strands. These tend to equate the entrepreneur with the small business venture (cf. McLelland, 1961; Dunkleberg and Cooper, 1982; Chell, 1985) and assume a successful entrepreneur equals a successful enterprise. Exceptions include Carland et al (1984) and Stanworth and Curran (1976) who seek to differentiate not only the entrepreneur from the enterprise but also differentiate an entrepreneur from an owner-manager. The underlying premise of this paradigm is that success can be explained in terms of the psychological set of the principal actors.

The demographic paradigm concentrates upon the background and lifestyle of the business founder and seeks to explain success in terms of the trigger event which leads to self-employment (cf. Cooper, 1981; Shapero, 1975; Birley, 1989).

The environmental paradigm focuses upon the physical and situational circumstances, in which the new enterprise is founded and seeks to explain success in terms of the networking of resources and support services and industrial/commercial sector (Stanworth and Gray, 1991; Foley and Green, 1989; Porter, 1980).

Some studies have sought to combine all or most of the aforementioned influences in creating an integrated paradigm to explain success. These range from cursory, surface analysis, to in-depth detailed research. For example, high-growth Japanese companies, according to the Nikkei Industrial Daily (reported in *Asiaweek*, 12 May 1993), use MAGIC! The mnemonic describes *m*edium size, *a*gility, *g*arage-shop (entrepreneurial) mentality, *i*nnovation and *c*oncentration (on a specific field). Ray and Hutchinson (1983) conducted a study of 'supergrowth companies'—i.e. companies which grew rapidly to a stock market quotation—compared with a matched sample of 'passive' small firms which did not grow to flotation. They found, amongst other issues, that the 'supergrowth companies' were considerably more focused in their objectives, with strong emphasis on forecasting financial data on a regular basis, particularly cash flow but also profit and sales. The changing style of management and organizational structure is also apparent as the companies develop.

Furthermore, the dynamics of the business environment suggest that the relative importance of influencing factors will ebb and flow in two key dimensions. Firstly, over time change in the general business environment will subtly alter the mix of dominant influences which impinge upon the overall level of success within the economy as a whole. Secondly, any situationally specific influences will alter as the organization itself develops. For any firm to remain successful over a sustained period there *must* be a capability to adapt to changing circumstances. Indeed, Greiner (1972) shows that failure to adapt to a series of 'crises' caused by growth is one of the principal causes of failure for all organizations. Hence, *one of the primary ingredients in small firm success must be the managerial competence of the owner-manager.*

What are these managerial competencies which underpin the successful small business? A useful guide may be to examine the contents of small business training and development programmes. There is a need to distinguish between training and development which might be necessary for employees within a small business and training and development which is focused upon the specific needs of the owner-manager(s) themselves. The small firm owner-manager requires specific, transferable, managerial skills directly related to entrepreneurship and professional management within the operating environment of the business, as shown in Figure 4.1. He or she needs to be able to initiate and implement change and improvement in services, products and systems.

It is very easy to note the obvious—that providing all the necessary skills and competencies are found across the whole team which makes up the small enterprise, the business should be capable of achieving success. However, adept management is still required to blend and bring out these abilities and as Jennings and Beaver (1993) illustrate, the personality and positional power of the entrepreneur often mean that latent talent within the team goes unrecognized or underutilized. This raises the question of whether small businesses fail through lack of managerial skills, which let down otherwise good skill and competence in providing the product or service, or through lack of competence in providing the product or service demanded by the customer, despite otherwise competent management in the organization?

## SMALL BUSINESS FAILURE

Small business failure rates vary according to the characteristics of the business and of those who own and manage it. Contemporary data such as that shown in Table 4.1 demonstrates that failure is endemic to the small firm sector.

Of the many surveys of contemporary small business survival and growth, both in the UK and the other developed economies, most seem to identify situational, operational and personality-driven reasons for failure (cf. Ganguly, 1983; Hall and Stark, 1986; LBS, 1987; Robson Rhodes, 1984; Stanford, 1982; Storey et al, 1987). It is interesting to note that in many respects the approach to researching small business failure has been very similar to the approach to researching entrepreneurs and entrepreneurship thereby establishing an inextricable link between entrepreneurial activity and small firm performance. According to Stanford (1982), the causes of small business failure may be:

**Table 4.1**   Businesses with Different Types of Support

| Types of business support | Proportion surviving at 3 years (%) |
| --- | --- |
| All registered businesses (1974–1984) | 64 |
| Worker cooperatives (start 1975–1983) | 66 |
| Worker cooperatives (start 1982–1983) | 56 |
| Enterprise allowance scheme (start from 1983) | 53 |

Source: Thomas and Cornforth (1989)

1.  inadequate accounting systems;
2.  poor location;
3.  lack of marketing skills;
4.  lack of capital budget;
5.  inadequate provision for contingencies;
6.  lack of management skills;
7.  excessive inventory;
8.  incompetency;
9.  lack of experience;
10. neglect;
11. fraud;
12. disaster;
13. poor record-keeping;
14. reckless money management;
15. lack of formal planning;
16. insufficient marketing talents;
17. indifferent employees;
18. inability to cope with growth.

Jennings et al (1992) point out that Stanford (as with most others) has not attempted to distinguish between *symptoms* and *causes* and the occasional exogenous event which may force a small business into liquidation. For example, a natural disaster may not be foreseen, and although it can be argued that managers should make provision for such events, in reality such preparations are seldom adequate. Alternatively, a prime business location may be rendered less than attractive—either temporarily or permanently—by the actions of others beyond the control of the owner-manager, for example the re-routing of a new motorway, or plans to build a new housing estate. Generally, it can be seen that whilst *symptoms* such as inadequate accounting systems, lack of a capital budget, excessive inventory, poor record-keeping or demotivated employees may be the *reason* for a small business failure, the root *cause* may be ineffective management.

However, this contention may be not only uncharitable it may also be without adequate support and justification. Ineffective management cannot simply be identified as the primary cause of small business failure without recognizing several factors which are peculiar to the small business operating context. The study by Grieve-Smith and Fleck (1987) using a case study approach to examining business strategies in small high technology firms in Cambridge raises several interesting managerial issues. Referring to one company they comment:

> A major factor in Domino's success seems to have been that the founder was conscious from the start of the need to bring in people with business or manufacturing experience to complement the technical expertise upon which the company was based.

They continue:

> Of concern to many companies was the establishing and keeping of an experienced management team. Many of the newer companies had recognised a need to complement their founder's technical skills and to appoint experienced managing directors and management specialists from large companies. This awareness, coupled with the willingness of professional managers to join a small company may be one of the crucial conditions for long term success.

Grieve-Smith and Fleck also point out that small enterprises can experience real difficulties recruiting such managerial skills as they cannot provide the salaries and recruitment benefits that managers could expect from larger organizations. Furthermore, their case studies highlight several other important issues. For example, they refer to the founders of certain companies being conscious, at the start, of the *need to recruit external managers and to appoint these individuals from larger companies*, presumably to facilitate business growth and development. Finally, they also refer to the need to attract managers with different additional skills to those already in the firm to complement the expertise on which the company was based. This would suggest that the business founder had the desire to construct a balanced managerial team as one of the prime drivers of sustained business expansion and performance. It is also a factor that may well dramatically reduce the risk of business failure.

Similar issues were raised by the Advisory Council on Science and Technology (1990) in its work on barriers to growth in small firms. It reported:

> From our case studies it is apparent that growth creates major management and organisational problems. The principal dimensions of this relate to the need to develop a balanced managerial team which combines appropriate marketing, financial and technical skills and the need to create an organisational structure which supports an appropriate delegation of decision-making.

It must be emphasized, however, that there are many types and categories of small business, each with its own particular operating context. Equally, there are also many different ways of organizing and managing in the search for competitive advantage and continued survival and an even greater diversity of small business owners and managers with varying motivations, expectations and abilities. It would, therefore, be unwise simply to focus on small high-technology firms as a basis upon which to make generalizations about management strategies for business growth and failure prevention. The analysis of the managerial contribution to small business failure must also acknowledge the factor of *disadvantage*, due not only to the size of the firm but also to the nature of the operating context and the relatively ineffective support infrastructure (Beaver and Harrison, 1994).

Nicholson and West (1988) illustrate the many significant differences between managers in small and large firms confirming both the presence and nature of disadvantage. Furthermore, there is some evidence provided by Handy et al (1988) in their international review of the education, development and training of managers that:

> Small companies are different. In no country do they take the same long term view of management development, nor are they prepared to spend time and money on any form of training which does not have an almost immediate pay-off.

This fixation with immediacy and short termism is probably as accurate a generalization about the managerial contribution to small business failure as we are likely to get. Put another way, small business failure is invariably caused through a lack of sensitive managerial strategic attention. This is confirmed in the research of Smallbone et al (1992) who examined the characteristics and (strategic) adjustments of surviving as opposed to non-surviving firms. They identified five broad types of adjustment:

1.   product and market adjustments;
2.   production process adjustments;
3.   employment and labour process adjustments;
4.   ownership and organizational adjustments;
5.   locational adjustments.

The basic hypothesis to be tested was that the firms which had been most active in making adjustments were the most successful in terms of employment change and survival. The research clearly confirmed the hypothesis. The second key finding was that of the five adjustment areas identified here, management development of markets was essential for most firms for both survival and growth, but achieving real growth required active market development in terms of both the identification of new market opportunities and increasing the breadth of customer care. It is interesting to note that the study identified internal organizational adjustment as the second most common type of adjustment characterizing surviving firms. Of particular note is that the high performing firms were most likely to identify organizational changes which had empowered top managers to delegate operational responsibilities and to manage strategically.

## CONCLUSIONS

Researching small business management failure is fraught with difficulties. Few, if any, entrepreneurs, owners or managers are willing to publicly admit to personal shortcomings. The links between organizational failure and management action (or inaction) are extremely tenuous and very difficult, if not impossible, to demonstrate conclusively. Only those persons immediately affected by organizational failure, or near failure, have sufficient knowledge of the precise circumstances to be able to suggest cause and effect relationships. Methods which rely upon self-reporting of information are likely to yield a distorted picture.

Studies which have sought to describe particular small business personalities in their organizational contexts, such as Jennings and Beaver (1993), illustrate the need for an appreciation of the nature of small business management which reaches beyond traditional management understanding. A number of interesting questions and issues have been highlighted. It is true that there are some owner-managers who see their organization as personal property to be used as a vehicle for satisfying personal ambitions. Equally, some owner-managers relegate organizational objectives to a position subordinate to their personal aims and therefore act in a misguided, mistaken and disappointing manner when faced with business difficulties. *This is not to say that these owner-managers are deliberately trying to destroy their organizations.* Rather, in their own minds they see their behaviour as being in the best interests of the organization at that point in time and would probably argue that they are indeed acting in a  manner compatible with professional best practice.

It is equally true to say that some owner-managers make deliberate decisions to avoid capitalizing upon opportunities which present themselves in order to constrain growth and, therefore, allow the owner-manager to retain control. Other stakeholders may interpret this as small business failure as it may prevent them from being able to satisfy their personal aspirations. However, to the owner-manager this may represent success in preventing the venture from developing beyond their personal capabilities.

In any given situation the interplay between the seven key roles identified earlier is fundamental to the adoption of a satisfactory course of action. The lack of any precise demarcation between the rights, responsibilities and duties of these roles creates confusion and overlap which prevents the role players from attaining a clear vision and articulating required outcomes. The demands of the seven roles constitute internal stakeholders within the unconscious mind of the small business practitioner and compete for dominance which will be manifested at the conscious level. When faced with a specific business problem the practitioner will unconsciously adopt the stance of the role which most closely conforms to their personal perceptions of the situation and provides the best vehicle for satisfying their personal expectations. These personal expectations may manifest themselves as strong needs for instantaneous self-gratification and lead to egocentric behaviour.

Nevertheless, *it is clear that sub-optimal performance and potential business failure are closely correlated with a lack of attention to strategic management.* Whether strategic management is readily visible as a formal process or is 'hidden' in informal systems of decision-making, the fundamental principles of needing to achieve organizational fit with the operating context to ensure long-term survival, growth and prosperity remains valid. Whether acting in a selfish manner intentionally, unintentionally or accidentally the consequences for the enterprise and its stakeholders of poor quality strategic decision-making are certain to result in failure in terms of the definition articulated earlier in this chapter.

The small business owner-manager may appear to be disinterested in creating an effective organizational system. Often, this task is left to subordinates to perform as best they can. This may well conflict with the expectations and demands of other external stakeholders and leads to the interpretation of behaviour as selfish, egotistic and destructive. A further level of complexity is added in situations where more than one key role player occupies a position of power and influence. Here the battle for dominance is not only restricted to unconscious conflict but is played out in the boardroom and/or amongst the management team.

In situations of organizational crisis there is a natural tendency for the small business practitioner to centralize control. Drawing responsibility inwards increases power by allowing the practitioner to deny the accuracy of information provided and reject the abilities of others who may be in a position to offer constructive help and advice. Such actions of owner-managers may be interpreted as despotism preventing the successful marshalling of organizational processes and people who must be trusted to implement leadership initiatives.

These conclusions have to be interpreted in the light of previous comments concerning the complexities of researching this area of small business management practice. The intention of this chapter is to promote thought and debate on what is a difficult and poorly researched area of management rather than to claim generally valid and reliable accounts of particular contexts of small business failure. An ethnographic research approach commends itself. However, researchers should anticipate difficulties in gathering information about potentially embarrassing and libellous issues. Additionally, researchers have the benefit of hindsight and it is relatively easy to be critical of managerial actions and decisions in the sure knowledge of their outcome. The question must be asked—if placed in exactly the same situation, with the same knowledge, experience and personality set, would any researcher act in any way different from the managers of small firms?

## REFERENCES

Advisory Council on Science and Technology (1990). *The Enterprise Challenge, Overcoming Barriers to Growth in Small Firms*, HMSO. London.

Andrews, K. R. (1971). *A Concept of Corporate Strategy*, Irwin, Homewood.

Anthony, R. N. (1965). *Planning and control systems: a framework for analysis*, Division of Research, Harvard Graduate School of Business, Boston.

Beaver, G. (1984). The entrepreneurial ceiling: a discussion of the small business management process, 7th UKEMRA National Small Firms Policy and Research Conference, Nottingham, September 1984.

Beaver, G. and Harrison, Y. (1994). TEC support for women entrepreneurs: help or hindrance? 17th National ISBA Small Firms Policy and Research Conference, Nottingham, September 1994.

Beaver, G. and Jennings, P. L. (1995). Picking winners: the art of identifying successful small firms. In: Hussey, D. (ed.), *International Review of Strategic Management*, Volume 6, John Wiley, Chichester.

Birley, S. (1989). The start-up. In: Burns, P. and Dewhurst, J. (eds), *Small Business and Entrepreneurship*, Chapter 2, Macmillan, Basingstoke.

Birley, S. and Norburn, D. (1986). Who are the high flyers? Strategic Management Conference, Singapore.

Bolton, J. E. (1971). Report of the Committee of Enquiry on Small Firms, Cmnd. 4811. HMSO, London.

Carland, J. W., Hoy, F., Boulton, W. R. and Carland, J. A. C. (1984). Differentiating entrepreneurs from small business owners: a conceptualisation, *Academy of Management Review*, **9**(2), pp. 354–359.

Carter, S. and Cannon, T. (1992). *Women as Entrepreneurs*, Academic Press, London.

Chaganti, R. and Chaganti R. (1983). A profile of profitable and not-so-profitable small businesses, *Journal of Small Business Management*, **21**(3), pp. 47–61.

Chell, E. (1985). The entrepreneurial personality: a few ghosts laid to rest? *International Small Business Journal*, **3**(3), pp. 43–54.

Chell, E., Howarth, J. M. and Brearley, S. A. (1991). *The Entrepreneurial Personality: Concepts, Cases and Categories*, Routledge, London.

Cohen, L. (1994). From Employment to Self-employment: Synthesis and Transformation, 17th National ISBA Small Firms Policy and Research Conference, Sheffield, November 1994.

Cohen, M. D., March, J. G. and Olsen, J. P. (1972). A garbage can model of organisational choice, *Administrative Science Quarterly*, **1**, pp. 1–17.

Cooper, A. C. (1981). Strategic management; new ventures and small business, *Long Range Planning*, **14**(5), pp. 39–45.

Curran, J. and Stanworth, J. S. (1973). *Management Motivation in the Small Business*, Gower Press, London.

Druker, P. F. (1977). *People and Performance*, Harper and Row, New York.

Dunkleberg, W. C. and Cooper, A. C. (1982). Entrepreneurial typologies. In: Vesper, K. H. (ed.), *Frontiers of Entrepreneurship Research*. Babson, Wellesley, Mass: Centre for Entrepreneurial Studies.

Faulkner, D. and Johnson, G. (1992). *The Challenge of Strategic Management*, Kogan Page, London.

Fayol, H. (1949). *General and Industrial Management*. Pitman: London (Fayol's book, *Administration Industrielle et Générale* (1916), translated from French to English).

Foley, P. and Green, H. (1989). *Small Business Success*, Paul Chapman Publishing, London.

Ganguly, P. (1983). Lifespan analysis of business in the UK, 1973–82, *British Business*, 12 August.

Greiner, L. (1972). Evolution and revolution as organisations grow, *Harvard Business Review*, July/August.

Grieve-Smith, A. and Fleck, V. (1987). Business strategies in small high technology companies, *Long Range Planning*, 20(2), pp. 61–68.

Gulic, L. H. (1937). Notes on the theory of organisation. In: Gulick, L. and Urwick, L. (eds), *Papers on the science of administration*. New York: The Institute of Public Administration.

Hall, G. and Stark A. (1986). The effects of the conservative government as reflected in the changing characteristics of bankrupt firms, *International Journal of Industrial Organisation*, 4(3), pp. 20–31.

Handy, C. (1987). *The Making of Managers*, London: NEDO.

Hofstede, G. (1981). Management control of public and not-for-profit activities. In: *Accounting Organisations and Society*, 6(3), pp. 193–211, Pergamon Press, Oxford.

Hornaday, R. W. and Wheatley, W. J. (1986). Managerial characteristics and the financial performance of small firms, *Journal of Small Business Management*, 24(2), pp. 53–67.

Jennings, P. L. and Beaver, G. (1993). The abuse of entrepreneurial power. In: *Small Business and Small Business Development Conference*, European Research Press, Leicester.

Jennings, P. L., Beaver, G. and Richardson, W. (1992). Improving the role of accreditation in the training and development of small business owner/managers, 15th National UKEMRA Small Firms Policy and Research Conference, Southampton, November.

Jennings, P. L. and Cohen, L. (1993). Invisible entrepreneurs, 16th ISBA National Small Firms Policy and Research Conference, Nottingham, November.

London Business School (1987). A study to determine the reasons for failure of small businesses in the UK.

Kelmar, J. H. (1990). Measurement of success and failure in small business—a dichotomous anachronism, 13th UKEMRA Small Firms Policy and Research Conference, Harrogate, November.

Marlow, S. and Strange, A. (1993). Female entrepreneurs: success by whose standards? Occasional Paper No. 2, De Montfort University, Leicester Business School.

McLelland, D. C. (1961). *The Achieving Society*, D. Van Nostrand, Princeton, New Jersey.

Mintzberg, H. (1973). *The Nature of Managerial Work*, Harper and Row, New York.

Mitroff, I. I. (1983). *Stakeholders of the Organisational Mind*, Jossey Bass, San Francisco.

Nicholson, N. and West, M. (1988). *Managerial Job Change*, Cambridge University Press, Cambridge.

Osborne, R. L. (1991). The dark side of the entrepreneur, *Long Range Planning*, **24**(3), pp. 26–31.

Peters, T. (1992). *Liberation Management*, Macmillan, New York.

Porter, M. E. (1980). *Competitive Strategy*, Macmillan, New York.

Ray, G. H. and Hutchinson, P. J. (1983). *The Financing and Financial Control of Small Enterprise Development*, Gower, London.

Robson Rhodes (1984). *A Study of Businesses Financed Under the Small Business Loan Guarantee Scheme*, DTI. London.

Rosa, P., Carter, S. and Hamilton, D. (1994). Gender and determinants of small business performance: preliminary insights from a British study, 17th National ISBA Small Firms Policy and Research Conference, Sheffield, November.

Schumpeter, J. A. (1934). *The Theory of Economic Development*, Harvard University Press, Cambridge, MA.

Shapero, A. (1975). The displaced uncomfortable entrepreneur, *Psychology Today*, November.

Smallbone, D., North, D. and Leigh, R. (1992). Managing change for growth and survival: the study of mature manufacturing firms in London during the 1980's, Working Paper No. 3, Planning Research Centre, Middlesex Polytechnic.

Stanford, M. J. (1982). *New Enterprise Management*, Reston Publishing Co., Reston.

Stanworth, M. J. K. and Curran, J. (1976). Growth and the small firm—an alternative view, *Journal of Management Studies*, **13**(2), May, pp. 5–110.

Stanworth, M. J. K. and Gray, C. (1991). *Bolton 20 Years On: The Small Firm in the 1990's*, Small Business Research Trust, Paul Chapman Publishing Ltd, London.

Storey, D. J., Keasey, K., Watson, R. and Wynarczyk, P. (1987). *The Performance of Small Firms*, Croom Helm, London.

Taylor, F. W. (1947). *Scientific Management* (first published in 1911), Harper and Row, New York.

Thomas, A. and Cornforth, C. (1989). The Survival and Growth of Workers' Cooperatives: A Comparison With Small Business, *International Small Business Journal*, **8**(1), pp. 34–50.

Thorpe, R. (1989). The performance of small firms: predicting success and failure, 10th UKEMRA National Small Firms Policy and Research Conference, Milton Keynes, November 1987.

Ward, R. (1991). Economic development and ethnic business. In: J. Curran and R. A. Blackburn, *Paths of Enterprise*, Routledge, London.

Wood, L. and Woodruff, N. (1993). Shattering the glass ceiling: barriers to growth within UK Enterprise Ltd. In: *Small Business and Small Business Development Conference*, European Research Press, Leicester.

# 5

# TRANSLATING BUSINESS STRATEGIES INTO ACTION: MANAGING STRATEGIC CHANGE

**Doug A. Stace**

*Stace Management Networks P/L, Sydney*

**Dexter C. Dunphy**

*Centre for Corporate Change*

In a volatile business environment, few would argue that the central task of management is the management of change. Yet how to formulate an overall change strategy, particularly one that has overall synergy with an organization's business strategies, has proven to be more difficult. This chapter describes the results obtained from an intensive and comprehensive field research study, which attempted to trace the linkages between an organization's business strategies, its organizational change strategies and its human resource (HR) strategies. We were interested to see if patterns of co-alignment could be identified between these three areas. The results of the study provide an alternate framework to the almost universalist prescriptions for incremental and consultatively based organizational change that is so dominant in management literature. We provide a situational model of change strategies, relating it with generic business strategies on the one hand and with a model of HR management strategies on the other. These models combined provide an integrated view of management strategies that are designed to ensure that business strategy repositioning is not only planned, but also effectively implemented.

*The Implementation Challenge*, Edited by D. E. Hussey
© 1996 John Wiley & Sons Ltd

## CRITICAL LINKS IN STRATEGIC REPOSITIONING

During the 1980s, much of the emphasis in strategic management literature was on the strategic repositioning of organizations in the face of globalization of markets, rapid technological developments and the effects of social change on changing patterns of client/customer need. Writers representing this strategic emphasis are Porter (1980, 1985), Miller (1986), Harrigan (1985), Murray (1988) and Ohmae (1987): their emphasis is on content, direction and repositioning rather than process. Yet a critical factor in the successful repositioning of an organization's business strategies is that of the internal capability of the organization, generated through appropriately chosen change and human resource strategies.

Whilst business strategy repositioning often requires radical organizational change, until recently large sections of management process literature, particularly represented by the fields of organizational development (OD) and human resource management (HRM) were dominated by an ideology of tender mindedness, fine tuning, and careful and collaboratively based microtechniques or interventions, such as team building, interpersonal skills training and effective communication strategies. Writers representative of this school include Sashkin (1986), Kanter (her earlier work reported in 1983) and Golembiewski (1979). More recently, however, there has been an emergence of other writers, such as Gagliardi (1986), Tushman et al. (1986), Miller and Friesen (1984) and Nord and Tucker (1987), who have developed some formative and valuable frameworks for understanding the processes of large-scale, radical, transformative change, which have been evident in many organizations during the past decade. The question arose: was it possible to take this more recent management process literature a stage further by developing a general contingency model of change strategies, to balance the almost prescriptive ideology of gradualism that is so characteristic of the earlier organizational change and human relations literature. The second question was to see whether patterns in these areas had an association with generic business strategies.

## RESEARCHING THE LINKS

During 1988/90, the authors conducted a major research study in the Australian service industry sector to explore the links between business strategy repositioning and management process (organizational change and HRM) strategies.

Figure 5.1 illustrates the overall conceptual model explored in the research. The figure illustrates the suggested relationship between an organization's human resource (HR) strategies with both the organization's business strategy and its change strategy. Organizational change strategy in this schema becomes

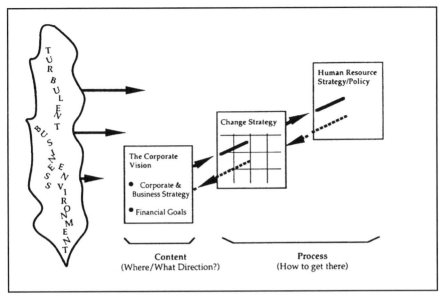

© Stace/Dunphy Research Project

**Figure 5.1**   Business Strategy—Management Process Linkages

a crucial process variable, and in fact a vital link and referent point between business strategy on the one hand and HR strategies on the other.

The study had several aims. Firstly, to see whether linkages between generic business, change and HR strategies existed in practice; secondly, to explore whether changes in an organization's business strategy led to a similar repositioning of its change and HR strategies; and thirdly, to look for any contrasts between higher and lower performing organizations, particularly in the area of organizational change strategies that are used.

Thirteen Australian organizations, five in banking/finance, five in insurance, two in aviation and one in international telecommunications, were included in a comprehensive field research study. High, medium and low performers were included in the sample, based on independent performance rankings by a panel of three industry market analysts. The research involved structured interviews with over 450 executives and managers, who as part of the research were asked to respond to several forced-choice instruments on business strategy, change strategy and HR practices.

## A NEW CONCEPT OF CHANGE STRATEGIES

The research provided confirmation and extension of the earlier theoretical contingency model of change developed by the authors (Dunphy and Stace,

1988). This model of change strategies (Figure 5.2) developed a situational model of organizational change strategies. It proposed that, in environments undergoing differing degrees of change, managements would pragmatically choose situationally based rather than universalist, prescriptive change strategies as a means of maintaining their organization's 'strategic fit' with the environment. The implication was that the change strategies of participative evolution and charismatic transformation, which were advocated in the OD and HRM literature, may be appropriate strategies for corporate change for some organizations. However, in a more volatile business environment, it was likely that more directive and even coercive change management strategies could be successfully used at the corporate level. Where radical change is needed to return an organization to environmental 'fit', there may be major conflicts between external stakeholders and/or internal interest groups, which make maintaining an ideology of collaboration and participation in the planning of change impossible. In such situations, directive or

|  | Incremental change strategies | Transformative change strategies |
|---|---|---|
| Collaborative/ consulatative mode | 1. Participative evolution<br><br>Use when organization is in fit but needs minor adjustment, or is out of fit but time is available and key interest groups favour change | 2. Charismatic change strategies<br><br>Use when organization is out of fit, there is little time for extensive participation but there is support for radical change within the organization |
| Directive/ coercive mode | 3. Forced evolution<br><br>Use when organization is in fit but needs minor adjustment, or is out of fit but time is available, but key interest groups oppose change | 4. Dictatorial transformation<br><br>Use when organization is out of fit, there is no time for extensive participation and no support within the organization for radical change, but radical change is vital to oraganizational survival and fulfilment of basic mission |

© D. Stace and D. Murphy

**Figure 5.2** The Dunphy/Stace Typology of Change Strategies and Conditions for Their Use

coercive change leadership may be essential for the organization to achieve its business objectives (though it will not *necessarily* achieve these ends).

The results of the research demonstrate that executives of firms that maintain medium to high levels of corporate performance successfully use a variety of approaches to change, rather than a universalist approach. As a result of the research (see Stace, 1989; Dunphy and Stace, 1990a, 1990b), our original two × two matrix of organizational change strategies (Figure 5.2) was refined to cover four scales of change and four styles of change leadership viz.

Scale of change (the characteristics of change):

• Fine tuning (Scale Type 1)
• Incremental adjustment (Scale Type 2)
• Modular (divisional) transformation (Scale Type 3)
• Corporate transformation (Scale Type 4)

Style of change leadership/management (the management of change):

• Collaborative (Style Type 1)
• Consultative (Style Type 2)
• Directive (Style Type 3)
• Coercive (Style Type 4)

In matrix form, these dimensions of change form a four-by-four contingency model (Figure 5.3). Overlaid on it are the percentages of organizational responses, indicating the areas on the matrix '*utilized*' by the sample organizations for their change strategies. This was based on self-ratings within each organization by executive and senior manager interviewees, using instruments on the scale and style of change characteristic of their organizations in two time periods: the modal score was utilized for this purpose.

Overall, the research evidence shows that at a corporate level of analysis:

• the two lower performing organizations in the sample were rated as using fine tuning change (one using a consultative, the other using a directive change style);
• no organization rated its executives as using a collaborative change style in any period;
• one organization used a combination of coercive change style and corporate transformational change as a means of regaining '*fit*' (the organization became a high performer within 3 years of this radical type of change intervention);
• eleven of the thirteen organizations had utilized a directive change style, associated with corporate transformational change, for periods of 12–24 months in the previous 3 to 5 years

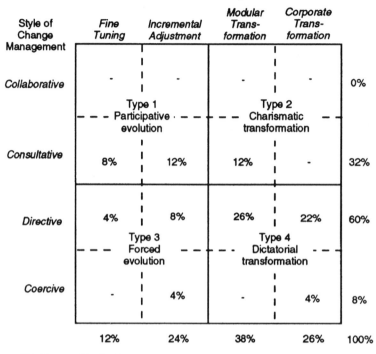

**Figure 5.3** Change Matrix Positioning of Australian Service Corporations. ($N = 13$ Organizations in Two Time Periods. Figures Given are Based on Modal Responses of Senior Executives in Each Organization and have been Converted to Percentages.)

This demonstrates that, even in higher performing organizations, more differentiated successful change strategies exist in practice than are often portrayed in management literature. Overall, the predominant approach to corporate change identified by the research was not that of participative evolution or even charismatic transformation, which were so widely advocated in the OD literature: we found that medium to high performance can be maintained by leading the corporation by either a consultative *or* directive management style. In the current business environment, a directive corporate management and leadership style is dominant in Australian financial and service organizations. A minimal level of change, or fine tuning, appears overall to be a non-viable change strategy, as it is unable to deliver enough adjustment for the organization to sustain high performance in a volatile business environment.

Examples of different corporate change strategies are plentiful. A change strategy will succeed in one organization where it will not elsewhere. The critical point for success of a change strategy is that it must be integrated with the business needs of the corporation. It must be capable of delivering the amount of structural, systems and cultural change necessary, within time, to deliver the emerging business imperatives of the organization. Traditionally, organizations such as IBM have been able to achieve this by our change strategy Type 1—participative evolution, but IBM has now adopted more transformative change strategies (probably a mix between change strategy Type 2—charismatic transformation and change strategy Type 4—directive transformation) under IBM President, John Akers.

In Australia, the transformation of Westpac Banking Corporation in the early 1980s under Managing Director Bob White could best be described by change strategy Type 2—charismatic transformation. Westpac's change strategy involved a major revolution in the business, but the process was assisted by organization-wide team building, internal communication and new MBO-type performance management strategies. As a result of widespread workforce support, Westpac's approach to change in the early 1980s became a hallmark for transformative change by consultation. The transformation of Honeywell Information Systems in the United States (US) under Renier is similarly an example of a Type 2 change strategy (Renier, 1987). Recent business events for Westpac have, however, led to an alteration in its corporate change strategies: a more directive if not coercive approach is now used.

However, in contrast to Westpac's early 1980s consultative approach, the directive, results-oriented approach in Australia's Lend Lease Corporation, under Stuart Hornery, has been successfully utilized for nearly 20 years and is characteristic of change strategy Type 3—forced evolution. Lend Lease is one of Australia's consistently high performers. Rupert Murdoch, the international media tycoon, has chosen change strategy Type 4—dictatorial transformation, with demonstrated success, at critical periods in News Corporation. The celebrated case of the introduction of new technology at Murdoch's Wapping Plant and breaking the power of the Fleet Street unions illustrates the success of this type of change strategy (Harris, 1987). Murdoch's approach was similar to that used by Jack Welch in General Electric, resulting in the retrenchment of 140 000 of the company's workers.

All of these strategies have been successful, in business terms, in their time, and yet some are contrary to the dominant approaches to change advocated in much of the management literature. In fact, we would go so far as saying that the near-universal advocacy of participative forms of leadership has left many executives confused and ill-equipped to handle the demands of leadership in a difficult business environment. We do not, however, suggest that participation or consultation should not be used. In fact, our research has shown that the following patterns of change leadership/management most typically emerge in medium- to high-performing organizations at two different levels in such organizations:

- *predominantly directive at corporate level.* Whilst some executive groups espoused a corporate value system of consultation and appeared to practise it, there was only one organization in our sample where executives and supervisors/managers agreed that the top group effectively used a consultative change management style as a means of effecting corporate change. A strongly directive/directional approach was the norm.
- *consultative between managers and employees at the business unit level, particularly in the process of strategy implementation.* This was true for all but two organizations. In one of these cases, a directive approach appeared to be an attempt by business unit managers to cope with a lack of direction from above; in the other case, the directive approach appeared to stem from a tough results-oriented philosophy consistently maintained at all levels in the organization.

Whilst these are the predominant trends from our research, we do not, however, espouse them as a universalist position. In fact, one of the highest performers in our sample, Macquarie Bank—a small, high value-added niche bank—had utilized incremental adjustment by consultation (change strategy Type 1)—participative evolution as its dominant corporate change strategy, with demonstrated success throughout most of the 1980s. Whilst this was atypical of the rest of the medium to high performers in the sample, it suggests that change strategies might be best chosen for their situational specificity and their linkage with the organization's business strategy, rather than their universalist appeal. This led to an examination of the relationship between an organization's generic business strategy and its change strategy.

## BUSINESS STRATEGY LINKS TO ORGANIZATIONAL CHANGE STRATEGIES

Using a typology of four generic business strategies (Miles and Snow, 1978; Snow and Hrebiniak, 1980), we asked executives in each organization to use these types to classify their organization's predominant business strategy. They were asked to do this for two time periods: 3–5 years before the study (1984–86), and at the time of the study (1988–90), to gain a wider point of reference in each organization. These business strategy categories can briefly be described as follows:

### Business Strategy: Basic Competitive Characteristics

| *Strategy type* | *Definition* |
| --- | --- |
| Defender | The low-cost producer of high-quality goods/services. Stable or monopolistic markets. |
| Prospector | The product-market innovator in changing markets. |

Analyser          A focused strategy. Cost containment in some areas of the business, product-market innovation in others.

Reactor           A non-viable business strategy that is a simple set of inconsistent reactions to environmental crises.

Responses to each of the financial service organization's business strategies were overlaid on the Dunphy/Stace change model to assess whether there was a relationship between business strategy and the kind of change strategy being used in the organization. The trends, summarized as gestalts in Figure 5.4, strongly suggest that there is a link between changes in an organization's business strategy and changes in its organizational change strategy. In all cases, where there was alteration in an organization's business strategy, there was a subsequent and corresponding shift in change strategy. The converse also held (with one exception), i.e. where there was no shift in business strategy, there was no shift in change strategy. This means that an identifiable change in business strategy (from, say, prospector to analyser) is almost always associated with the adoption of a different change strategy or different change management style.

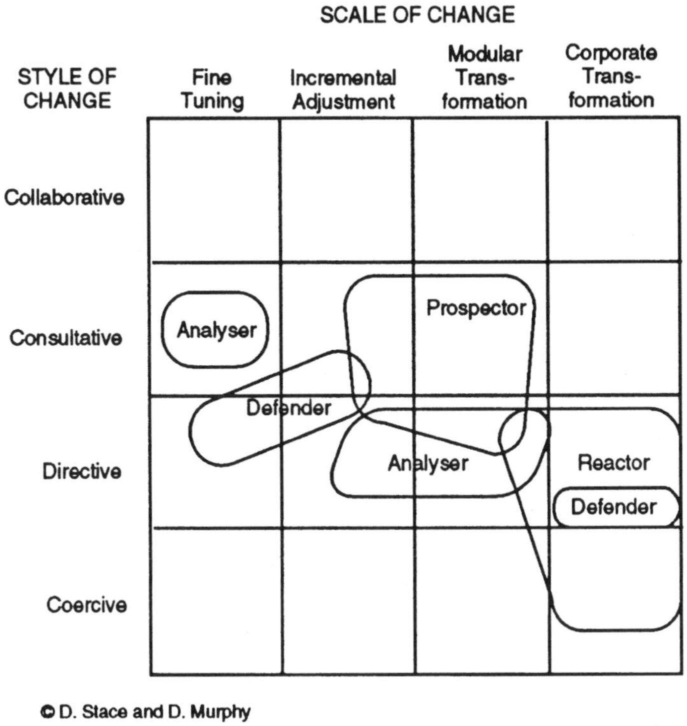

© D. Stace and D. Murphy

**Figure 5.4**  A Schematic of Generic Business Strategy Types and Their Association with the Change Matrix

We were able to trace some relationships between specific business strategies on the one hand, and, on the other, positions on the change model that represent different approaches to implementing organizational change. Firstly, the defender business strategy is primarily associated with incremental organizational change, that is, change by fine tuning or incremental adjustment, and with a consultative or directive style of change leadership (particularly the latter). Defenders generally do not undertake transformative change as their near-monopoly situation or price leadership in the market makes major changes unnecessary.

On the other hand, both the prospector and analyser strategies are associated with mid-range change strategies, that is, with incremental adjustment or modular transformation. However, they are differentiated by their styles of management and leadership. Organizations that are analysers have corporate executives who predominantly use a directive change leadership style because of the need to redirect the organization's energies rapidly to value-producing niches. Prospectors, however, have executives who predominantly use a consultative corporate leadership style because of the teamwork necessary to maintain an innovative organizational climate.

Finally, the reactor business strategy is insufficient to maintain business effectiveness, unless the organization is in a monopoly situation. To move from a reactor position to a viable business strategy demands corporate turnround, often involving large-scale restructuring, massive cultural change, workforce reductions and targeted retrenchments. As turnround requires major reallocations of power and resources, these changes are not normally achievable through consultation or collaboration as the processes of negotiation can often be so extended as to endanger the survival of the organization.

The research indicates that as organizations change their business strategies, there appears to be a complementary and subsequent alteration in their organizational change strategies. Executives must therefore be alert to the need to choose an appropriately customized change strategy to embed new business strategies, rather than relying on consultant-packaged or ideologically based solutions to change, which may be inappropriate to their organization.

## LINKING HUMAN RESOURCE STRATEGIES TO THE CHANGE 'GAME PLAN'

Our research then examined the relationship between business strategy and HRM, the important finding being that it is not as direct as previous writers have suggested. For example, Miles and Snow (1984), Smith (1982), Tichy et al. (1982) and Collins (1987) attempted to trace a direct correspondence between the strategic direction and business strategy of an organization and its HR strategies. However, this search for a direct business strategy/HR link can often neglect the vital role that an organizational change programme has on HR strategies. In our view, HR strategy is most strongly affected by the kind of '*change game plan*' run by management in moving the organization back into strategic fit. We can therefore predict more about which HR strategies should be used from knowing the degree and type of change leadership exercised than we can by knowing the corporate or business strategies pursued by the management of an organization. It is the degree of internal change and repositioning required that makes the most powerful impact on which HR strategies will be chosen. This means that change theory is the missing link in the business strategy/HRM model. Business strategy has the potential to affect HR strategy, but the organizational change programme is the important intervening variable that modifies the relationship.

When we looked at the evidence from the research, two broad sets of phenomena were identified. The first was that across all the medium- to high-performing organizations in our sample, there emerged several strong common trends in HRM, irrespective of their business or change strategies. The second phenomenon was that there were some distinct variations in HR strategies between organizations positioned on different parts of the change matrix. Both of these phenomena are explored below.

## Common Trends in HR Management

The trends in HRM that were common to all the medium- to high-performing organizations in our sample were:

- a decentralization of operational HR functions to divisions/business units, away from centralist HR departments.
- a trend for organizations to adopt, at the corporate level, a more strategic approach to HR policy and its links into the business planning process of the organization. This was evidenced in the reporting of the most senior HR executive directly to the chief executive and by the strategic importance of 'human capital' issues to the business planning process. This was occurring concurrently with the decentralization of operational HR functions.
- the development of comprehensive performance management systems as an integrated approach to MBO-type goal setting, appraisal, development and reward structures.

These trends (see also Stace, 1987) constitute a strong, common thrust to any study of differences in patterns of HR policy/strategy between organizations.

## A Differentiated Model of HR Strategies

Apart from these common trends, there were also important differences in the HR strategies of organizations. For example, two large banks in the sample had different business strategies (prospector and analyser) and different change strategies. However, the question remained as to whether both organizations would also have a distinctively different emphasis in their HR strategies. Intuitively, a major initial difference appeared to be amongst those organizations that were developmentally oriented and those that tended to use radical structural solutions in HR strategies, as a means of maintaining or regaining strategic fit (see also Curtain and Mathews, 1990). The former organizations appeared to emphasize team concepts and to be more oriented toward staff training and development, career development and culture development. The latter organizations appeared to be more aggressively managed, less team oriented and more reliant on organizational restructuring and lateral recruitment. This initially suggested two distinct types of HR strategy, which we initially termed developmental and structural.

A rigorous process of analysis was undertaken to test this perception by systematically checking to see whether organizations with similar change strategies also had similar clusters of HR practice. We found that they did. However, we identified not two but four different and distinct generic HR strategies (Table 5.1). They cover the following four HR strategy types:

- Task-focused HR strategies
- Developmental HR strategies
- Turnround HR strategies
- Paternalistic HR strategies

The *task-focused HR* strategy type (earlier referred to as a structural HR strategy—see Dunphy and Stace, 1990b; Stace and Dunphy, 1990, 1991) was characteristic of most organizations in the sample. The HR emphasis of these organizations appears to involve business unit, work-team and job redesign; functional skills training; lateral recruitment was common rather than the exception; and more relative emphasis on business-unit oriented HR systems than corporate HR systems. The approach appears to be more oriented to structural solutions, role definition and technical skill development and is less concerned about involving employees in planning personal, professional or corporate-level organizational change. In all cases, this type of HR strategy was associated with a directive management style at the corporate level.

The second strategy type, the *developmental HR* strategy, appears to be compatible with the central thrust of much of the mainstream HRM literature, and was characteristic of three medium- to high-performing organizations. These organizations placed strong emphasis on workforce and organizational development in areas such as personal development, management

**Table 5.1**   Four Human Resource (HR) Strategy Types

---

*Task-focused HR strategies**
HR strategy is strongly focused on the business unit—
*Features:*
- Strong bottom-line orientation
- Emphasis on workforce planning, job redesign and work-practice reviews
- Focus on tangible reward structures
- Internal or external recruitment
- Functional skills training and formalized multiskilling
- Strong business unit culture

*Developmental HR strategies**
HR strategy is jointly actioned by the corporate HR unit and the business units—
*Features:*
- Emphasis on developing the individual and the team
- Internal recruitment, where possible
- Extensive developmental programmes
- Use of 'intrinsic' rewards
- Corporate organizational development given high priority
- Strong emphasis on corporate culture

*Turnround HR strategies*
HR strategy is driven for a short period by the executive leadership, characterized by challenging, restructuring or abolishing HR systems, structures and methodologies
*Features:*
- Major structural changes affecting the total organization and career structure
- Downsizing, retrenchments
- Lateral recruitment of key executives from outside
- Executive team building, creating a new 'mindset'
- Breaking with the 'old' culture

*Paternalistic HR practices*
HR practice is centrally administered
*Features:*
- Centralist personnel orientation
- Emphasis on procedures, precedent and uniformity in HR practice
- Organization and methods studies
- Inflexible internal appointments policy
- Emphasis on operational and supervisory training
- Industrial awards and agreements set the HR framework

---

*Both of the above give high priority to performance management systems
© D. Stace/D. Dunphy

development, career management and culture management (internal marketing, culture surveys, employee communication strategies). In each case, this type of HR strategy was associated with the consultative style of corporate change leadership.

However, the research also demonstrated that the task-focused and developmental HR strategies were not discrete categories: organizations with a dominant task-focused HR orientation would often include some elements of developmental HR policy in the overall HR strategies. Similarly, organizations with a dominant developmental HR orientation would often include some elements of task-focused HR practices in their overall HR strategies. Thus, the task-focused and developmental HR strategies did not represent absolute differences in HR practice, but rather a different balance of emphasis. The implication is that even when pursuing a strongly oriented task-focused HR strategy, some culture building and management development will be necessary. Similarly, a strongly oriented developmental HR strategy should not avoid the difficulty of workforce and job restructuring, although large-scale downsizing would be inimical to an organization following a developmental HR strategy thrust.

Two other HR types were also identified. The *turnround HR* strategy type was characteristic of six of the organizations 3 years before the study, a time when these organizations were undergoing a period of business redefinition and corporate transformation. These organizations had substantially downsized, redefined or abolished their central HR departments; were radically reviewing their HR systems and policies; were effecting voluntary or forced retrenchments, and had opened their recruitment to outside appointees at key executive and other levels.

The final HR strategy type, *paternalistic*, was associated with the lower performing organizations making change by fine tuning. A paternalistic HR strategy exemplifies the traditional mechanistic HR policies of the 1960s and 1970s. It is strongly influenced by scientific management, standard industrial relations practice and a desire to maintain the status quo. This HR type featured a strong centralist HR role, an emphasis in HRM based on procedures and precedents, heavy reliance on productivity work studies as a form of personnel control and frequent resort to formalistic employer–employee industrial relationships.

What this analysis suggested was that the orientation of HR policies/ strategies in the sample organizations cannot be solely explained by a developmental–structural dichotomy, as we had initially thought. Figure 5.5 shows a more differentiated set of HR strategies with four generic HR strategic types superimposed on the change model. The evidence shows that HR strategies are altered subsequent to alterations in organizational change strategies, which indicates that an organization's change strategy tends to drive its HR strategy rather than vice versa.

The implication is that executives and HR strategists must correctly choose the HR strategy that has most synergy with the organization's change strategies. A loose collection of non-customized HR interventions and gimmicks will not suffice if the organization is to develop the necessary internal synergies for high performance.

Scale of Change

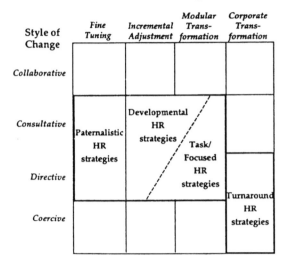

: D. Stace/D. Dunphy

**Figure 5.5**   Human Resource (HR) Strategies and Organizational Change

Figures 5.3 and 5.5 demonstrate that both task-focused and developmental HR strategies are associated with medium- to high-performing organizations; turnround HR strategies are associated with organizations attempting to regain strategic fit, where this requires major change in the organization as a whole; and paternalistic HR strategies are associated with lower performing organizations.

## STRATEGIC IMPLEMENTATION: AN INTEGRATED APPROACH

What we have described overall is a set of models for identifying an organization's management process strategies (change and HRM) and their linkage to its business strategy. This pattern of relationships is summarized in Table 5.2.

The models advance our understanding of the way in which an organization's business strategy influences its organizational change strategies, which in turn influences the choices made in selecting HR strategies and policies. In our view, there is a critical need for such an integrated view of how different areas of strategic choice relate to each other. This is particularly important for those who seek to implement

**Table 5.2**    Business Strategies and Their Links with Strategic Change Implementation

| Business Strategy Type | Corporate Change Strategy Type | Human Resource (HR) Strategy Type |
|---|---|---|
| *Defender* (Low-cost producer, or monopoly) | *Scale:* Incremental adjustment/ fine tuning<br><br>*Style:* Consultative/directive | A mix of types<br>• Paternalistic HR<br>• Developmental HR<br>• Task-focused HR |
| *Prospector* (Product-market innovator) | *Scale:* Modular transformation/ incremental adjustment (mid-range change)<br>*Style:* Consultative | Dominantly developmental HR, with lesser aspects of task-focused HR |
| *Analyser* (Focused, niche strategy) | *Scale:* Modular transformation/ incremental adjustment (mid-range change)<br>*Style:* Directive | Dominantly task-focused HR, with lesser aspects of developmental HR |
| *Reactor* (Inconsistent business strategy) | *Scale:* Initially fine tuning, then corporate transformation (usually forced)<br>*Style:* Coercive/directive | Paternalistic HR, followed by turnround HR |

© D. Stace/D. Dunphy

business strategy through organizational change and HR programmes and strategies. Both organizational change and HR strategies are currently being translated into a wide range of interventions in organizations, sometimes in non-complementary ways. For instance, we see frequent use of major organizational structuring interventions, as part of an overall business and change strategy instituted by senior management: however, some in-house trainers will try to distance themselves from such draconian measures. They prefer to focus on interventions such as interpersonal skills training, whether or not that form of intervention represents the most appropriate and focused use of the organization's resources in actioning its business strategies at that particular stage of the business cycle. The opposite, of course, may apply if a major radical structural intervention is utilized by corporate strategists when a more appropriate team development intervention should be used.

This chapter therefore provides a basis on which change and HR strategies can be conceptualized and mapped as complementary and synergistic components of the overall strategic management process, concerned with the implementation and influencing of business strategies in a changing business environment.

# REFERENCES

Collins, R. (1987). The strategic contributions of the human resource function, *Human Resource Management Australia*, **25**(3), pp. 5–20.

Curtain, R. and Mathews, J. (1990). Two models of award restructuring in Australia, *Labour and Industry*, **3**(1), pp. 58–75.

Dunphy, D. C. and Stace, D. A. (1988). Transformational and coercive strategies for planned organisational change: beyond the OD model, *Organisation Studies*, **9**(3), pp. 317–344.

Dunphy, D. C. and Stace, D. A. (1990a). Transformational and coercive strategies for planned organisational change: beyond the OD model. Published as a chapter in Advances in Organisational Development, Massarik, F. (ed.), Ablex Publishing, Norwood, N.J., pp. 85–104.

Dunphy, D. C. and Stace, D. A. (1990b). Under New Management: Australian Organizations in Transition, McGraw Hill, Sydney.

Gagliardi, P. (1986). The creation and change of organisational cultures: a conceptual framework, *Organisation Studies*, **7**(2), pp. 117–134.

Golembiewski, R. T. (1979). Macro-level interventions and change-agent strategies. In: Approaches to Planned Change; Part 1A, Golembiewski, R. T. (ed.), Marcel Dekker, New York.

Harrigan, K. R. (1985). *Strategic Flexibility*, Lexington, Massachusetts.

Harris, R. (1987). Rupert Murdoch: media tycoon, strikebreaker and citizen of the world, The Listener, 27 January, p. 7.

Kanter, R. M. (1983). *The Change Masters: Innovation and Entrepreneurship in the American Corporation*, Simon and Schuster, New York.

Miles, R. E. and Snow, C. C. (1978). *Organizational Strategy, Structure and Process*, McGraw Hill, New York.

Miles, R. E. and Snow, C. C. (1984). Designing strategic human resources systems, *Organisational Dynamics*, Summer, pp. 36–52.

Miller, D. (1986). Configurations of strategy and structure: towards a synthesis, *Strategic Management Journal*, **7**, pp. 233–249.

Miller, D. and Friesen, P. H. (1984). *Organizations: a Quantum View*, Prentice-Hall, Englewood Cliffs, New Jersey.

Murray, A. I. (1988). A contingency view of Porter's generic strategies, *Academy of Management Review*, **13**(3), pp. 390–400.

Nord, W. R. and Tucker, S. (1987). *Implementing Routine and Radical Innovations*, University of Kentucky Press, Lexington, Kentucky.

Ohmae, K. (1987). *The Mind of the Strategist*, Penguin, Harmondsworth, Middlesex.

Porter, M. E. (1980). *Competitive Strategy*, Free Press, New York.

Porter, M. E. (1985). *Competitive Advantage: Creating and Sustaining Superior Performance*, Free Press, New York.

Sashkin, M. (1986). Participative management remains an ethical imperative, *Organizational Dynamics*, Spring, pp. 62–75.

Snow, C. C. and Hrebiniak, L. G. (1980). Strategy, distinctive competence and organisational performance, *Administrative Science Quarterly*, No. 25, pp. 317–335.

Smith, E. C. (1982). Strategic business planning and human resources, *Personnel Journal*, Part I and Part II, **61**, 89, pp. 606–610, 680–682.

Stace, D. A. (1987). The value-added organisation: trends in human resource management, *Human Resource Management Australia*, **25**(3), pp. 52–63.

Stace, D. A. (1989). *Strategic Change and Human Resource Policy in Australian Service Industries*, Unpublished PhD Thesis, University of New South Wales.

Stace, D. A. and Dunphy, D. C. (1990). A new paradigm: human resource strategies and organisational transitioning in Australian service industries, Published as a chapter in *Research in Personnel and Human Resources Management*, Suppl. 2, JAI Press, Connecticut, pp. 37–51.

Stace, D. A. and Dunphy, D. C. (1991). Beyond traditional paternalistic and developmental approaches to organisational change and human resource strategies, *The International Journal of Human Resource Management*, **2**(3), December, pp. 263–283.

Tichy, N. M., Fombrun, C. J. and Devanna, M. A. (1982). Strategic human resource management, *Sloan Management Review*, Winter, pp. 47–61.

Tushman, M. L., Newman, W. H. and Romanelli, E. (1986). Convergence and upheaval: managing the unsteady pace of organisational evolution, *California Management Review*, **29**(1), pp. 29–44.

# 6

# SOCIAL NAVIGATION: INTERPRETATION AND INFLUENCE OF THE CULTURE CHANGE PROCESS

**Christopher Parker**
**Robin Neff Lorenzini**

*IMD Lausanne*

## INTRODUCTION

The phrase 'culture change' has become part of management vocabulary like cash flow and profit. This is good on the one hand but bad on the other; it is good that managers have the word in their vocabulary, but it is bad in that many managers do not understand the underlying processes and time frames involved when they embark on such a process. Like profit, culture change can be an elusive hope because the surface statement is not supported by a deeper structural understanding.

Many managers know what they want but would prefer a quick fix rather than develop a meaningful understanding of what is required and an appreciation of the time frames involved. This is like the alcoholic who keeps on doing 'cold turkey' but does not do anything about changing the causes of the underlying lifestyle. Like repeated cold turkey, quick fix approaches to culture change probably take away more energy than they put back in to the 'patient'. The primary reason for this is that there is often only a 'surface understanding' of how a culture is defined and maintained. This can sabotage any change efforts because without this understanding, a company cannot

*The Implementation Challenge*, Edited by D. E. Hussey
© 1996 John Wiley & Sons Ltd

correctly analyse its current culture; and if it does not know where it is, it is impossible to direct itself to where it wants to be.

## GETTING TO THE ROOTS OF CULTURE

### Culture and Action

The main assumption in many corporations is that their culture consists only of the actions of its members. Therefore, management believes that culture can be 'trained' and that changing culture simply means changing individual actions. Great effort has been put into developing the right seminars and quickly disseminating teaching aides throughout the organization. Within the past 15 years, large scale 'quick fix' programmes became the order of the day. Predictably, it has since become clear that

> . . . the greatest obstacle to revitalization (in an organization) is the idea that it comes about through company-wide (taught) change programs, particularly when a corporate staff group such as human resources sponsors them. (Beer et al, 1990.)

These programmes fail to produce sustained change because they fail to give any new meaning to the way that people do their actual work.

Behaviours are part of organizational culture, but they are not all of it. They are only the surface; and culture goes much deeper than the surface level. In order to get at the primary force or core of the culture, we have to ask two questions: what drives these observable behaviours; and when enacted, how are these behaviours interpreted (or given meaning) by the actors and the rest of the organization? Here, we are adapting a more systemic view to culture (à la Prigonene and Stengers, 1984; Senge, 1990), viewing it more as a cyclical/ organic process rather than a static description.

The answers to such questions helped us to develop a framework in which culture can be understood and analysed. Specifically, culture is multi-levelled and is interpreted through the assimilation of many subtle signals and has different degrees of penetration within the organization. We will discuss all of these issues beginning with the 'levels' of culture.

### What You See is Not All You Get

The dimensions of culture can be described on a continuum, ranging from the external and recognizable to deeper and more concealed (see Schein, 1985). For the purpose of explanation think of an outdated culture as a weed (Figure 6.1). Behaviours comprise the easily observable dimensions of this 'culture weed'— the leaves and flowers of the plant. These also represent the organization's day-to-day language as actions and words are continually tied together. What people say influences what they do and vice versa. In other words, the actions,

**Figure 6.1**    Visible Characteristics

knowledge and language of an organization are inseparable (Pondy, 1978; Stubbs, 1983).

Moving deeper down, we have the roots of the plant, where much of the nourishment is transferred. We liken the roots of a weed to the intrinsic *values* of the organization's culture; they give a sense of grounding to people's actions, and help to feed the visible parts at the same time.

Finally, we have the weed's environment: its soil, air, rain and sun. Without these, the plant could not exist (at least not in its present form). The roots would have nothing to grab hold of and the leaves would not get oxygen or sunlight for photosynthesis. The elements of organizational culture, which have a similar fundamental control, are the core assumptions of its members. They are the building blocks that drive all values and behaviours. Like the forces of nature, assumptions come from all around, which makes them particularly difficult to manage or change. However, as they are the most fundamental part of a culture, they *must* be adapted to meet the desired change context.

Using the weed analogy further helps to illustrate this point. Everyone knows that if you simply cut off the foliage of a weed, another will soon grow in its place. So too will old behaviours, which 'pop up' soon after they have been cut. If you pull the weed from the roots, then you kill the weed (or the culture) but you are left with a hole, which may be suitable only for a similar plant. To be able to successfully 'plant' your new culture, you may have to adjust people's underlying assumptions (just as you may have to cultivate the soil by adding chalk or alkaline, giving it more water, and/or moving objects that affect the amount of sunlight). In other words, great attention must be given to making the context as suitable for the new culture as possible; otherwise, it will not take root (Figure 6.2).

The main point is that people's actions can usually be explained by some underlying influences. If their behaviours are manipulated, and these influences are not adapted accordingly, extreme tension develops, which is eventually alleviated by pushing the new behaviours out and pulling the old ones back in. People have an unerring capacity to detect fakes, and if they do, not only do

**Figure 6.2**   The Whole Context

**Table 6.1**   The Levels of Culture. (Adapted from: Schein, E. H. (1985). *Organizational Culture and Leadership*. Jossey-Bass, San Francisco)

1. Visible characteristics: these are the overt behaviour and language or surface characteristics

   Exception: seeing that people only perform those duties that are in their own job description

2. Values: these constitute people's sense of how things should be

   Exceptions: you should not be concerned if a fellow worker needs help or go out of your way to offer assistance

3. Basic assumptions: these are the building blocks of what people take for granted as being true. This is the deepest level on which people define their reality

   Exception: you have to look out for number one

---

they not support a change in culture, but they become cynical (see Table 6.1 for summary and a working example).

**Adding Motion: How the Levels Interact**

What we have described is a good start but there is something missing; in practice, it is too static or linear. It does a good job of describing what a culture is, but it does very little to describe how it is developed or how it is maintained. Until this is understood, the ability to intervene in a change effort is handicapped.

   At this point, we need to draw upon open systems ideas to help us conceptualize the model in a more dynamic manner. Let's start with the linear framework:

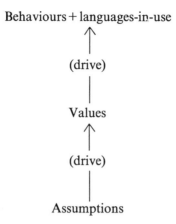

Starting in this way is acceptable, but the model is not complete until you understand how behaviours and languages-in-use can feedback to affect people's assumptions and values. *In fact, this is how assumptions are originally formed through how people interpret specific behaviours.*

For any given situation, people will develop a repertoire of responsive actions. If any behaviour proves to have a *consistent* outcome, then people will begin to form a strong association between the action and the result.[1] If this continues across time, then the association will become an assumption or what Argyris and Schön (1974) refer to as a 'theory-in-use'. It then becomes part of a person's core reality or his or her definition of the culture of his or her organization.

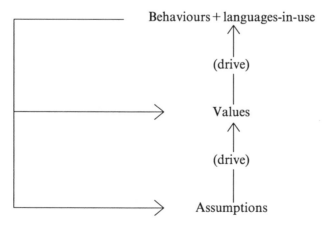

---

[1]Schein (1985) contended that only positive reinforcement would create the link between behaviours and assumptions. These authors believe that the result can be positive or negative, as long as it is consistent across time

## We are Rarely Aware of Our Assumptions

Ironically, as these behaviours and values transform into assumptions and become a stronger driving motivation for actions, people become less aware of them. In other words, they take the form of tacit or intuitive knowledge, as opposed to explicit or conscious knowledge. People do not think about them or question their relevance or usefulness, they are completely accepted; debate is unnecessary and sometimes inconceivable.

Examples of this phenomenon are endless. Every culture contains a number of rules or beliefs that have this *assumed usefulness*. In other words, no one questions why things are done in a certain manner, it is simply accepted as 'the right thing to do' or 'the way it has always been done'. If people have the insight to stop and think about the effectiveness or relevance of their actions, it is not uncommon for them to find a flaw in the reasoning behind the practice and a better way to approach the situation.

By getting rid of practices that have *assumed usefulness*, an organization increases its productivity and performance by 'working smarter' (Drucker, 1991; Taylor, 1911). Fundamentally, this involves asking two questions: 'what is the outcome we want to accomplish?' and 'how is this best done?' The challenge is to find critically objective answers which add value and are not simply based on prior assumptions.

Take, for example, the situation in which a corporation discovers a large cost problem. Traditionally, organizations have reacted to this by first revealing the amount of debt (say $10 million) to their stakeholders, particularly the employees. Next, it is announced that soon there will be implementation of 'major cost reduction plans'. The *assumption* is that this announcement will instil a sense of urgency in the organization's workers and that they will become motivated to accept some lean times in order to save the company (i.e. using cost problems as a justification for reductions has assumed usefulness). Instead, what can happen is that when the employees are informed of the amount of the cost problem they immediately start calculating how many jobs will be lost. At this point, they begin to feel betrayed by their company. This leads to a decrease in productivity, a loss in profits and an increase in the cost problem.

The damage is compounded over time as the management debates (mostly behind closed doors) the details of the required 'cost reduction plans'. The employees' sense of relief about still having their jobs soon gives way to cynicism and resentment. They feel angry, powerless and degraded. By this time, serious damage is done to employee relations, the cost of which cannot be easily measured but which is very great. *Goodwill takes years to mould and weeks to destroy.*

# SOCIAL NAVIGATION: THE CHANGE PROCESS

'Social navigation' is a term that we use to describe the process by which culture is formed and culture change is implemented. As the word 'navigation' implies, change involves first figuring out where you currently are (i.e. your culture climate), then plotting and following the markers that will get you where you want to go. It is the navigator's (i.e. leaders) job to keep 'the boat' on course and to make sure that key players are on board. This paper discusses this process by addressing three key areas:

1. Culture interpretation and perception: surfacing of underlying assumptions;
2. Identifying 'natural' initiates of change;
3. Implications for leadership practices.

## CULTURE INTERPRETATION AND PERCEPTION: SURFACING OF UNDERLYING ASSUMPTIONS

The driving force behind 'social navigation' is that in order to achieve sustained change, an organization must have a clear understanding of its current reality. This is done by surfacing the underlying assumptions on which actions, behaviours and decisions are founded. In other words, we need to hold a mirror up to the company and its members. Unfortunately, assumptions are not something that you can ask someone to list. By their very definition (embedded and tacit) people are blissfully unaware of them and usually need help to identify them, even if they are not consciously trying to block them.

Rather than study assumptions directly, we look at the visible manifestations that people use to build their assumptions. These are summarized in Figure 6.3

## CULTURE INTERPRETATION AND PERCEPTION DIAGRAM

This diagram has helped managers to understand their culture by drawing attention to three challenging questions:

1. What are the manifestations of our culture?
2. How are these factors interpreted?
3. What metaphor is used to classify our culture and how deeply is this culture embedded?

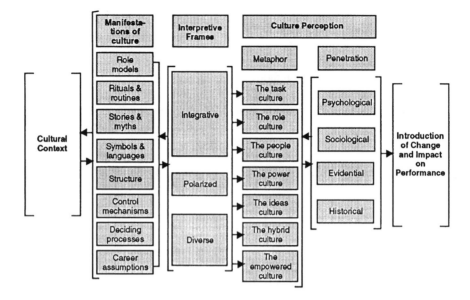

**Figure 6.3** Social Navigation Chart © 1992 by The International Institute for Management Development (IMD), Lausanne, Switzerland. Not to be used or reproduced without permission. IMD retains all rights

### What are the Manifestations of Our Culture?

Organizational culture is not something people immediately grasp upon entering into a company. Instead, understanding is achieved over time through a process of constantly assessing and calibrating visible manifestations of the culture. As we assess where we are, we need to trace these same manifestations, in order to 'map out' people's culture perceptions and allow the underlying assumptions, which are driving individual behaviours, to surface.

*Role models*

One of the most powerful indicators of an organization's culture is the characteristics of people's role models.

Which traits are rewarded in the company?

Which traits are strictly forbidden?

Which traits are discouraged, but practised anyway?

People intuitively pick up on these questions by studying individuals who have been targeted for promotion or who have been recently promoted. They then use this person's behaviours as a model for their own. Most typically, this person will eventually be rewarded for these preferable actions, and the behaviours are cycled into assumptions and become a powerful part of the culture. Derr (1986) has suggested that role models in organizations not only send signals about behaviour at work, they also send signals about lifestyles. He denotes four styles of career success that signal to everyone in the company not only the way to be 'seen' at work, but also prescribe elements of one's personal life. His 'getting ahead' type is 'driven' for status and power, his 'getting high' by professional excellence, his 'getting balanced' by balancing work, home and leisure and his 'getting secure' by security and belonging.

When role models are 'framed' in these subtle ways, they become a 'totem' in tribal terms and begin to represent the values, styles and behaviours to which the organizational tribe should aspire. Heroes are made and outlaws are defined in this way.

## Rituals and routines

An organization's rituals and routines are practised daily and in many different forms. Greetings such as 'Good morning' and 'Ca va?' have ritual responses. When taken to an extreme, organizational life can be viewed as an enactment of rituals by people with specific roles (Goffman, 1974; Berne, 1964; Boje, 1989). However, this rather fatalistic viewpoint has its advantages when an organization is attempting to enact change. As behaviours become routine they can be neatly identified. This classification can be used to accelerate change by people recognizing the rituals that they practise and questioning their validity and usefulness.

> Do current rituals and routines add value or are they just
> assumed to add value?

> Does the way that you do things around here add value for your customers?

> What are the benefits and limitations of these routines?

A classic example of this comes from Wallace Co., a Houston-based distributor of industrial pipes and valves. This company was awarded the coveted Baldridge award in 1990. Yet in early 1992, it had to declare chapter 11 bankruptcy. Why? Because the owners had placed too much emphasis on the award and had accepted so many speaking engagements that their attention to the business had suffered. The moral is that no rituals or awards, no matter how commendable, should be allowed to run, or ruin, your company. You have to pay attention continually to what makes sense at that point in time.

The way in which rituals and routines are transmitted from long-service members to new rookies is in itself a part of an organization's culture. Some companies practise paternalistic policies, where rookies are 'taken under wing' and patiently taught the guidelines. Others have more brutal rites that are designed to tear people down. These 'rites of passage' are the prelude for acceptance; most consulting firms, investment banks, and MBA and PhD programmes are classic examples of this practice.

### Stories and myths

Explicit communications, such as written language, do not completely represent the organizational messages transmitted as part of a culture. It is also necessary to identify the 'words' behind the words.

In every company, there is a repertoire of stories that has a powerful influence on individual behaviour. Stories are the verbalization of a deeply felt human history within the organization and a shared picture of a company culture. This leads them to be more memorable than any other type of communication (Martin, 1982). Stories, more than any other organizational communication, are shared with freedom and trust, without fear of ridicule.

Some scholars consider stories to be the basis from which people define their reality. Words get their meaning only when they are put in the context of a story. People define their own organizational role as it fits into current stories and use these cues to help reduce any ambiguity that they perceive. As Wilkins (1984) said,

> . . . stories . . . are often all we have to go on (p. 48).

Therefore if you change the story, you change people's reality, or at least their reality within their organization.

In addition, stories can be used to help release the power of an emergent organization. Change cannot be done by treating individuals as ingredients in a cake recipe. Instead, you have to give them enough information about where the organization needs to go and let them use their creativity to get there. As Paul Allair, Chief Executive Officer (CEO) of Xerox, said,

> . . . To win, we need to find ways to capture the creative and innovative spirit of the . . . worker. That's their real organizational challenge. (Dumaine, 1991.)

Stories give the right amount of direction, while still allowing people to feel like independent contributors within a short space of time. This is the essence of empowerment.

Strong stories provide a common background for a group. *Good leaders know this!* Stories or scripts guide people in a forceful way to understand the variety of complex skills necessary to complete their jobs and at the same time give flexibility in order that they can adapt the prescriptions to their own distinct situation, within the range of their own style and current competencies.

Martin (1982) argues that the power of stories comes from their core or script. This is the setting, organizational context, sequence of events, plot and roles. The script is what remains after the specific details have been stripped away. The strongest stories usually signal values, power relations and feelings. To illustrate this point, consider two similar stories from two different organizations. Both involve a situation where a female line employee confronted the male president of the corporation because he was not following a rule that was her responsibility to uphold. The first involves Thomas J. Watson, Founder and Chairman of the Board of IBM. As the story goes:

> . . . a twenty-two-year-old bride weighing ninety pounds whose husband had been sent overseas . . . had been given a job until his return. Every wife of a serviceman received a week's pay each month during these absences, and they were a super-loyal contingent of employees. The young woman, Lucille Burger, was obliged to make certain that people entering security areas wore the correct clearance identification.
>
> Surrounded by his usual entourage of white-shirted men, Watson approached the doorway to an area where she was on guard, wearing an orange badge acceptable elsewhere in the plant, but not a green badge, which alone permitted entrance at her door.
>
> 'I was trembling in my uniform, which was far too big,' she recalled. 'It hid my shakes but not my voice.' 'I'm sorry,' I said to him. I knew who he was all right. 'You cannot enter. Your admittance is not recognized.' That's what we were supposed to say.
>
> The men accompanying Watson were stricken; the moment held unpredictable possibilities. 'Don't you know who he is?' someone hissed. Watson raised his hand for silence, while one of the party strode off and returned with the appropriate badge. (Rodgers, 1969, pp. 153–154).

The second story involves Charles Revson, the head of the Revlon Corporation. Concerned that corporate hours were not being respected, Revson required all company employees to sign a confidential registration book to ensure that they were arriving at work on time. As the story goes:

> . . . One day, when Revlon was in the process of moving from 666 Fifth Avenue up to the General Motors Building, in 1969, Charles sauntered in and began to look over the sign-in sheet. The receptionist, who was new, says 'I'm sorry, sir, you can't do that.' Charles says, 'Yes, I can.' 'No sir,' she says, 'I have strict orders that no one is to remove the list; you'll have to put it back.' This goes back and forth for a while with the receptionist being very courteous, as all Revlon receptionists are, and finally Charles says, 'Do you know who I am?' And she says, 'No sir, I don't.' 'Well, when you pick up your final paycheck this afternoon ask 'em to tell ya.' (Martin et al, 1988.)

Two similar situations with similar characters, yet the outcomes create two divergent sets of assumptions about the rules of the organization. One in which everyone in the company is equal and the rules apply to all. A second in which there is a privileged elite who are above reproach and have complete power over those who do not. Clearly, this will serve to foster very different cultures and ensuing behaviour amongst the employees of IBM and Revlon.

### Storytelling—fact or fiction?

People who are good storytellers have been shown to be more powerful communicators and leaders (Boje, 1989; 1991). The other side of this, however, is that such individuals can use the power of stories to further their political intentions. Stories can give the impression that sectional interests are universal throughout the organization, or they can be designed to create 'purposeful mystification' (Fisher, 1984) whereby intent or blame is hard to assign.

It is critical to make sure that the stories that are circulated are positive, healthy and constructive towards the change that the organization desires rather than representative of specific political factions. One part of the social navigation process is to essentially un-script and re-script an organization. As we navigate new waters, we need to be attuned to the stories that we hear and the stories that we tell. In successful change situations, we see that key people have thought about the way that they will script the future, who is in the play for what reasons and how the denouement unfolds.

Successful sales and marketing people have been doing this for years by scripting and rehearsing new product and service launches. We need to start applying this common sense by treating the change process as a product with internal and external customers. The change process can be scripted, at least in the beginning.

### Symbols and language

Every organization has its own language. It consists of the national, industrial, technical and individual jargon, which has developed over time. Long-service executives speak it fluently, and newcomers must learn it in order to gain credibility and legitimacy.

An organization's language is considered by many scholars to be a direct indication of its culture. The content of company annual reports can be linked to propensity to enter into joint ventures (Fiol, 1989) and the level of risk aversion (Bowman, 1984). In other words, the actions, knowledge and language of an organization are inseparable (Pondy, 1978; Stubbs, 1983).

Language introduces an interesting challenge in any change effort because the communication of an organization's restructuring goals creates a couple of interesting paradoxes. On the one hand, 'language' is essential before any change can begin (i.e. the people must be informed). On the other hand, introduction of change can immediately instil a sense of fear and cynicism, which can cause people to resist or block the change process. In fact, use of the word 'change' can produce negative physical reactions. In contrast, the term 'continuous improvement', used widely by most Japanese firms, is given a much more positive reaction. It instils a sense of prideful persistence more than of unwelcome disruption. (However, we recognize that some psychological disturbance is a necessary precursor to 'internalized change'.)

Conflict also arises in relation to the clarity of the change message. Management's language needs to have a clear and consistent purpose and to be translatable to every level of the organization. *Yet*, leaders often make the message too clear, which can inhibit ownership by other members of the company and restrict the flexibility that is so necessary in today's business environment (Eisenberg, 1984). We have seen a number of situations that use 'hard' cost reduction numbers to instil a motivation for change. This strategy, however, has a negative impact on the quality of thinking that is necessary to produce innovative and sustainable cost-cutting processes.

Language is the fundamental building block of communication and its impact cannot be underestimated or ignored. If people do not speak the same language, they simply cannot communicate. Today, this is a potential problem not only across countries, but within the walls of many companies. Managers do not understand scientists; manufacturing does not understand marketing. As Ronald Willis, Chief Scientist at Hughes Aircraft, said,

> You can't have four people describing the same defect four different ways. You have to make common sense. (Stewart, 1992.)

The notion that social navigation brings to companies is sensitivity to language difficulties, which helps individual companies to build a common language.

Traditional research on organizational language has concentrated on written documents, using methods such as semiotics and content analysis. However, in the future, social navigation research will focus on language-in-use groups, through video- and audio-taping of individual interviews, natural work teams and customers. The goal will be to trace how language, and its emotive content, exemplifies

> . . . the rules that regulate meaning . . . (and) defines the values embedded in the system (of the organization). (Fiol, 1989, p.279.)

## Structure

An organization's structure is the most easily observable manifestation of cultural assumptions. For instance, something as concrete as the physical shape of the building(s) offers powerful clues. What are the layouts of the offices? What is senior management's proximity to the shop floor? Where are the buildings in relation to the customer? How comfortable are the working conditions and how do they vary across levels? Decades ago, the Hawthorne studios (Mayo, 1933) showed that simple manipulations of a plant's physical layout could have dramatic effects on worker motivation and productivity; mostly because they made people feel that others were paying attention to them.

Major corporations such as Nike, Trinova, Becton Dickinson, Rhône-Poulenc Rorer and Chrysler have recognized the effect of structure on organizational culture. Each has dedicated major funds to the construction of new office centres and/or research facilities that are designed to be more friendly, less monstrous and to promote more communication and contact amongst their employees (see Alpert, 1991). The result is the creation of a sense of community, which enhances trust and supportive risk taking.

A hierarchical structure has a concrete and symbolic impact on employees' assumptions, particularly on what they believe to be their purpose and position within the company. Many organizations are currently attempting to 'invert the pyramid' in order to empower their workers by taking away most of the bureaucratic blockages to productivity and job satisfaction. This is the expressed mission of such leaders as Xerox, Cypress Semiconductor, Becton Dickinson, General Electric, Hewlett-Packard, Ericsson and Ciba-Geigy.


*Control mechanisms*

Bill Hewlett of Hewlett-Packard fame said, 'you get what you measure' and as we navigate new social realities we need to be aware of this axiom. Intelligent human beings seem to forget too easily the principals of classical and operant conditioning, i.e. that we adapt our behaviours to what is positively reinforced. Instigators of change need to have a clear idea of what has been measured historically, what needs to be maintained of the old system and what new measures need to be conditioned into the system.

The relevance of this issue can easily be seen for multinational corporations. Traditionally, differences created by geography, currency differences and governmental trade regulations have controlled the performance of the company as a whole. People have been 'conditioned' to think in terms of divisions. Now with these barriers being removed, a more systemic frame is needed.

One factor that few companies consider is how do you control and measure the actual change effort? How do you know if your organization is 'on course'? Early warning signals of recidivism need to be built into the company's social/ change navigation 'radar system' and markers must be put in place to keep the effort from washing ashore. It is for this reason that companies are making serious efforts to gather 'soft data' from surveys and internal interviews with individuals and groups as a way of tracking process and feedback mechanisms. Ericsson of Sweden uses its OPUS system as well as other sophisticated systems to track perceived penetration of new policies and principles (e.g. Total Quality Management (TQM) in their Italian subsidiary Fatme).

*Decision processes*

How decisions are made within an organization can reveal the roots of many elements of a culture. This is particularly true if the decision processes are inconsistent with espoused practices. For instance, the current trend of flattening hierarchical levels and inverting the pyramid automatically has implications for how decisions are made within organizations. This can be summed up in one word—consensus. Managers have come to realize that no matter how quickly a decision is made, if it is not accepted by everyone then it will either not reach its potential or it will fail.

Although there is usually consensus around the necessity for consensus, problems still arise during the process of trying to reach an agreement. Why? Managers typically want to reach consensus by telling the workers what they should agree about. In other words, nothing has really changed. Reaching an agreement takes time, and lots of it. This is one of the major differences between Japanese and American companies. The Japanese spend time to reach consensus in a product's planning phase. Americans go more by the trial and error rule. The result is that many American products have far more errors during development and after they have reached the customer.

Not only does consensus decision-making take time, it involves a number of other steps, which are not a part of outdated authoritative leadership. Firstly, managers must learn how to gather *relevant* information, not just what they want to hear. Processes must be implemented to allow the free exchange of non-threatening ideas. Communication patterns must be developed to allow these ideas to be accurately distributed throughout the organization, so that people are able to contribute.

Secondly, managers need to learn how to incorporate this diverse and complex information into their solutions. Opening up the pipe lines to new ideas can be overwhelming and many managers react by simplifying the information into more manageable forms: graphs or two-by-two matrixes. They then use this simplified version for the basis of their decisions. This often leads to incorrect decisions because they are based on incomplete information. The real damage, however, comes when employees become aware that their input was not used in the actual decision process. The net result is an increase in cynicism towards management, a decrease in the level and quality of information sharing and a regression into old top-down decision systems. In fact, the real power behind the TQM movement is in the use of 'problem-finding' and 'problem-solving' techniques. When TQM works, there is universal acceptance of the seven quantitative and seven qualitative quality tools that become the way to structure data into information and transform such information into new knowledge about doing business. The undeniable message is that everyone should be contributing to decision-making.

*Career assumptions*

Contracts get made between leaders and their people about why and when they may be promoted. In turbulent times, it is becoming difficult to offer 'career promises', yet most leaders send signals of 'possibilities' on a one-to-one basis, which can be difficult to uncover. These promises have a deep influence on how and why work gets done.

Many difficulties associated with multifunctional teamwork come from the career pacts that function leaders make with individuals in order to 'protect their turf' from outside interference. This limits the ability of people to inform other functions in time, on time and with good information.

Working with a major global chemical business, we found that its efforts to increase multifunctional teamwork had achieved only 60–70% of aspirations after 5 years. The major blockage came from career deals concluded between functional chiefs and their subordinates. These deals were made in order to protect data and keep the functional turf free from intrusion, but on a larger scale they significantly hindered the organization's growth. This company has now changed its promotion criteria to include a significant portion on effective cross-functional cooperation.

### How are these Factors Interpreted?

Identification of these manifestations is only the beginning of how organizational members interpret their culture. The next natural step is to form these impressions into some sort of associative network. To do this, people naturally use what we refer to as an 'interpretive frame'. These frames can be thought of as the base equation that people use for calculating their culture; they are how bits of information are put together into 'complete thoughts' (see Goffman, 1974).

Figure 6.3 lists three interpretive frames: integrative, polarized and diverse (see Martin and Meyerson, 1988). With an integrative frame, various cultural manifestations are 'framed' in a way that they support and validate each other to form the perception of activities and functions. For instance, if you are using an integrative frame and you have identified a role model who is person-oriented rather than a task-driven individual, then you will most likely look for other manifestations that support this observation. You will listen for stories about how this role model spends time with his/her workers, and notice ways in which the organization has supported these behaviours. The primary focus is on finding similarities in manifestations that support a common theme, or metaphor (see below).

The opposite of this is a polarized frame of reference. Here, you are driven to look for contradictions and oppositions amongst the manifestations. For example, a common experience is seeing an organization that has changed to a relatively flat organizational structure, yet still has rituals and routines that support a class division such as reserved parking spaces. If this exists in organizations moving to 'new ways', it can lead to increased cynicism, as it highlights certain inconsistencies within an organization. People use these inconsistencies to confirm their polarized perspective.

The last frame is one that we call 'diverse'. This frame is unique because it does not concentrate on any one kind of relationship amongst cultural variables. Here, you value the diversity that is apparent; you are not looking for ways that manifestations support or contradict each other; simply what they are. Players and policies in an organization are not explicitly connected to one another in any particular fashion. They complement each other in the delivery of customer satisfaction. It is similar to looking through a kaleidoscope. As you watch the changing patterns of light and shapes, you do not analyse how the pieces fit together, you simply admire the designs for what they are.

In our discussions about interpretive frames, we are usually asked a primary question: whether one frame is more 'correct' than the other. It is very difficult to judge the relative superiority of these frames. It is only when placed in the context of a specific organization, and/or industry that a comparison can be made. For an individual company (or perhaps industry), each frame can produce very different observations, some of which may be more accurate than others for that particular company. For instance, it has been argued that a diverse frame is most appropriate for a highly innovative organization because of its high levels of creativity and ambiguity (Martin and Meyerson, 1988) or when process or product diversity is needed to 'shake out' an industry or sector (Anderson and Tushman, 1991). All three frames exist and all three can be appropriate at different stages of business development. However, it is difficult to really *know* what is the most correct interpretation—as it is usually in the eye of the beholder. What we believe to be more important is to help people realize how their interpretive frame affects their perception of their organization's culture and how that perception can be changed simply by changing their frame of reference. This helps people to understand how others could come to very different conclusions given the same information. The result is a broadening of their perspective and a 'bigger' view of the system leading to less nervousness and paranoia about the actions and intentions of others.

## What Metaphor is Used to Classify Our Culture and How Deeply is this Culture Embedded?

Details of the culture chart have been outlined in order to show how these manifestations can be used to find clues about the underlying assumptions in an organization's culture. We then discussed how interpretation of these clues can be affected by an individual's interpretive frame. This results in a perception of the organization's culture.

In order to bring coherence to all of this complicated and ambiguous information, people connect this perception with a metaphorical label (Boland and Greenberg, 1988; Kuhn, 1970; Morgan, 1980). In other words, people use these metaphors to translate information into understanding (see Figure 6.3 for examples). Our use of metaphorical structure is not new to organizational analysis; it has been used by workers, managers and scholars for years. The two most prominent examples of this are the organization as a machine and the organization as a part of an organic system (Morgan, 1980). Phrases like 'the group worked like a well-oiled machine' and 'information overload' were constructed because of the images that these metaphors brought to mind. Survival of the fittest is a common metaphor applied both internally and externally.

Clearly, the metaphor used to describe an organization is going to have a significant impact on how it is viewed (Boland and Greenberg, 1988). Metaphors not only frame perceptions, but also 'feelings' about the organization. This is what makes metaphors so powerful. The machine metaphor leads to a belief that a company has, and should optimize, its level of control. The object is to make sure that all the parts are working together efficiently and productively. Biological or living system metaphors give much more emphasis to the environment, co-dependence, synergy, feedback loops and organic structures.

We find it helpful to view culture under the metaphor of a spider's web: a large number of manifestations connected to each other in an elegant yet recognizably complex and intertwined way. Our conception of a company as largely symbolic—but subject to the content of its repertoire of stories, scripts, language and rituals—has strong implications for how and in what way we perceive and analyse the organization. The culture web metaphor is useful in change efforts, particularly for the way it helps identify factors that are responsible for the assumptions that drive individual and group behaviours.

Numerous metaphors that can be applied to an organization at any given time are representative of the various subcultures within the company. One cause of this variety is their different *levels of penetration* (see Figure 6.3). In order to understand how an organization's metaphors (and the assumptions and behaviours on which they are based) are representative of the culture, we also have to understand its level of penetration (Saffold, 1988). If penetration is at the psychological level, then metaphors used by *unconnected individuals* are representation of their own culture. Examples are:

Working here is like being a cog in a big machine (task culture).

I like working here, it's like being at a tennis camp. I get the coaching and resources I need to perform at my best (people culture).

Working here is like being in the army, and I guess I feel like a corporal squashed between the other NCOs and the mass of soldiers (role culture).

Sociological penetration is formed by a group of people to describe their own particular associations. For example:

The production people here are consistently the underdogs. The marketing guys have all the power just because the CEO is a marketing guy (power culture).

At NEC we are working like the human brain. We want active neural connections between people to get the best ideas (ideas culture).

We at NUR systems are like university professors compared to our business unit partner TEKALUR. We make customized instrument solutions whereas TEKALUR produce mass, easy for measuring equipment. But both of us can sell the full range of our SBU output to complimentary customers (hybrid culture).

At Kiste Chemicals I am one of 500 managers, but I feel like an owner or partner in my business (empowered culture).

If a culture metaphor is consistent across the *current* organization as a whole (i.e. across functions, countries, etc.), then it has penetrated to the evidential level. This is historical penetration at the deepest position, meaning that the metaphor has become part of the archival stories of the organization. At this point, it has been 'written' into fact within the minds of the employees (and possibly the external environment) and can have either positive or negative effects.

When attempting to bring to the surface existing culture perceptions and metaphors (in order to facilitate change), it is essential that you ascertain their level of penetration. Psychological penetrations are, in some ways, the easiest to approach, as only one person or small groups are dealt with. If at the other extreme you are confronted with a historical penetration you will find that it is much more difficult to change. To illustrate this point, the following four scenarios can be considered:

*One*: You are the general manager of a regional toy manufacturer. Although all of your line workers are good, there is one in particular, Jim, who consistently has produced excellent work, has had numerous excellent ideas for quality improvement and has demonstrated strong leadership initiative over the past 5 years. Although he is an average of 7 years younger than the other workers, his peers clearly like and respect him. That is why they named him 'The whiz kid'. As a reward for his obvious talent, you decide to promote Jim to a supervisory level, and everyone in the group agrees that this is a great idea.

Two weeks into Jim's new position you start to notice difficulties with his area. Production is down and there is a certain disorderliness with the otherwise smooth process. You decide to have a talk with him. It does not take you long to realize that the problem is coming from Jim's belief that he is too young to be able to manage the group. The fact that they have called him a 'kid' and have treated him as if they were proud parents has made him assume that he has no right to give them orders, or have any authority over them at all. Then there was Paul, the 54-year-old veteran of the plant who was on his way to retiring. He had been Jim's mentor and trainer when Jim first started; now Jim was his boss—and that did not seem right. He regretfully asked to be demoted as he was obviously the wrong person for the job.

*Psychological penetration.*    In this case the only problem with Jim's ability to supervise his group is his belief that he is not qualified to do so. No one else in the company shares this opinion. This is because of his assumption that his peers really view him as a kid and that they could never take him seriously. Jim needs to be helped to make the transition to boss by talking through his assumptions and finding a new personal metaphor other than the 'whiz kid'. Realizing that Paul wants nothing more than to see his protégé excel will help greatly, but he needs to rescript his part in the old team. This rewriting involves working out the reality of the role, some personal style feedback and behaviour change. But is it also the creation of a new 'story' for Jim, which builds positively on his whiz kid history. A growing, maturing metaphor would help, real or imagined. For example, a story on how the 'local boy makes good'.

*Two*: You are the manager of the engineering department of an American semiconductor chip manufacturer who has just set up a production division in Western Europe. This is the first attempt that the company has made at coordinating the sales/marketing efforts in four countries: Germany, France, Italy and the United Kingdom (UK). As a first step you decided to have a joint meeting with all of these groups. Your goal is to set up a coordinated effort between your facility and these sales forces and to look for ways to reduce the obvious costs that have occurred due to duplication of effort. In fact, one of the motivations for creating your division came from customer complaints that they were being bombarded by too many of your sales people.

Before you can begin speaking, a representative of the German group hands you a paper outlining the exact chip specifications that are necessary for his customers. You notice, with amusement, that there are even technical calculations included (which are wrong) and it is written in language that a

7-year old could understand. Still, the German proceeds to go over it with you, step by step.

After listening patiently for a few minutes, you politely interrupt saying that this is something that can be discussed later. But once again you are side-tracked by each of the other countries with their specific requests and instructions.

Finally, you stand up and ask everyone to take their seat. The purpose of this meeting, you explain, is to work on a unified process across all countries, not to delineate individual needs. You are met with blank stares. You realize that since their creation, 8 years ago, these four divisions had always worked as separate units. It had been 'natural' to do it that way, given the language, geographical and regulation differences. In fact, when asked not one of the people present could ever remember speaking to someone from outside their division, unless it was at the yearly sales meeting.

'We are different, that's all,' explained one of the UK representatives. 'France has their customers, we have ours. Why would I want or need to coordinate with them?'

You knew you had a long meeting ahead of you.

*Sociological penetration.* Because there has never been an attempt to coordinate these four countries, they have been free to create their own assumptions about how to run their businesses. Control mechanisms as obvious as geography, currency and governmental regulations have helped to foster this division; not to mention the language barrier. Each group has its own culture, and sees coordination with the other divisions as full of potential problems rather than opportunities. Joint process analysis and coordination work can help, but no one should be surprised at the amount of effort that needs to go into getting these 'tribes' to work with each other. Groups like this often 'scale-up' the problem to a national level. This serves to add to the hopelessness of the change effort. By far the best approach is to find small projects on which people from different countries can 'pair up on' to solve. This is a small step, but it can be very effective.

*Three*: You have just been hired as the President of a small shoe manufacturer in North-east America after completing a successful turn-around of a family-owned clothing company. On your first day at work you have a meeting with your two vice-presidents and your secretary to get a feel for the current organizational climate. You notice that the meeting begins on a very formal note, with your colleagues referring to you as 'Mr Jensen' as they sit very stiffly in their chairs (at a safe distance). Your efforts to loosen up the conversation only meet with blank stares and obvious discomfort. So you ask them why they are so distant.

Your secretary replies, 'We thought this is how you preferred to be addressed by your subordinates.' The obvious emphasis on the last word could not be missed.

Rather than be taken aback you ask her to explain further, and being a woman who loved to talk, it did not take much prodding to get her to open up further. Your reputation, it appears, has preceded you to this company. Apparently, one of the men in marketing had been a summer intern at your last company. Upon hearing that you were to take over here, he immediately recounted a dispute he had overheard in which you were involved. The details were fuzzy but he did remember you saying rather angrily '. . . and from now on call me MR JENSEN!' You remembered the situation, and in fact it had been a joke between you and one of your colleagues.

The story had made sense to the company as you had been hand picked by its last president, of 6 months, Mr Vanders (or Scrooge as everyone called him). Everyone knew that Vanders' role model was Howard Hughes, and that he insisted on having total control over your company. He believed in top-down management, executive perks like reserved parking and paid vacations, and absolutely insisted on having the largest corner office in the building (even if that meant remodelling).

Finally, and this part was true, during your interviews with the company you had plainly stated that you did not have a definite plan for career progressions for the rest of the employees. 'I have enough trouble keeping track of myself, let alone 200 other people' you had quipped.

Your secretary stopped, looked furtively at the vice-presidents who had gone pale and bowed her head. 'That's about the sum of it,' she mumbled.

*Evidential penetration.*    Even though Jensen had been at work for less than a day, he already had a reputation. It was based on two stories, only one of which was correct, and some strong associations made between him and the man who had formerly held his place. The good news is that Vanders had not had very long (only 6 months) to instil these assumptions on the organization. If Jensen's actions in the next few months consistently denied this false reputation, he could have a strong impact on the culture of this promising company. Active and energetic denial through positive actions is the order of the day.

*Four*: You are a newly appointed CEO of a large multinational corporation, called Forman, which is based in the UK. Since its origination 25 years ago, your company has had as part of its charter the phrase '. . . and dedication to growth through acquisition'. Forman has honoured this by purchasing 18 companies in the past 15 years.

Unfortunately, 12 of these 18 companies failed and Forman was forced either to sell the companies or close them all together. The company has retained as many of these laid-off workers as possible. As a result, Forman consists of a hotchpotch of employees from a number of its failed ventures. Each is a constant reminder of a failed attempt at acquisition. Four of the 18 are barely breaking even, and the remaining two (the only UK companies in your portfolio), which were essentially left to themselves, have continued to prosper.

You have had your eye on a medium-sized Swedish company, Serport, which you expect to do very well in the next decade but is currently struggling for capital. Preliminary meetings with the president of Serport have gone well, but you both agree that Forman's history with acquisitions is a major hurdle. Forman's employees are tired of having to take on these 'catch-22s' and the Serport employees would view a merger as a punishment.

You have spent a great deal of time analysing why most of these acquisitions failed and are positive that this Swedish deal would be a success. But how do you get your people to believe in it? In addition, as your only two prosperous ventures have been within the UK, why would you want to go to Sweden? You know that in order to make this a success, you must have the support of your organization.

*Historical penetration.*    As we move down the change process from adjustment through transition to transformation, the more we find ourselves influenced by history. This is the deepest level of an organizational culture. History is extremely difficult to change, but it can be edited and built upon. Whereas the other three levels could actually be uncovered and to some extent modified— this is often not the case with historical penetration. You cannot rewrite each individual's mental history of the company. Instead, you have to build upon it, showing why and how things are going to be different. This is a slow and gradual process, as you cannot ask people to give up their history; this is a part of their identity. It is important to concentrate on the positive aspects of the culture and the management processes currently in place to find out what adds value and what does not. Good analysis will unearth the historical core capabilities/competencies of the business. Once people are made aware of these, they can be helped to adjust their practices and processes by dropping those things that are no longer useful. Margaret Thatcher was very good at getting people to change working practices in the UK by demanding that 'We have to get back to the things we were good at'. This appeal to history has led to quite revolutionary change.

However, this process takes time, in some cases 5–10 years before people will adjust their picture of history. This time frame is not unrealistic. To accelerate it, you may have to change some of the people or rotate internationally. But you have to be careful not to lose some of the 'embedded knowledge' that you need to make things work. Drastic changes among top people do not necessarily wipe out history, they only take out historic symbols. This does provide an opportunity to staff for a new history, but this has to be built up through the other three levels of penetration and the celebration of a successful future.

The above scenarios were designed to show how culture (and its assumptions, manifestations and metaphors) can penetrate an organization at numerous levels. It is necessary to understand the level from which these assumptions are emanating in order to know how and where change efforts should be targeted.

The remainder of this chapter will deal with two issues that are relevant to potential culture intervention techniques. The first deals with the element of time, and how it 'naturally' affects change; the second addresses new focuses on the leadership of change.

## 'NATURAL' INITIATES OF CHANGE

Most people will agree that change is difficult; that it feels awkward at best and devastating at worst. Part of our research has been devoted to finding situations in which this is not true. Was there anything that caused a 'natural' change in people? More directly, could this be used to help accelerate a change process?

This led us to do some research on the timing and pace of the culture and change processes within an organization. In a study of group development, Gersick (1988) noted that groups consistently progressed through a series of predictable phases—marked by their perception of the available time. For the first half of the time allocated to a project, the team makes no significant progress towards completion. Instead, it is stuck in a phase of inertia, in which it spends its time generating ideas, but does not attempt to integrate or direct the information towards completion of the task. Then at the midpoint,[2] as it notices that half the time has gone, it makes a dramatic transition. This is what gives teams direction and helps them to focus on finishing projects. Gersick contends that it is only at the midpoint that groups are able to make this transition. Any attempt to make this break early will be unsuccessful. Furthermore, if the group passes the half way mark without making this shift, the task will never be completed (Gersick, 1989).

Gersick's model seems to point to some 'natural' pace that people follow when given an unfamiliar project. They appear to use time as a guidepost. If they feel that they have more rather than less of it, they do not feel a compulsion to move themselves out of an information-generating mode.

---

[2]The midpoint is defined as the half time of a group's allotted schedule. If the group meets for 1 hour, the midpoint is 30 minutes, if it meets for 1 year, it is 6 months, etc.

Having less than half the allotted available time, is an understood, automatically accepted trigger to change the focus of attention towards task completion.

The interesting question is what does time pressure do to our capacity to navigate new social realities? Can we accelerate the point at which people are destabilized and willing to let go of history. This is evident from the impact of time-based strategies. Many global organizations are demanding the halving of time for manufacturing, then halving again and again on the basis of retaining value-added processes only. The positive results of this use of time reduction are remarkable, with many organizations attaining up to 90% time reductions with significant quality, cost and working capital improvements. Sophisticated use of time targets may be one of the most powerful social navigation tools available if they are used as organizational mileposts. Our belief is that these findings can be applied implicitly to a process of change within organizations.

## IMPLICATIONS FOR LEADERSHIP OF THE CULTURE AND CHANGE PROCESS

Success depends on leadership. (Michael Walsh, CEO, Tenneco. Former CEO, Union Pacific Railroad.)

As the need grows to develop and communicate a corporate culture that is aligned with change efforts, the role of the leader becomes increasingly important. Leadership styles and behaviours are one of the largest determinants of the cultural climate; the signals and symbols created are critical to the change effort. If a leader's position is ambiguous, this can cause great confusion and conflict within the organization. In major change cutting across functions and levels, the bridge building power of the CEO is critical.

Yet, as with the communication of change, there is a fine line between specificity and restriction. Popular terms like 'transformational' and 'empowerment' speak of the need to give employees the resources (both internal and external) to excel in their jobs, not just to perform them. In fact, the notion of empowerment is a paradox for leaders because with empowerment people want direction and independence at the same time. They want the direction of a vision and the independence to act within it. But what are the values and behaviour of a successful change leader?

Scholars have been addressing the question of leadership for the better part of this decade. As Burns (1978) said, 'Leadership is one of the most observed and least understood phenomena on earth' (from Van Seters and Field, 1990). Table 6.2 summarizes the development of leadership theories. Early leadership theory (late 1920s) attributed successful versus non-successful leadership to the personality or charisma of the leader himself. It was not until the late 1950s that the concept of a relationship between leader and follower was introduced, as well as the influence of the organizational and external environment. Leaders need followers in a particular context. Since that time, the perceived nature of the relationship between leader and follower has changed (i.e. from influence to transformation), and the environment has become more complex (i.e. situation to contingency). However, there has not been a fundamental shift in the assumptions regarding the role of leadership. It is still primarily concerned with what leaders or managers should or should not do to others (Streufert and Swezey, 1986). The theories attempt to identify correct or incorrect behaviour and actions. Unfortunately, although each has something to offer, when these theories are applied, they show major flaws and inconsistencies (Argyris and Schön, 1978).

**Table 6.2**   Summary of Predominant Leadership Theories. (Adapted from: Van Seters, D. A. and Field, R. H. G. (1990). The evolution of leadership theory. *Journal of Organizational Change Management*, 3(3), pp. 29–45)

| Stage | Assumptions |
|---|---|
| Personality (e.g. great man theory) | The first leadership theories; leadership involved imitating personalities and behaviour of great leaders |
| Influence (e.g. five bases of power) | Leadership involved the relationship between boss and subordinate |
| Situation (e.g. environment approach) | Leadership involved dealing with other factors rather than intra- and interpersonal matters. 'Appropriate' styles depend on recognizing particular situational cues |
| Contingency (e.g. path-goal theory) | Leadership cannot be put into a 'pure' form. Successful leadership depends on numerous internal and external factors |
| Transactional (e.g. vertical dyad linkage) | Leadership was based on role differentiation and social interaction |
| Culture (e.g. theory Z) | Leadership is omnipotent in the culture of the whole organization; quality began to take over quantity |
| Transformational (e.g. transforming leadership | Leadership is based on tapping the intrinsic motivation of organizational) members |
| Force for change (i.e. Kotter, 1988) | Leadership is based on opportunistic capacity for change |

## Connecting Leadership Behaviours to Values

Good leaders empower their people. Empowerment is a feeling, and for that feeling to be sustained leaders need to display coherence and consistency at a number of levels, not simply at the behavioural level. Koestenbaum (1988) has identified four leadership capacities that are associated with a powerful leader. He emphasizes that in order for a leader to be successful, all four need to be in evidence. The 'leadership diamond' is as follows:

VISION

RATIONALITY                     ETHICS

COURAGE

Vision is not simply ideas, but ideas that win commitment. Ethics are not only morality, but also treating people with respect and dignity. Courage is the capacity to go against the 'common view'. Rationality is the process of managing using data and information, rather than by opinion.

Using these dimensions, a large multinational pharmaceutical company has asked its employees to rate over 500 managers on 50 leadership practices that exemplify these values and to give them a feeling of empowerment. The list includes promoting co-operation, delegating authority, developing people and encouraging innovation. The results are being used to teach individuals and groups of managers to help others to feel empowered by connecting effective leadership values to appropriate behaviours. This presents a believable message, which is transmitted in a believable way.

## Dealing with Complexity

Successful leadership is more than the right behaviour, it is seen as the ability to:

> . . . focus on the interrelationships or interactions, that is, the integration of multiple thoughts, attitudes or actions in the service of a more overall perspective . . . (Streufert et al, 1988, p. 78.)[3]

---

[3]Researchers at IMD, Pennsylvania State University College of Medicine and the University of Geneva have implemented the use of a computer simulation model, which is designed to test cognitive complexity.

Dr Siegfried Streufert has used this research method on entrepreneurs for over 10 years. His findings show a strong correlation between successful entrepreneurs and high levels of cognitive complexity. It is our belief that this trait is also associated with the ability to manage change in today's global business environment, and that it is this component that will add the newest insights to research on the leadership of change.

This is the aptitude to deal with dynamic complexity or the

> ... situations where cause and effect are subtle, and where the effects over time of interventions are not obvious. (Senge, 1990, p. 71.)

Why is this ability so critical to successful leadership? As the uncertainty of business environments increases, the direct effects of a firm's decisions become less obvious. What was previously routine has become exceptional. Consequently, there are numerous details demanding a leader's attention, and the probability that he or she will lose focus on the organization's mission and direction increases. Yet the consequences of this confusion range from market share loss to bankruptcy.

## CONCLUSION

How can we use the ideas behind social navigation to accelerate change? Simply using the social navigation chart to ask some questions is a great help in becoming aware of the areas that we need to influence in any change effort. We need to help people to become aware of their underlying assumptions and how these create the current culture and accelerate or block the desired culture change. This process illuminates the organization's 'social system' in a non-threatening user friendly way, so that they can decide what needs to be maintained, what needs to be changed and at what level the change should be enacted. This helps to develop 'systems thinking' and helps individuals and teams to understand the 'dynamic complexity' of their working environment.

Leaders work simultaneously as champions, sponsors and orchestrators of change. The pace and targets of each of these roles varies and we must be able to monitor how the results of one impact on the others. The social navigation charting process forces leaders, and other organizational members, to think hard about the soft side of change.

## REFERENCES

Alpert, M. (1991). Office buildings for the 1990s. *Fortune*, November 18, pp. 76–80.
Anderson, P. and Tushman, M. L. (1991). Managing through cycles of technological change. *Research Technology Management*, **34**(3), pp. 26–31.
Argyris, C. and Schön, D. A. (1974). *Theory in Practice*. Jossey-Bass, San Francisco.
Argyris, C. and Schön, D. A. (1978). *Organizational Learning: A Theory in Action Perspective*. Addison Wesley, Reading, Massachusetts.
Beer, M., Eisenstat, R. A. and Spector, B. (1990). Why change programs don't produce change. *Harvard Business Review*, November–December, pp. 158–66.
Berne, E. (1964). *Games People Play: The Psychology of Human Relations*. Grove Press, New York.

Boje, D. M. (1989). Postlog: bringing performance back in. *Journal of Organizational Change Management*, **2**(2), pp. 80–93.

Boje, D. M. (1991). The storytelling organization: a study of story performance in an office supply firm. *Administrative Science Quarterly*, **36**, pp. 106–26.

Boland, R. J. and Greenberg, R. H. (1988). Metaphorical structuring of organizational ambiguity. In: L. R. Pondy, R. J. Boland and H. Thomas (eds) *Managing Ambiguity and Change*. John Wiley & Sons Ltd, New York.

Bowman, E. H. (1984). Content analysis of annual reports for corporate strategy and risk. *Interfaces*, **14**, pp. 61–71.

Burns, J. M. (1978). *Leadership*. Harper & Row, New York.

Derr, C. B. (1986). *Managing the New Careerists*. Jossey-Bass, San Francisco.

Drucker, P. F. (1991). The new productivity challenge. *Harvard Business Review*, November–December, pp. 69–79.

Dumaine, B. (1991). The bureaucracy busters. *Fortune*, June 17, pp. 26–36.

Eisenberg, E. M. (1984). Ambiguity as strategy in organizational communication. *Communication Monographs*, **51**, 227–42.

Fiol, M. C. (1989). A semiotic analysis of corporate language: organizational boundaries and joint venturing. *Administrative Science Quarterly*, **34**, pp. 277–303.

Fisher, W. R. (1984). Narration as a human communication paradigm: the case of public moral argument. *Communication Monographs*, **51**(March), pp. 1–22.

Gersick, C. J. G. (1988). Time and transition in work teams: toward a new model of group development. *Academy of Management Journal*, **31**(1), pp. 9–41.

Gersick, C. J. G. (1989). Marking time: predictable transitions in task groups. *Academy of Management Journal*, **32**(2), pp. 274–309.

Goffman, E. (1974). *Frame Analysis: An Essay on the Organization of Experience*. Harper & Row, New York.

Hannan, M. T. and Freeman, J. H. (1977). The population ecology of organizations. *American Journal of Sociology*, **32**, pp. 929–64.

Koestenbaum, P. (1988). Developing leadership: corporate survival in the third millennium. *Work Link*, June, pp. 79–81.

Kotter, J. P. (1988). *The Leadership Factor*. Free Press, New York.

Kuhn, T. S. (1970). *The Structure of Scientific Revolutions*. University of Chicago Press, Chicago.

Martin, J. (1982). Stories and scripts in organizational settings. In: A. H. Hastorf and A. M. Isen (eds) *Cognitive Social Psychology*. Elsevier/North-Holland, New York, pp. 255–305.

Martin, J. and Meyerson, D. (1988). Organizational cultures and the denial, channeling and acknowledgment of ambiguity. In: L. R. Pondy, R. J. Boland and H. Thomas (eds) *Managing Ambiguity and Change*. John Wiley & Sons Ltd, New York.

Mayo, E. (1933). *The Human Problems of an Industrial Civilization*. The Macmillan Company, New York.

Morgan, G. M. (1980). Paradigms, metaphors and puzzle solving in organization theory. *Administrative Science Quarterly*, **25**, pp. 605–22.

Pondy, L. (1978). Leadership is a language game. In: M. W. McCall, Jr and M. Lombardo (eds) *Leadership: Where Else Can We Go?* Duke University Press, Durham, North Carolina, pp. 87–99.

Prigogine, I. and Stengers, I. (1984). *Order Out of Chaos: Man's New Dialogue with Nature*. Bantam Books, New York.

Rodgers, W. (1969). *Think*. Harper & Row, New York.

Saffold, G. S. (1988). Culture traits, strength, and organizational performance: moving beyond 'strong' culture. *Academy of Management Review*, **13**(4), pp. 546–58.

Schein, E. H. (1985). *Organizational Culture and Leadership*. Jossey-Bass, San Francisco.

Senge, P. (1990). *The Fifth Discipline: The Art and Practice of the Learning Organization*. Doubleday/Currency, New York.

Stewart, T. A. (1992). A master of the megillah. *Fortune*, January 27, pp. 50–1.

Streufert, S., Nogami, G. Y., Swezey, R. W., Pogash, R. M. and Piasecki, M. T. (1988). Computer assisted training of complex managerial performance. *Computers in Human Behavior*, **4**, pp. 77–88.

Streufert, S. and Swezey, R. (1986). *Complexity, Managers and Organizations*. Academic Press, New York.

Stubbs, M. (1983). *Discourse Analysis: The Sociolinguistic Analysis of Natural Language*. University of Chicago Press, Chicago.

Taylor, F. W. (1911). *The Principles of Scientific Management*. Harper & Brothers, New York.

Van Seters, D. A. and Field, R. H. G. (1990). The evolution of leadership theory. *Journal of Organizational Change Management*, 3(3), pp. 29–45.

Wilkins, A. (1984). The creation of company cultures: the role of stories and human resource systems. *Human Resource Management*, **23**(1), pp. 41–60.

# 7

# VISION INTO ACTION: A STUDY OF CORPORATE CULTURE[1]

**Michael Mainelli**

*BDO Consulting*

## INTRODUCTION

Large organizations that have evolved over time to become successful in their target markets refine their strategies, business and systems to match their environment and to contend effectively with their competitors. They become perfectly adapted—so perfectly, in fact, that sudden, unexpected and continuous change, of the kind that we are currently seeing in global markets, must inevitably kill them, unless they change their behaviour.

In responding to this problem, organizations are variously described as engaging in the management of change, organization development, corporate renewal or total quality management. These are, in essence, all attempts to produce in organizations the fundamental capacity to redirect business rapidly to secure some competitive advantage. The common thread linking these initiatives seems to be the phenomenon called 'organizational culture'.

The interest and vigour with which organizations have pursued culture change at times seems ill-matched to its capacity to really produce cost-effective and positive change. Yet, the fashion for culture change continues unabated—given voice in academia, the media and the pronouncements of chief executives. Perhaps the strongest impetus was provided by Peters and

---

[1]This is the full text of a report published in 1992 by BDO Consulting from fieldwork conducted in 1991

*The Implementation Challenge*, Edited by D. E. Hussey
© 1996 John Wiley & Sons Ltd

Waterman (1982) in the now famous *In Search of Excellence*. One of their central findings was that

> the dominance and coherence of culture proved to be an essential quality of the excellent companies.

Over the past decade, the main concern of managers and consultants has been how this concept can be used as a tool—in short, how it can change an organization. Indeed, there is no shortage of managers and consultants who will swear that culture change dramatically improved the functioning of a particular organization.

However, at first blush, there appear to be as many approaches to culture change as there are consultants.

It is because of this complexity and confusion that BDO Consulting initiated this study. Our intention in conducting the research was to focus on culture change from the point of view of what large organizations were actually doing—that is, the practical considerations and processes of culture change. Some of the guiding principles we adopted were:

- to sample a wide range of large organizations;
- to understand the patterns or themes common to organizations engaging in culture change;
- to emphasize a qualitative approach in order to capture the essence of culture change in individual organizations.

The results of this undertaking are set out in the following pages. Firstly, however, we must mention the participants (Appendix) in the research who freely gave their time to a series of interviews between February and August 1991, and made the findings meaningful by their considerable candour and openness. We are indebted to them.

## OUR APPROACH

The research consisted of in-depth person-to-person interviews of 1–4 hours duration with individuals who were involved in undertaking, leading or planning large-scale change initiatives in their organizations. As can be seen from the list of participating organizations, the 28 interviewees were all senior managers who could provide a detailed view of change programmes in their organizations.

We intended to draw together a sample that covered a wide range of business sectors, including recently privatized organizations. Another consideration was that the organizations should be large—either in terms of turnover or numbers of employees. Our focus on large organizations was based on the belief that large organizations are necessarily complex and that the challenges of implementing change are equivalently complex and therefore instructive.

The final list of participating organizations therefore covered the following business sectors:

- manufacturing;
- electricity generation and supply;
- transport (public and private);
- retail;
- mining;
- entertainment;
- financial services;
- telecommunications;
- construction.

Interviews followed a predetermined schedule of questions that sought to expand on the following areas:

- the meaning of culture and culture change (in an operational sense);
- trigger events;
- methods of culture change used in the organization;
- issues arising out of culture change.

The interview discussions covered these areas and usually considerably more. An important feature of the research was the verbatim comments of participants—many of which have been incorporated in this report. Indeed, it is the words that senior managers use to describe their organizations' cultures and change efforts that truly capture the essence of the phenomenon.

Finally, the interview data was qualitatively analysed to examine trends and common themes, differences of opinion and differences of approach.


## THE FINDINGS

Ten primary themes emerged. They were:

1.   Direction from the top.
2.   Emphasis on incremental change.
3.   The crisis point as trigger.
4.   Culture change as an act of faith.
5.   Involvement of staff.
6.   Visibility of leaders.
7.   Living with change.
8.   The management development spiral.

9.  Alignment of terms and conditions.
10. Decentralization and delayering.

This list seems, at first glance, to have something of the 'how to' about it. This is encouraging. It suggests that different organizations face similar challenges and deal with them in similar ways. But this is also misleading. If there is an overarching truth to be learnt from this research and from our own experience of culture change assignments, it is that culture change should be determined primarily with reference to the nature of the organization involved. If this sounds circular, then that is the essence of culture.

Comparisons across organizations are useful but merit caution. Different organizations emphasize different things. Culture seems extraordinarily resistant to formula and mechanism and highly responsive to conviction and leadership. As Nietzsche wrote:

Men believe in the truth of all that is seen to be strongly believed in.

In short, it would be dangerous to think of the 10 themes as a simple flow chart to success.

## KEY FINDINGS—I

Change cannot be divorced from the personalities that lead it.

The trouble with mission statements and statements of values is that all companies aspire to the same things. But you still need them! They're the starting point for action.

Some business leaders just have an instinctive feel for the right things at the right times—they understand whether something is going to work or not.

Vision or direction is the chief executive's main job in managing change. Otherwise the whole programme would end up going 45 degrees to where it should be going.

The need is to be single-minded about change. Forget the scars. Just keep going.

### Direction from the Top

It seems a truism to suggest that culture change programmes need steerage from the top management of an organization. However, it was startling to learn that in almost all the participating companies, change was frequently driven by a single person. Often, a new chief executive had taken over the reins or had determined, virtually single-handed, that a new strategic agenda was called for. As can be seen from some of the verbatim comments below, much of this role is about setting the broad vision. As one managing director put it:

> My philosophy about change is straightforward: I'm the boss. I'm right. This is my view and this is what we're going to do.

However, at least as much of the role is concerned with managing the ongoing process as simply setting the agenda. This means being seen to be part of the change process—demonstrating in behaviour the new values and beliefs of the desired culture. Many of the participants pointed out how isolated the leader of change becomes and how frequently he or she must defend against both criticism and legitimate concern for the short-term difficulties that inevitably accrue once a change programme begins.

It is typical of organizations that most managers, even those at senior level, find it difficult to keep thinking strategically, to strike the balance between reacting to pressing problems of immediate impact and driving forward with long-term changes that are often neither popular nor well understood. The success of a senior figure in carrying colleagues with him not infrequently rests on his willingness to clear the field of antagonists.

Indeed, on more than one occasion participants hinted at the progressive early retirement of those senior directors either opposed to change or holding diametrically opposed views. Unanimity of vision is clearly vital as change proceeds.

## KEY FINDINGS—II

One of the first questions we asked ourselves was: How much organizational energy do we have to make this massive change?

The problem we faced was setting change targets that were sufficient to get us to our overall final objective but not mega-targets of such a magnitude that no one would believe they were achievable.

We saw the change programme as a series of incremental changes to the behaviour of people that ultimately achieved a critical mass. Once the critical mass was there, we started to see real change.

It's critical to make changes of an order of magnitude. Don't do salami-slicing—a bit of this, a bit of that. Does not work. Confuses people. Allows them to adapt to change without changing.

**Emphasis on Incremental Change**

There has been much debate over the issue of evolution versus revolution in organizational change. It is unsurprising therefore that the debate was also a theme amongst the participants.

Most argued strongly for a phased approach to change, but simultaneously stressed the need for objectives that were highly challenging and that would effect substantial change. Getting this balance right is difficult. There is the danger of simply taking too long, with the result that people 'adapt to change without changing'.

Likewise, there is the mistake that one organization made during the planning stage:

> We had no idea, at first, just how deep the culture was and how pervasive.

The result? An unacceptable delay, whilst senior management had to start from scratch and faced the considerable problem of lost credibility. People had begun to say,

> Oh, it's just another fad . . .

This anecdote suggests that getting the pace of change right is initially dependent on understanding the organization's culture and subcultures. Hofstede (1991), writing about cultures and organizations, has warned against senior management assumptions about how well they know their organization's culture. Organizations, of course, look very different from the top than they do where the work is done. Indeed, several participants commented on the wishful thinking of senior managers during the early phases of change programmes.

Alternatively, rushing through a change initiative (or at least accelerating the pace) can have both positive and negative outcomes. One participant described how the blistering rate of change was essential in itself to achieve the overall objectives. It left people in no doubt that senior management were serious and that those who fell by the wayside would not be part of the new culture. Brutal and pragmatic, yes, but it was appropriate for the organization at that time.

Within a very different context, a senior manager commented:

> When the top management team is highly stable—in other words there are no changes in the key figures for many years—then change is also slow.

Given an organization of this type and the culture that surrounds it, it is understandable that massive changes at high speed are likely to be unacceptable and that the casualty list is very high.

Again, it is instructive that in those participating organizations where large-scale change was fastest, demanning was usually greatest.

# KEY FINDINGS—III

Culture change was considerably easier when we had our backs to the wall.

The truth dawned that it was *not* all sweetness and light. It was about hard facts and often unpalatable decisions—grasping nettles, if you like.

We used privatization as a way of telling staff that if we didn't change we wouldn't survive.

Management gimmicks like TQM and culture are useful in the sense of providing a new trigger for change at an appropriate time.

The HR function should be the catalyst for the Board's change initiatives.

## The Crisis Point as Trigger

Why do organizations change? Do they start the process or are they pushed into it? We might answer that it's a bit of both. Yet several of the participating organizations seemed, on occasions, to have deliberately created crises for the purpose of triggering radical change. The reason for this is that people in organizations are good at hiding from the need to change. They need a justification for change. They need to be pushed.

In the 1980s, the UK had its share of crises—the government's privatization plan, which forced the power generating organizations and others into the new reality of competition; the impact of Big Bang on financial institutions; the globalization of markets and increasing international competition. These themes continue in the 1990s.

'One of the triggers,' confessed a participant, 'of the fad for change management is that Britain managed to isolate itself so effectively until about 15 years ago that it has only recently woken up to the real competitive world. Culture change offers a panacea that seems to have rescued other organizations from the brink elsewhere in the world.'

But external crisis points are still external and not all large organizations rely on such events to provide them with the need to change. A crisis point is a trigger *and* a justification. In fact, amongst the participants it is more a justification than a trigger. It is true that people respond more favourably to change when there is a compelling reason to do so.

Deliberately inducing a crisis has a lot to do with forcing staff to operate above the comfort zone. The crisis is about offering a reason or incentive to take the step that brings change. This immediately places people above the comfort zone where further change can be sustained. A crisis, whether real or manufactured, creates uncertainty (if not fear) and seems, at least amongst the organizations participating in this study, to enable senior management to lever the cultural boulder that single inch that gets it moving.

An induced crisis may take many forms, but frequently it appears to be a clear enunciation, from the top and down throughout the organization, of imminent decline in comparison to competitors, even if this is untrue. This supplies the justification for 'sub-crises'—the appointment of a new business unit head to shake things up, redundancies or overhead cost reductions.

There was also a strong belief amongst some participants that the role of human resources (HR) in the 1990s must become more strategic, must start to force new, often radical ideas into line management under the stewardship of the senior executive team.

## KEY FINDINGS—IV

---

A 'strategic' decision to change is usually nothing more than gut-feel dressed up in numbers and rubber-stamped by some committee.

Culture change means changing people. People are fallible. That's why culture change isn't as easy as it should be.

Evaluating success in culture change is like measuring goodwill in the balance sheet.

In a long-established, stable organization really fundamental change can be very dangerous—the downside risk is much greater than you might anticipate.

---

### Culture Change as an Act of Faith

Most large organizations would be right to ask, 'Where will culture change take us?' Most come to the conclusion that the entire venture will be an expensive best guess—an act of faith.

One of the reasons for the interest in change management, and the 'learning organization', is to try to tackle the act of faith by making organizations much more reactive. If the organization responds rapidly to external pressures and demands, and is liberated internally from bureaucracy, then long-term culture change becomes unnecessary. The conundrum is how to become a learning organization without going through fundamental culture change. There is not an answer to that. Clearly, one must follow the other.

The participants were unanimous in saying that there were no guarantees of a positive outcome of any particular change programme—'positive' being loosely defined as, at minimum, some payback on the investment, evidenced in improved overall business performance, reduced costs and higher quality products. However, there was a keen awareness that culture change itself needs to be justified, even if it is an act of faith. One participant, with only a touch of cynicism, cautioned:

> It's not just about change. It's about trying to make more money.

It is a comment on the difficulty of measuring success in culture change, even indirectly, that few of the participants had set in place any evaluation mechanisms. Those who had, emphasized that direct costs can be tracked fairly tightly; estimates of the management and staff time involved are possible; and it is feasible to attach a negative cost to failure.

However, in the participating companies, the focus was more frequently on qualitatively assessing things like:

- the preparedness of managers for more senior appointments;
- customers' perceptions of improvements in service;
- greater control over unions;
- is the whole organization pulling in the same direction—i.e. *one* culture rather than warring subcultures?

## KEY FINDINGS—V

---

You need to make people obsessive about change: show them the new values then nag them persistently until change has happened.

In implementing change we worked on the rule of thumb that it was a good thing to have as many change initiatives going *up* the organization as *down*. This generates both the commitment and momentum crucial to success.

A great problem has been the 'Mafia subculture'—a sort of informal network of resistance based on the principle: 'You cover my back and I'll cover yours'.

Change doesn't happen because top management want it to happen. It only occurs when it is deeply embedded in the people you want to change.

---

### Involvement of Staff

Participants agreed that changing culture was about changing the people involved. Some had been more systematic in this endeavour than others. For example, there was the view that it was important to create a network of change agents in key positions at all levels and by this means to build up sufficient momentum to overwhelm resistance. Most participants also identified the role of consultants as indispensable in providing either an objective diagnosis of culture and change requirements or assistance with downstream implementation of new values and systems.

A salutary note was also sounded by a senior personnel figure:

> There is at least as much danger in copping out and letting consultants dictate culture change as there is in doing it yourself . . . You need aid from consultants, not substitution of staff and management effort.

In fact, several participants expressed concern about vast information technology (IT) implementation projects that absorbed the full-time use of large numbers of consultants. Such projects clearly required the expert assistance, but were seen to be in danger of unwittingly fostering a new culture—not of self-sufficiency and initiative, but of dependence and uncertainty.

Getting everyone in an organization involved in change is something to which most organizations, and all writers in the field, will pay lip service. The benefits are obvious, practical implementation is not quite so easy. More than two-thirds of the participants mentioned the difference between an intellectual involvement and a true commitment to change:

> What you tell me makes sense, but why should I change?

Alignment of terms and conditions to support the new cultural values (discussed later) is part of the solution. However, a number of participants pointed to the difficulty that incentive schemes tend to degrade over time as staff learn how to manipulate them.

Where participants felt change had so far been successful, this had frequently involved the widespread communication about, or even inducement of, a crisis-point, as we discussed earlier. It seems that getting things started by providing a need to change is largely the key to the process.

Resistance to change was handled in different ways. Several participants discussed circumventing the resisting factions. Few had tackled them head-on and a number partially resolved the problem with early retirements and redundancies.

## KEY FINDINGS—VI

> For top management, and ultimately all managers, culture change is about learning to 'walk the talk'—that is, being consistent to the espoused values.
>
> We found that training wasn't very effective except where management behaviour was in harmony with the training.
>
> On reflection, the key facet of success in the programme was the style of the MD—in other words, 'Get out and do it!'
>
> We changed our culture by being highly consistent in management action—doing what we said we'd do.

**Visibility of Leaders**

'Do as the boss does' is perhaps one of the primary mechanisms of acculturation in organizations. New employees are influenced by both the formal and informal behaviour of their bosses. The impact of peers should not be underestimated either, but managers usually possess an automatic authority to sanction (sometimes unwittingly) or punish certain patterns of behaviour.

Certainly, participants felt very strongly that managers, first at the very top then lower down the hierarchy, should be the primary change agents. But achieving a real change in behaviour (learning to 'walk the talk') is not easy. It requires continuing, visible adherence to a new set of behavioural norms. 'Do as I say, not as I do' is no longer good enough. Old values such as 'information is power' need to be *seen* to be replaced by the real sharing of information.

Nonetheless, old habits die hard. This is why a singleminded focus on the new culture by the chief executive is so important. If the signs and symbols distinguishing the new values are seen to waver at the top, how much greater is the wavering down the rest of the organization.

In one participating company the statement was forcefully made that employees had a *right* to *expect* certain behaviour from managers—behaviour that embodied the new values. Seeing the evidence of changed behaviour in senior managers builds the conviction that the new behaviour is right. We come back to Nietzsche's words again that people will have faith in the truth of those things that are seen to be strongly believed in.

As distasteful as it may be to British managers and British organizations, there is enormous power in the almost evangelical adoption of new cultural norms by senior management. Undirected leadership training is not the answer—though many companies still try this.

At the heart of culture change must be a core of values that are truly held and provide the backbone of the organization.

## KEY FINDINGS—VII

---

Continuous change is about anticipating problems.

Culture change isn't something you can drop and then take up again when you wish! It needs constant managing.

You must keep the organizational 'strain' up above the comfort zone. This is essential. Without 'strain', jobs get into a rut. And the maintenance of strain is equivalent to ongoing change.

People like comfort and hate displacement—even something as simple as having to move their desk!

---

### Living with Change

Today, we have all become aware of and concerned about change. Contemporary organizations face a highly competitive business environment. Public sector organizations have been thrust into increasing accountability. Affecting all of us is the accelerating rate of technological change, and we find ourselves in a physical and social environment that has become highly volatile, subject to both political and ecological imbalances.

To remain competitive, organizations cannot stand still. As a point of comparison, it is estimated that the total accumulation of scientific knowledge is doubling every 10 years. The impact of this on society is dramatic. Yet most participants in this study believe that employees dislike change. How then are organizations to cope?

The process of organization development (OD) was defined by Bennis (1969) as:

> a response to change, a complex educational strategy intended to change the beliefs, attitudes, values, and structure of organisations so that they can better adapt to new technologies, markets, and challenges, and the dizzying rate of change itself.

That was in 1969, but the description still applies perfectly in 1991. So are organizations any closer to dealing effectively with the pace of change? Have the methods of OD had an impact?

Well, at least half the participants in this study felt that an acceptance of continuing change had been inculcated into their organizations, where previously stability was the order of the day. In addition, there was a growing belief that the imposition of sufficient organizational strain was necessary to keep employees operating above their comfort zone. Such strain might take the form of increasing standards of performance, shifting work groups, and doing more with less.

Perhaps this is a result of a new realism. A participant admitted:

> We thought of ourselves as highly sophisticated. We were arrogant about our success and reckoned our competitors were useless. We were only ever used to an expanding market. That was our Achilles' heel—we were, in fact, naive. In the world markets of the 1990s we know we have to be radical, pragmatic, even brutal. It's not enough for people just to understand the intellectual argument; they actually have to *do* those things.

## KEY FINDINGS—VIII

> Most large organizations like ourselves spend great sums of money on outplacement counselling. The question we've started asking ourselves is why we don't spend the same on career development counselling when people are still with us!
>
> Management development stops people thinking just about *activity* and starts them thinking about *achievement*. Achievement is what makes the company successful!
>
> Our prime process of change has been management development—not simply the provision of training courses but hard, factual analysis of the people and skills the business requires and a long-term strategy for developing them. This had to be company-wide rather than divisional, so that a company culture was fostered and not a series of warring subcultures.

**The Management Development Spiral**

In Japan (and in many Japanese companies outside that country), young management trainees are moved from one job to another every 2 or 3 years and may be transferred to other offices or plants.

In a national culture that values and promotes service longevity (as in Japan), it is sensible to expose managers to as many new organizational and business experiences as possible and also to ensure that they have solid grounding in every function—finance, production, marketing, personnel, sales and research and development. The long-term objective is to develop managers who will be more valuable as they go up the organizational hierarchy. This can be represented as an upward development spiral across different experiences and functional departments.

In the West, we often lament the shortage of true general managers. Organizations in the UK in particular have tended to develop managers as functional specialists who, in the current business world, are poorly equipped as they reach senior positions.

There was a growing recognition amongst the study participants that the long-term development of general managers was crucial to sustained competitive success. At least a third of the participants saw management development as one of the main initiatives to change the organizational culture. The focus was not so much on training managers to be better in their current jobs, but on identifying management talent and developing the general managers of the future. Such a strategy must be very long term. It necessitates forward-thinking and succession planning, as well as the establishment of competencies against which individual development can be measured within the development spiral. It is categorically not about short-term training initiatives, but rather about the merit of experience.

## KEY FINDINGS—IX

We want to be able to fine-tune the organization in an ongoing fashion—not have to do major surgery every so often. This means the culture has to be one that accepts change, isn't bureaucratic, isn't tied down to tradition and history.

A great danger is that operating management believe they know what the existing culture is—without finding out in some objective way. Then they wind up not understanding the vested interests of staff and have no idea how to change this. They simply end up out of touch. . . .

To get staff to provide good service we have to show that management has regard for them.

### Alignment of Terms and Conditions

Once the agenda has been set or change has begun to happen, maintaining it becomes an issue.

Most of the participants spoke of modifying terms and conditions as part of this process. Still, organizations do this in small ways all the time. But success in building and sustaining more effective 'high wire' performance amongst employees as part of wide-ranging and deep culture change, demands that personnel terms and conditions owe as little as possible to historical factors and as much as possible to the new, desired values. In other words, the appraisal system, bonus and incentive schemes, policy statements, remuneration, and promotion all must have a role in helping to support and drive the new cultural values. They are themselves mechanisms to change behaviour, not simply organizational baggage.

Meshing cultural drive-wheels with the cogs of HR systems is never easy. Nonetheless, the lesson would seem to be to do it fast. Long drawn out modifications to HR systems, delayed by poor industrial relations or by fears of too much too soon, frequently enable employees to adapt to change without changing. The aim here is to institutionalize the changes by means of HR systems, to begin to synchronize individual and organizational values. However, it scarcely needs to be said that HR systems or the structure of the organization are not the only mechanisms of sustaining change. Management style and leadership are the elements that establish the social context within which the HR systems motivate employees. A number of the participating organizations had overhauled their HR systems in less than 18 months—not without considerable pain, but with a high degree of success.

## KEY FINDINGS—X

---

We want a race-horse culture. Those people who can't run fast enough are simply in the wrong race—they need to go.

Moving people about helps to reinforce the new decentralized culture.

The legitimate interests of staff are not always the same as the organization's. This means that some people get left behind. . . . It's inevitable.

In this company and in many others, the role of the middle manager hangs in the balance. IT is both changing their traditional communication or buffer role and replacing them.

One or two of the old top team objected to my style. They've gone.

**Decentralization and Delayering**

One of the trends in assessing the success of culture change is to ask:

Are we doing more and better with less resource?

In almost all of the participating organizations, culture change had produced delayering—that is, the stripping out of one or more management levels, with the consequent redundancy of many of those managers. None of the participating organizations ruled out redundancies in the future as part of their culture changes. It is important to note that this was viewed not as a response to recession but to the need to be more competitive and, though brutal, to remove individuals unsuited to the new culture or unwilling to adapt quickly.

Delayering was closely related to decentralization and the shift of autonomy and accountability to operating units. As operating units get more authority and accountability, so head office functions shrink.

But why do this? Centralization used to work. The primary reason is that decentralization places strategy and operations closer to the market, or rather the market closer to strategy and operations. This has to be a good thing: it forces managers and employees to be more attuned to the real world and competition.

In the UK, this has become very fashionable. It was not true, however, of all the participating organizations. Those that had always been decentralized were somewhat amused by the rush to decentralize. In fact, the decentralized companies were keen to exert more central control—particularly on activities such as management development, purchasing and some overarching areas of policy such as personnel, IT and finance.

## CONCLUSION

The idea of organizational culture first took the stage in the 1960s. At that time, there was confusion about its meaning, a problem not helped by its rapid adoption in business and media parlance.

In the 1990s, we cannot deny that culture has become a fad. Fads come and go with the generations of managers who populate organizations. On this count alone, we might be tempted to dismiss the idea. But that would be a mistake. All but one of the participants in this study stated that they believed culture was both important and useful. The point was made eloquently by one person:

Describing an organization in terms of structure and finance is rather dead. Culture brings it to life.

In this sense, corporate culture is an attempt to deal with all those aspects of organizational life that are irrational and paradoxical but no less important for it.

Our opinion, having completed over 60 hours of interviews and three times that time sifting through the data, is that major UK organizations are making good use of the concept. It is both possible and desirable to change the culture of organizations. The difficulties, of course, can easily be underestimated and careful thought needs to be given to the strategic objectives of such an endeavour.

We hope that the 10 themes discussed in this report will demonstrate the practical and ambitious initiatives that large UK organizations have undertaken, their concerns and indeed fears, and sometimes even their failures. Beyond all that, however, we hope that it shows the commitment of senior managers in choosing to take control of culture and implementing their vision.

## REFERENCES

Bennis, W. G. (1969). *Organisation Development: Its Nature, Origins and Prospects.* Addison-Wesley, Reading, Massachusetts.

Hofstede, G. (1991). *Cultures and Organisations: Software of the Mind.* McGraw-Hill, London.

Peters, T. and Waterman, R. H. (1982). *In Search of Excellence: Lessons from America's Best-Run Companies.* Harper and Row, New York.

## APPENDIX

### The Participating Organizations

Alfred McAlpine Group
AT&T Istel
BAA
Balfour Beatty Group
Barclays Bank
British Steel
The Burton Group
Eastern Electricity
London Underground
National Power
The Nestlé Company
P&O Group
Prudential Corporation
The Rank Organization
Rank Xerox

Rolls-Royce
The RTZ Corporation
Smith Kline Beecham Pharmaceuticals UK
Southern Electric
Vickers Defence Systems
Westpac Banking Corporation
WH Smith Group

# 8

# 'PROJETS D'ENTREPRISE' AND MISSION STATEMENTS: COMPARATIVE ANALYSIS OF CONCEPTS AND PRACTICES, IN FRANCE, GREAT BRITAIN AND THE UNITED STATES

**Dominique Peyrat***

*Professor, Groupe ESC Nantes Atlantique*

The study of the development of mission statements incorporating the concepts of strategy, values and objectives began receiving increased attention in the early 1980s. In France, this has developed under the descriptive phrase 'projet d'entreprise'. Literally translated, this means 'project of the enterprise', and involves an integrative process stressing collaborative involvement of multi levels in a firm. The concept was first addressed in professional literature and was first put into significant practice in the mid 1980s (Brabet, 1989). The attention in the literature has dwindled since the late 1980s but it is still being installed today.

During this same period, attention to mission statements for business organizations in the US and Great Britain was developing. These efforts were incidentally related to the French concept.

*Now Dominique Peyrat-Guillard

*The Implementation Challenge*, Edited by D. E. Hussey
© 1996 John Wiley & Sons Ltd

However, no significant comparison between the approaches taken in the three countries has been made. This is starting to change, particularly in France and Great Britain. The work of Campbell et al (1990a) about 'a sense of mission' has recently been translated into French. However, the bibliography of this book includes no French article or work on the 'projet d'entreprise'.

The central aim of this chapter has been to compare the concept of 'projet d'entreprise' with one of mission statements and the firms' practices in France, with those in Great Britain and in the US. It is based on the results of a study (Peyrat, 1993) conducted in France with 82 firms (41 with a written 'projet d'entreprise' and 41 without such a 'projet'). Firms were paired up according to their sector of activity and size, and then compared on a wide range of variables. Results were then compared to results of research carried out in Britain and in the US.

## 'PROJETS D'ENTREPRISE' IN FRANCE, MISSION STATEMENTS IN GREAT BRITAIN AND IN THE US: SIMILARITIES AND DIFFERENCES

In the US, Pearce's (1982) contribution about mission statements is recognized as one of the most significant.[1] He has listed six elements of a mission statement:

- product or service, market and technology;
- aims for survival, growth and profitability;
- business philosophy;
- competitive strengths and advantages;
- corporate image;
- the responsibility of the parties involved.

In Great Britain, another important research about the sense of mission and mission statements was started in November 1987 by the Research Committee of the Ashridge Strategic Management Centre. The committee was formed of planning managers of the biggest British firms.

In their book, Campbell and Tawadey (1990, p. vii) set out this research, in which they took part. They stressed two conclusions: to have 'the sense of mission' is not necessarily linked to having written this mission and mission statements are useful only if firms have also a sense of mission.[2] That is why

---

[1]W. R. King and D. I. Cleland, in their book *Strategic Planning and Policy*, p. 124, had previously, in 1979, underlined the importance of writing the mission
[2]A *Financial Times* article (11 January, 1989) took up Campbell's ideas to question itself about mission statements' efficiency

their research has moved towards the sense of mission instead of mission statements (Campbell and Tawadey, 1990, p. viii). They collected mission statements from approximately 200 different firms in Europe, the US and Japan. The names of the documents thus gathered varied a lot ('Our Mission', 'Vision, Values and Philosophy', 'The Five Principles of . . .'). David (1989) and Campbell et al (1990b) analysed the contents of these statements. In the second stage of their research, they conducted semidirect interviews in some firms which had or had not written their mission (Campbell and Tawadey, 1990). Their definition of the mission is schematized by the 'Ashridge model of the mission' in Figure 8.1.

This model really reflects their main concern—the focus on mission *contents*. (A questionnaire that can be found at the end of their book, intended to test an organization mission statement quality, also attests this fact.) The super-ordinate goal is the entire reason for the being of the firm. This should go beyond the mere intention of making shareholders rich. Rather, it should reflect an ideal: for example, to put on the market products that protect the environment. Strategy is meant in the usual sense. Values represent the firm's beliefs, its ethics, the right way of acting. Finally, norms and behaviours are the translation of strategy into action. It can be said that a 'strong' mission exists when these four elements are strongly linked (Campbell and Tawadey, 1990, p. 5).

One can establish the connection between the term of 'mission' and the one of 'vision'; indeed, they are sometimes used interchangeably (Fry and Killing, 1989). Collins and Porras (1991, p. 31) observed that most organizations respond to the need for vision in creating what they call a 'mission statement'. They set out the 'mission' as one of the elements of the 'vision', the other ones being 'values and beliefs', 'final aim' and 'vivid description' that must represent what the firm will be when the mission is accomplished (pp. 46 and 47). One can thus find some elements of the 'mission' in the Ashridge Management Centre sense.

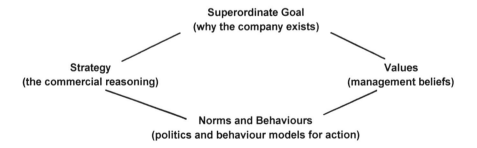

**Figure 8.1**   The Ashridge Model of the Mission

As in the French literature about the 'projet d'entreprise', Campbell and Tawadey (1990) underline that the main advantage of a mission is employee commitment.

This British approach of the mission seems closer to the 'projet d'entreprise', because of its strategic and cultural contents, than the American approach. Concerning contents, the main difference between American and French statements is that the texts of American statements are heavily oriented towards values statements (D'almeida, 1987, p. 134). On the academic plane as well, the different standpoints about mission contents between the Ashridge Centre and Pearce can perhaps be explained by the fact that the first one groups together British researchers whereas the second one is American. However, these differences are recognized as being minor (Campbell and Tawadey, 1990).

Lastly, the British Campbell and Tawadey, or Klemm, Sanderson and Luffman and David who is American, ascribe the origins of the mission statement idea to Drucker. The French authors also do. All things considered then, are those two approaches so different and are they really different from the French concept of 'projet d'entreprise'?

The British and American concepts are very close together—and therefore far from the French—in that they define the mission only by its *contents*. Thus they do not involve participatory collaboration; the process is less important than the content and is mainly developed by upper management. *This is the fundamental difference with the concept of 'projet d'entreprise'.* The French authors agree that the process is far more important than the contents.[3] Schwebig (1985, p. 78) makes this clear when writing that

> what distinguishes most philosophies from 'projets' is the process of development chosen. Here, the values system is not the creed of the founder father; the code of ethics is not necessarily a crude expression of power. It is the entire social corps that participate in defining its identity and its design. There is thus a repeated process between the different components of the firm. This iterative process tends to answer important questions: who are we, where are we going, what are our strengths, our weaknesses, which values must we develop, in which direction?

Possibly, this emphasis in the 'projet d'entreprise' is more suited to the French culture. The more Latin temperament is less adapted to these real gospels, filled with moral, even religious values, where a veritable concept of world and of work progress are explained. But there must be no mistake, French reservation towards these written and imposed codes must not hide their de facto acceptance of philosophies that are often not written, but just as mind coercive (Schwebig, 1985, p. 77).

---

[3]See particularly Monteil (1986, pp. I–11), Schwebig (1985, p. 78) and Ribette (1988, p. 322)

On that subject too, Gondrand (1989, p. 178) noticed that Thomas Watson Junior (son of IBM's founder) defines the reason for being of the mission statement, i.e. essentially, values and action principles, far more than objectives and challenges that are naturally changing.

These words can be explained by the fact that IBM has what is more appropriate to call a code of ethics than 'projet d'entreprise'. This is revealed both by a declaration established by the limited circle of managers and by the content which puts forward moral values that employees commit themselves to respect when going into the firm. Gondrand (1989, p. 178) thinks that the statement of these objectives is yet essential if one wants to arouse dynamism in the firm, because men can be carried away only by a challenge that surpasses themselves.

However, a recent article about vision makes us think that the importance of collaboration is now better perceived in some areas. Collins and Porras (1991, p. 32) have written that vision must be elaborated at each level of the firm and every group must decide on its own vision.

The study of contents and development process of mission statements and 'projets d'entreprise', related to organizational practices, will allow us to specify the similarities and differences mentioned above.

## 'PROJETS D'ENTREPRISE' AND MISSION STATEMENTS: THE CONTENT

Following publication of his article (1982), Pearce made an empirical study about mission statements, in collaboration with David (1987). They questioned the top 500 *Fortune* firms and made a contents analysis on the basis of 61 mission statements. Their aim was to check what percentage of statements included the main elements of Pearce's model and to test differences between higher and lower performing firms. Although the study does not show consistent patterns, it does show that mission statements actually include the different elements suggested by Pearce. Some 40% of the firms that answered stated that they had not written their mission. A survey of the same type was then conducted by David (1989). On the basis of 181 answers, he obtained 75 documents formalizing the mission, which represented 41% of the firms. He saw two main reasons explaining that the majority of the firms had not written their mission statement: one is the risk of revealing disagreements about mission and the other one is too much focus on the short term.

Considering that these reasons were in fact disadvantages for a firm's functioning, David affirmed that mission had to be written. Results obtained on the basis of a statistical analysis of contents of the statements led him to add a further element to the list: attention to employees. He also tried to differentiate the content of industrial firms' mission statements from those of services firms, the latter being, according to him, less comprehensive than the others (p. 93).

Campbell and Tawadey (1990, p. 261) do not entirely agree with elements of the mission quoted by Pearce and consider that he pays too little attention to superordinate goal and to norms and behaviours. They also do not agree with the importance that Pearce attaches to growth and profitability.

Klemm et al (1991), in their study mentioned earlier, observed that literature is not very explicit about what mission content should be. On the basis of their own experience of working with British firms, they suggest the following typology, making a distinction between a document focused on values and documents describing the current or planned activities of the firm:

*Document 1:* values[4]
A statement of the firm's long-term superordinate goal.

*Document 2:* strategic objectives
A statement of long-term strategic objectives.

*Document 3:* quantitative estimates
A document projecting quantitative predictions for a given period.

*Document 4:* activity definition
A document about activity areas of the firm and its geographical field of action.

They showed that these types of documents are more and more fashionable: the two-thirds of the firms that answered the questionnaire (59 firms) had both type 1 and type 2 documents and 80% had published a type 4 document. Amongst the firms, 70% had established their document in the last 4 years and some of them were writing it at the time of the survey. Therefore, it seems that the initial development of mission statements in Great Britain took place approximately at the same time as in France. One can criticize their typology as being somewhat oversimplified; for example, the authors commonly found in one document the contents of their type 1 and 2 statements.

Other studies about mission contents can be found (Cochran and David, 1986; Want, 1986). The study carried out by Purcell (1987), in collaboration with other researchers (Marginson, Edwards, Sisson and Martin), is a particular case. Although mission statements is not the object of the study, they use them in their analysis of management styles.

---

[4]They call it 'mission'. However, in order not to get confused with what mission means for other authors, we chose 'values'

**Table 8.1**  Comparison of the Contents of 'Projets d'Entreprise' and Mission Statements

|  | France | USA | Great Britain |
|---|---|---|---|
| Concept | Projet d'entreprise | Mission statement | |
| Main authors | Entreprise et progrès (1984), Schwebig, Giroire (1985), Boyer and Equilbey (1986) | Pearce, David | Campbell and Tawadey |
| Elements of mission statements contents | | | |
| Mission | Dessein, réflexion sur la vocation et le métier (Schwebig) Dessein volonté (Giroire) Vision du futur, dessein (Boyer et Equilbey) | Institutional image, responsibility towards the parties involved | Superordinate goal |
| Principles | Système de valeurs (Schwebig, Giroire, Boyer et Equilbey) | Business philosophy (Pearce, David) Attention to employees (David) | Values |
| Objectifs généraux | Stratégie et politiques poursuivies (Schwebig) Choix essentiels (Giroire) Priorités et axes majeurs pour l'action (Boyer and Equilbey) | Product or service, market and technology The aims for survival, growth and profitability Forces and competitive advantages (Pearce and David) | Strategy, norms and behaviours |

Table 8.1 summarizes the contents characteristics of the different 'projets' and mission statements. Whatever the country, we can see that a statement is composed of the same three elements; however, they have different importance in different countries (for example, business philosophy in the US) as mentioned earlier.

Even if British and American authors have focused their attention on the statements' content, it is possible to find some references to the mission statements' development process.

## 'PROJETS D'ENTREPRISE' AND MISSION STATEMENTS: THE PROCESS

Campbell and Tawadey (1990, p. 9) distinguished three approaches to develop a mission statement. The first consists of a progressive development from some messages of management, which have both strategic and cultural content, and will then be progressively reinforced and illustrated. The second approach, more intellectual, according to them, consists in writing the mission statement, in which case it is more difficult to lead to a consensus of management opinions. The last option is more 'practical': it is from an agreement about how to solve a number of problems that the mission statement evolves.

They (pp. 10–12) drew from this a number of principles: it requires years and not months; a real consensus of management opinions is necessary; actions promote communication better than words; 'visibility' of the management team is essential (it must be accessible); continuation of the management team is also very important; the documents that formalize mission must reflect the firm's identity; an 'echo' between strategy and values must exist; and emphasis has to be placed on the link between behaviour and values.

Further, they do not consider participation in development as important as statement content. The management team alone is invited to take counsel together in order to come to a consensus. The figures of the postal survey launched in Great Britain by Klemm et al (1991, p. 75) prove it: amongst 59 statements, 60% had been written by the firm's management team, whereas the others had been written by the founder or the manager. Moreover, the questionnaire appended to their working paper includes no question about the development process.

Frohman and Pascarella (1987), management consultants, are a little more interested in the development process than the researchers are. They described six stages for the writing of a mission statement. The first stage consists of determining management commitment to define the mission. The second stage is an outline of the mission content, based on the opinions of the founder, previous management and present management. It is underlined here that employees who have been with a firm for a long time can help to define its history. Collection and interpretation of information are the subject of a third stage, which consists of an internal and external audit through interviews, group discussions and questionnaires. The fourth stage is formulated in a very basic way: it is a matter of 'anticipating the future'. One will then deal with writing the mission statement. It is noticed here that five methods of writing can be successful: by the manager, by the management team, by a working group, by a team of specialists (each of them writing a part), or by external consultants. The management must, however, have charge of the final writing. Finally, the last stage involves presenting one's opinion about the mission for internal and external scrutiny.

The process is thus noticeably different from the one that is advocated by French researchers, consultants and managers. To wit: Frohman and Pascarella cite

a mission elaborated using a bottom-up approach

as ineffective.

# 'PROJETS D'ENTREPRISE' AND MISSION STATEMENTS: THOUGHTS COMING TOGETHER

At the conclusion of this review, it seems to us that, despite the differences that remain on the concept plane as well as on the organizational practices plane, an evolution of the thought about mission statements is appearing. Evidence of this is the fact that David (1989, p. 97) questioned whether the development process of a written mission statement was not more important than the document itself.

This reflection, added to the joint works of the researchers cited at the beginning of this article will perhaps contribute towards concepts and practices of 'projet d'entreprise' and mission statements in France, Great Britain and the US coming together.

## REFERENCES

Boyer, L. and Equilbey, N. (1986). *Le Projet d'Entreprise*, Les Editions d'Organisation, Paris.

Brabet, J. (1989). *Le Projet d'Entreprise*, Communication aux journées des I.A.E. de Strasbourg.

Campbell, A., Devine, M. and Young, D. (1990a). *Du Projet d'Entreprise à l'Engagement Personnel—Le Sens de la Mission*, Les Editions d'Organisation, Paris.

Campbell, A., Devine, M. and Young, D. (1990b). *A Sense of Mission*, The Economist Books Ltd.

Campbell, A. and Tawadey, K. (1990). *Mission and Business Philosophy—Winning Employee Commitment*, Heinemann, Oxford.

Cochran, D. S. and David, F. R. (1986). Communication effectiveness of organizational mission statements, *Journal of Applied Communication Research*, **14**(2), Fall, pp. 108–118.

Collins, J. C. and Porras, J. I. (1991). Organizational vision and visionary organizations, *California Management Review*, **34**(1), Fall.

D'almeida, N. (1987). *La voie du projet d'entreprise—le problème de la construction d'une identité et d'un avenir partagés*, Thèse de doctorat de 3ème cycle, Université de Paris IV Sorbonne, CELSA.

David, F. R. (1989). How companies define their mission, *Long Range Planning*, **22**(1), pp. 90–97.

Entreprise et Progrès (1984). *Le projet d'entreprise*, Paris, Juillet.

Frohman, M. and Pascarella, P. (1987). How to write a purpose statement, *Industry Week*, 23 March.

Fry, J. N. and Killing, P. J. (1989). Vision-check, *Business Quarterly*, **54**(2), Autumn.

Giroire, J. (1985). *La Volonté Stratégique de l'Entreprise*, EME, Paris.

Gondrand, F. (1989). *Quand les Hommes Font la Différence (Cent Exemples de Participation à la Gestion)*, Les Editions d'Organisation, Paris.

Klemm, M. et al (1991). Mission statements: selling corporate values to employees, *Long Range Planning*, 24, June.

Monteil, B. (1986). Le projet d'entreprise: revitaliser les hommes et l'organisation. In: *Projet d'Entreprise et Management Participatif: la Pratique Quotidienne*, I.G.S., dossier technique, Centre d'Etudes, de formation et d'assistance, 27 Mai.

Pearce, J. A. (1982). The company mission as a strategic tool, *Sloan Management Review*, Spring, pp. 15–24.

Pearce, J. A. and David, F. R. (1987). Corporate mission statements: the bottom line, *Academy of Management Executives*, **1**(2), pp. 109–116.

Peyrat, D. (1993). *Participation et implication des salariés: le projet d'entreprise, approche comparative*, Thèse de Doctorat, Université-I.A.E. de Poitiers, Janvier.

Purcell, J. (1987). Mapping management styles in employee relations, *Journal of Management Studies*, September.

Ribette, R. (1988). Approche systèmique de la dimension personnel dans l'entreprise et gestion stratègique des ressources humaines. In: D. Weiss et collaborateurs, *La Fonction Ressources Humaines*, Les Editions d'Organisation, Paris.

Schwebig, P. (1985). *Communication, identité et pouvoir*. In: annexe A of R. Reitter, B. Ramanantsoa, *Pouvoir et Politique (au-delà de la Culture d'Entreprise)*, MacGraw Hill.

Want, J. H. (1986). Corporate mission: the intangible contributor to performance, *Management Review*, August, pp. 46–50.

# 9

# THE SUCCESSFUL DOUBLE TURNAROUND OF ASEA AND ABB—TWENTY LESSONS[1]

**Staffan Brege**
**Ove Brandes**

*Linköping Institute of Technology*

The double turnaround at ASEA and ABB is one of the most spectacular renewals of large and complex industrial firms in Europe during the last decade. However, we did not know that we had picked a winner when we started in-depth, longitudinal studies of ASEA in 1982 and ABB in 1987. We consider the change of CEO as the starting point of the turnaround process which can be divided in five phases from retrenchment to international expansion. The lessons cover issues as the CEO's role, the initial situation, the climate for change, the turnaround process, the grand plan and learning. In comparison with earlier studies we have found that the deep involvement of CEO and the top management team in the implementation of the turnaround strategy is of decisive importance for success.

## INTRODUCTION AND PURPOSE

Success stories are always appealing to managers and consultants looking for new ideas to improve the performance of their firms and their own records.

[1]This study has been supported by a grant from the Bank of Sweden Tercentenary Foundation

Also from an academic standpoint deep studies of single cases are interesting if the cases are chosen in a context which shows that it can improve our knowledge of the complexity and dynamic aspects of corporate strategy. If there are several case studies undertaken in parallel within a well-motivated plan for comparison between the firms studied the chances for interesting results are even greater.

The purpose of this chapter is to draw the managerial conclusions of general interest with empirical illustrations from the most spectacular of our five in-depth case studies—the double turnaround at ASEA and ABB (ASEA Brown Boveri). Even though the other four case studies are not presented in this chapter, they have played an important role in the analysis, e.g. in comparisons and the search for general patterns. The ASEA/ABB case is described in five phases and the analysis is presented as short lessons which are discussed from a managerial viewpoint.

When we started our case study of ASEA in 1982 and ASEA Brown Boveri Ltd (ABB) in 1987, both firms were in critical situations (in the latter case the Brown Boveri part) and a new CEO, Percy Barnevik, had been appointed. In each case, most experts gave the CEO less than 50% chance to turn the complex heavy electrical equipment manufacturer around. What we started to study turned out to be the beginning of a double turnaround. A turnaround is defined as the process that takes the firm from a position of weak performance to a position of sustained good performance.

We did not know that we had picked a winner, a CEO who would receive several international awards for outstanding leadership and a firm which would become one of the most exciting in Europe at the beginning of the 1990s. A case like this is a rich source for other big, complex firms in trouble to get ideas from for managing a turnaround, even if it is impossible to copy exactly a success either as a whole or in detail. There are many specific factors behind it, e.g. strong personalities, good teams, good luck with the timing and a hundred years of technological core competence in the industry. Still, there are so many new ideas and experiences of general interest in this process that there is a reason to present the managerial conclusions of this success story separately.


## THE STRATEGIC DOUBLE TURNAROUND OF ASEA/ABB

In 1980, ASEA was amongst the 10 largest companies in heavy electrical industry, i.e. generators, turbines, transformers, electrical motors, railway engines, etc. ASEA's technical level was world-class, but in a market characterized by excess capacity and a weakened demand, its growth and profitability had declined. (By 1990 ABB was three times larger than its closest competitor within its core businesses and showed good profitability considering the rapid growth and the extensive internal structuring.)

In the late 1970s, ASEA found itself on a downhill course with declining profits and stagnating growth. ASEA considered itself one of the major 'all round' suppliers in the world within heavy electrical equipment, but its position was threatened. Internationalization was still unsatisfactory and did not meet the company's internal goals although approximately 50% of turnover was exported. The large dependency upon the domestic market, in terms of sales, profits, production and R&D, was a significant problem with the poor demand and high relative costs in Sweden. Excess capacity strained the profits within certain areas which represented a large portion of ABB sales, and heavy losses in steel production were incurred. However, the picture was not completely dark, as ASEA had numerous product areas which were both growing and profitable.

ASEA had high functional competence. The production unit was a leader with its modern Manufacturing Planning and Control Systems. A very high level of technical and, toa certain extent, also marketing competence existed within ASEA. The problems were weak integration and poor cooperation between the different functional departments as well as between headquarters and the international parts of the organization. In general the organization was centralized, authoritarian and bureaucratic.

ASEA had advanced accounting and cost calculation systems, but only a few persons were able to interpret the information generated by these systems. Furthermore, the systems were not used for any planning purposes. The long-range planning that existed was primarily a centralized investment plan.

The corporate culture was technocratic. It emphasized technical development, contracting and production at the expense of market orientation. Common values based on the importance of technology kept the organization together. When candidates were sought to fill managerial positions, evaluations were based on technological competence, and this created many 'legendary managers and engineers'. Another important ingredient in the corporation's culture was employment security. ASEA had not discharged personnel since the 1930s and had maintained this policy during the difficult years of the late 1970s.

### Phase 1: Barnevik Accepts the Position of CEO

The ASEA Board of Directors' choice of Percy Barnevik as the new CEO was both surprising and unconventional. The Board chose a person that represented a very different way of thinking, both strategically and organizationally. However, the developments of the late 1970s, indicated the need for radical changes. A new CEO with strength and skilfulness was needed to change the large and inert organization.

At this time, Barnevik was one of the vice-presidents of Sandvik, a multinational company with its base in steel and powder metallurgy, but was virtually unknown within the Swedish business community. His experience included a managing position with Sandvik's US subsidiary and from work in an international matrix organization. Barnevik was characterized by a strong analytic ability, and an exceptional capacity for work and a restless and insistent attitude towards his fellow managers.

Barnevik accepted the offer, but only first after having obtained the Board of Directors' promise of total support for the extensive and radical changes he deemed necessary. He prepared intensively prior to assuming the CEO position.

### Phase 2: Structuring One's Way out of the Crisis, 1980–1982

Barnevik's appointment as CEO of ASEA caused a great deal of surprise and scepticism internally and generated a high level of expectations regarding potential changes. How could an externally recruited graduate economist manage this extremely technology-oriented and complex corporation? Yet, a large number of top and middle managers as well as representatives of the trade unions realized that radical change was necessary.

Barnevik took over on 1 June 1980. Directly after the summer holidays, the plans for the first reorganization were presented and implemented. The central plant engineering sector was split up and built into the new product divisions. For the first time production and contracting had been brought together with the marketing function in units with one division manager for each product area.

Several members of the top management team (TMT) considered Barnevik's initial ideas too much oriented towards short-term profits. They felt that the company's core competence was put at risk by scattering and disintegrating its plant engineering and functional competence. Nevertheless, managers were loyal towards both the company and its CEO, in accordance with the ASEA culture. Furthermore, there was at least one person in the TMT who was in complete agreement with Barnevik's visions, namely the vice-president marketing, Mr Arne Bennborn. He had himself earlier presented his plans for a reorganization but had been turned down. Barnevik's political and communicative skill was proofed when he had to get the trade unions' support for the many severe decisions regarding the reorganization and reductions.

Concurrent, Barnevik focused upon the corporation's excess production capacity in Sweden. The first step was to either painfully shut down or substantially reduce the steel operations. This was motivated by the need for short-term profits and the new priorities of ASEA's product portfolio. This decisive action was in direct contrast to ASEA's traditional strategy of backward integration for securing the special steel supply. From now on each business would primarily be judged according to its own merits. Furthermore, another established ASEA principle was altered: guaranteed employment regardless of the economic situation.

This principle had led to a series of unprofitable contracts and marginally priced business deals with the purpose of maintaining production volume and, thereby, employment. One of Barnevik's immediate short-term measures was to stop marginally priced business deals, review the pricing system and renegotiate a number of unprofitable contracts. These decisive and successful actions strengthened Barnevik's position within the company and attracted media attention which further strengthened his position internally.

In parallel with these short-term actions, Barnevik presented his long-term strategic visions regarding ASEA's future toward the 1990s. The necessary market orientation of the entire corporation was to be achieved by means of reorganizations. Yet, this was not enough. The increasing costs of maintaining a leading R&D position required growth in both volumes and profitability. This had to be achieved through stronger positions in selected international markets in face of fierce international competition.

The vision was that, in order for ASEA to remain within the 'power equipment industry's highest division', it would be necessary to change from an export-oriented corporation to a multinational corporation with strong international positions in both marketing and production. This demanded an acquisition strategy, especially if ASEA was to compete in industrialized countries with large and government-protected markets. Organic growth was considered insufficient. Barnevik had, in the light of his experience from the US market, visions of strengthening ASEA's position in North America through acquisitions.

Barnevik showed his conceptual ability and began early to preach a number of strategic principles: 'spearhead' products, choice of international niches and dominance within these niches. Priority businesses were, from the very beginning, given resources for expansion. The slogan 'To be an insider, not an invader', was created within the company at this early stage and eventually came to be the foundation of ASEA's attitude towards foreign markets. Barnevik took every opportunity to spread his message of 'The New ASEA'.

For the first time there were profit centres with practically total responsibility for their performance. Divisional managers were chosen amongst the earlier sector managers but were given new responsibilities based on an evaluation of their capacity and competence.

An important ingredient in the divisionalization of the corporation was to provide increased resources for economic control and strategic planning. A central group of young academics acted as internal consultants to the division management. The motto was 'Give Those Responsible the Planning Tools'. The TMT demanded immediate action, and time-consuming investigations and reports were abandoned. Formal strategic planning became an important means of communication between the TMT and division managers and was an

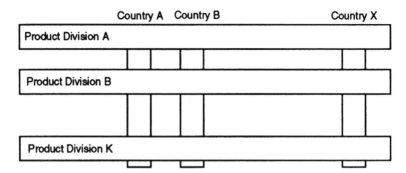

**Figure 9.1.**   ASEA's International Matrix

important instrument in facilitating the delegation of the strategic initiative to the divisional level.

The international matrix, a second reorganization, was introduced in 1981. The subsidiaries abroad were tied closer to the divisions of the parent company and other product subsidiaries within the ASEA group's eight business areas. Barnevik had, since the beginning, striven to make the organization 'transparent', i.e. make it possible to follow profit results from the point of purchase to the final delivery. The division and product subsidiary managers were given the responsibility for the very important task of allocating production resources in the international network of manufacturing units. In the new matrix organization, overlapping responsibility and high demands were set for coordination between the managers of the divisions and the managers of the national subsidiaries. The TMT had the assignment for coordinating activities within the matrix through its 'Parent Company Responsibility' (PCR) function, i.e. through its work (and responsibility for profits) on the various internal Boards. With the organizational changes, considerable resources were invested towards developing a new accounting system.

Many professionals, both internally and externally, criticized the matrix. The TMT felt that this design was necessary, considering amongst other things the complex interdependencies and demands for coordination that the plant engineering operations required: 'The matrix was there whether one acknowledged it or not.' The pressure placed upon managers was great. Division managers had to adapt from being mainly functionally based specialists to being general managers with profit responsibility. The international subsidiary managers had to better coordinate their resources with the division managers. There was a high turnover amongst managers initially. A group of young engineers, 'Percy's Boys', grew to be general managers of important units. Capability and competence rather than seniority became the guiding light for promotion to managerial positions. The matrix also permitted the TMT the possibility of playing a partially operative role. It was of critical importance that they did not just abdicate, but rather intervened to keep the organization together.

On the whole, the first years, 1980 and 1981, were a period of upheaval and revolutionary changes. In closing the accounts for 1980, a continued weak profitability was published—a result that Barnevik had only limited responsibility for and consciously played down in order to lay the groundwork for a future upswing (which came already in 1981). The Board received letters from its personnel and from those external to the company demanding the dismissal of Barnevik. The divisionalized organization and profit orientation could only, according to them, lead to short-term solutions as well as a separation and disintegration of ASEA's technological competence. However, the Board stood its ground and continued to give Barnevik its support.

**Phase 3: International Expansion, Mainly by Organic Growth, 1982–1984**

At the beginning of 1982, ASEA's performance improved, primarily as a result of the internal structuring. However, the Swedish currency had been devalued by 10% during the autumn of 1981, and this contributed to the strengthening of ASEA's competitive advantage.

Up to now the large staffs had not been reduced, this being postponed whilst other more important structuring was done. Barnevik wanted to attain additional benefits from decentralization by transforming each division into a legally independent subsidiary with its own profit/loss statement and balance sheet. Opposition from trade unions facing new risks in employment security (inasmuch as each major division would be an employer without backing from the parent company) caused Barnevik to halt halfway, and he put the idea on the shelf for a few years. In order to strengthen ASEA's financial operations, an additional business area was created by moving the financial function 'in house'.

ASEA's corporate portfolio strategy with the exception of the incorporation of Fläkt (environment protection) consolidation could be characterized as a 'fine-tuning strategy' with emphasis on market and performance orientation. Unlike its competitors, the new ASEA management continued to refrain from unrelated diversifications. CEO/TMT preached the strategic principles of dominance and market leadership within niches. Priority was given to strengthening the international sales and production organization in the industrialized countries and some selectively chosen developing countries. No large company acquisition had been implemented yet, but negotiations had been initiated.

Towards the end of 1982 and at the beginning of 1983 trade conditions improved when, amongst other things, the Swedish currency was further devaluated by 16%. This gave ASEA enough 'wind in their sails' to finalize the structuring of the domestic operations. In many cases the excess capacity of mature businesses had been reduced, and those businesses were now profitable. Performance improved rapidly, and prior to ASEA's centenary anniversary in 1983, Percy Barnevik was the undisputed leader. Internal as well as external criticism had more or less quietened down. The results had occurred relatively quickly and were sufficient. Barnevik took maximum advantage of the aniversary celebrations to profile ASEA by emphasizing spectacular products, e.g. robots and engines. Thousands of international guests arrived in Västerås, Sweden, and were able to view closely the successful corporation and its products. A very skilful PR move that bolstered ASEA's international good will.

A closing of accounts for the first years of the Barnevik epoch could now be done. Technology still had a leading position, even if R&D operations were more goal-directed and controlled. A certain insecurity still existed with respect to the long-term effects, but on a short-term basis, no catastrophe had occurred. Critics pointed out that priority was not given to technological questions within the executive management and that ASEA, after divisionalization, had extensive technical problems in coordinating large plant engineering projects. For example, the earlier centralized works with the development of technical standards had been discontinued. The 'new ASEA' could be characterized as a much more market- and profit-oriented organization.

**Phase 4: Strategic Development From 'The Nordic Strategy' to 'The Multi-domestic Company', 1985–1987**

ASEA's positive development at the beginning of the 1980s was in contrast to the development of its competitors. The internal structuring, with help from the Swedish devaluation, gave ASEA good results. The general international trade conditions improved steadily but demand within the power industry continued to be weak. The medium-sized companies especially showed weak profit growth, and many were bought by larger competitors. Despite signals of deregulation, e.g. in the USA and the UK, these and many other markets still remained closed to import.

Where geographically could ASEA expand? The strategy within industrialized countries was to become 'multidomestic' by means of acquisitions. The goal of 10% annual sales growth demanded that approximately half of the growth be created through acquisitions. The strategy that ASEA had for the Nordic countries, its home market, was fulfilled during 1986–1987 by the purchase of the Finnish firm Strömberg and the Norwegian firm Elektrisk Bureau. The Strömberg deal has been seen as a notable example of an ASEA-managed turnaround.

During this period the financial function became increasingly important from both a profit and competitive point of view. Competence in this area was needed to support the acquisition strategy and the increasing amount of barter trade. Barnevik's visions became more and more influenced by the discussions concerning the EEC's inner market, and the idea of a 'European company' began to take form.

The divisions of the parent company were eventually made into legally independent companies with separate profit/loss statements and balance sheets. Thereby 'the last 10% of efficiency was squeezed' from the newly built profit centres.

The new organization, with business areas/product subsidiaries and national subsidiaries within the matrix, was not free from problems. Internal price negotiations were required between the divisions, an effect of the new structure. According to some, ASEA's ability to coordinate large plant engineering projects had also deteriorated, but they were much better at marketing them. There was a great need for coordination, and 'centres of excellence' were created to strengthen functional competence.

## Phase 5: ABB—Combined Structuring and Expansion, 1988–1991

The preparations for creating ABB began in the utmost secrecy in the spring of 1987. The structures of Brown Bovery Company (BBC) and the ASEA of 1980 were very similar, both were driven by technology whilst market and profit orientation was weak. Furthermore, each had a small domestic market and was typically dependent on exports. The 1980s were becoming 'a lost decade' for BBC; as compared with ASEA, BBC's position had considerably worsened. In 1980 BBC's turnover was twice as large as that of ASEA and its stock market value was four times larger, but by 1986 the turnover of the companies was approximately comparable whilst ASEA's value was twice as large as that of BBC. Technological competence was still comparable, and in some areas, BBC's technical expertise was even greater. The difference lay in each corporation's management and marketing competence, the degree of decentralization and their international marketing organization.

Percy Barnevik was the undisputed CEO for the newly formed ABB. It has been said that one of BBC's key motives for the merger was its wish to have Barnevik as CEO. The role of Chairman in ABB's executive managing committee was shared by Curt Nicolin, ASEA, and Fritz Leutwieler, BBC. The top managers' positions were first divided equally between the managers of ASEA and BBC, but after a short period, ASEA's managers took over most top positions. Barnevik's change of strategy was primarily the same as with ASEA in 1980. ASEA's 'record', especially the Strömberg acquisition in 1986, created a sense of trust in the plans. For BBC, the transition to the international matrix, with its extensive rationalizations, coordination of production, and cuts in central staffs, was certainly 'bitter medicine'.

Barnevik followed the principle of his previous plan: take all the difficult decisions as early as possible in the change process.

As before, the tempo was fast-paced. The link to the Board and also the new TMT was relatively simple compared with how it had been at ASEA in 1980. On the other hand, the implementation of the changes in the new, multinational environment was essentially more difficult than anticipated. In addition to the issues of national prestige and cultural differences, it is important to note that ABB was five times as large as the ASEA of 1980 in terms of both number of employees and turnover. ABB's structure consisted of eight business segments, 50 business areas and approximately 5,000 profit centres. Also the national trade unions met the plans for change with scepticism and opposition. A Swedish top manager commented on the difference between the ASEA and ABB turnarounds as follows: 'Its like comparing a quiet jog with the New York marathon.'

Despite the opposition, ABB's structuring was implemented at a fast pace, and after a couple of years, profits from the rationalizations began to be realized. The attitude of the employees and trade unions also became more favourable as results improved. The turnaround put large demands upon the managers' ability, and many were replaced. According to Barnevik, ABB needed approximately 500 'global managers' who had the ability and the capacity to think multidimensional and that considered the corporation as an integrated entity. These persons should counteract the 'centrifugal forces' that are present in an organization with a large number of profit centres. Critics felt that ABB had gone too far in its decentralization efforts, and that the subsequent internal price negotiations were costly. Furthermore, it was pointed out that disintegration of plant engineering operations involves the risk of losing the know-how that comes from centralized competence.

With a turnover of nearly USD 30 billion in 1990 and with approximately 220,000 employees, ABB dominated the heavy electrotechnical equipment markets in terms of turnover and market shares. One of the driving forces underlying the merger was Barnevik's wish to obtain a stronger foothold within the EEC. For Swiss BBC had its largest business in former West Germany and considered Italy, Austria and former West Germany as its 'home markets'. ABB's product portfolio was initially more diversified than that of ASEA, including telecommunication and powerlines. Within their core business, ABB had achieved a globally dominant position. For example, ABB's market share of the global transformer segment in 1988 was 25%, which was three times larger than that of its closest competitor.

ABB's management chose ASEA's strategy 'one more time': focus upon a number of core businesses and avoid unrelated operations. In an area of priority, e.g. energy, railway engines, and environmental protection, competitiveness should be attained through a combination of:

- being closest to the customer;
- having products with the highest quality and leading technology;
- producing at a low cost.

ABB had become a global actor with a widely integrated network of production units in many markets (multidomestic) combined with international sales and service organizations. In this particular respect, ABB differed from its foremost competitors, who typically manufactured in their domestic market and exported to other geographical markets. ABB achieved low-cost production via ambitious programmes, and via competition amongst the various production units within the same segment. The merged specialities of the two corporations soon proved to be complementary to an extensive degree that was unexpected, and their competitive power was increased by the shared assortment.

The structuring work was not completed when the opportunity for acquisitions in the USA appeared, e.g. Westinghouse Transmission and Distribution and Combustion Engineering. These opportunities were judged to strengthen further the corporation's globally dominant position. However, the acquisitions strained the corporation's finances and management's capacity. Profitability diminished, hurting the balance sheet. The most important strategic tasks for the beginning of the 1990s are to structure the operations in North America and consolidate operations in Western Europe. The highest expansion priorities are Eastern Europe and Asia.

## LESSONS FROM THE SUCCESSFUL DOUBLE TURNAROUND OF ASEA AND ABB

What is meant by a double turnaround in ASEA and ABB? The initial situations at ASEA and at the BBC part of ABB were both similar and different in 1980 and 1987, respectively, when the processes started. In both cases the incumbent CEO's position was weak, performance records were unacceptable to the owners, a new and externally recruited CEO and his team started the process, the technological core competence was strong. The new CEO at ABB was the same person as the new CEO of ASEA seven years earlier, Percy Barnevik, who also brought several of his top managers to the new ABB headquarters in Zürich. The most important difference was that he also brought a 'blueprint' of a turnaround process to ABB which strengthened his credibility and power position from the very beginning. Both the similarities and the differences have led us to label the process 'the double turnaround', since the ABB merger involved a new turnaround situation with many patterns that were similar to the case of ASEA.

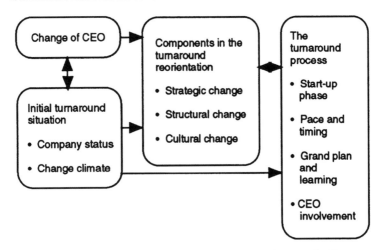

**Figure 9.2.**  A Conceptual Framework for Analysis of Strategic Turnarounds

The presentation of the managerial conclusions from the case study of the double turnaround in ASEA and ABB is structured according to a model with four categories of explanatory variables (Figure 9.2): the change of CEO, the initial turnaround situation, the turnaround reorientation and the turnaround process. Our analytical model can be seen as an inductive result from our empirical studies in combination with other empirically based findings from turnaround changes (cf. Schendel et al, 1976; Hofer, 1980, 1988; Bibeault, 1982; Robbins and Pearce, 1992).

- The first two categories constitute the starting point of the turnaround process: change of CEO and the initial situation in terms of management, strategic and financial status and the change climate of the organization.
- The third category is the content aspect of the turnaround reorientation, i.e. change in strategy, structure and culture from the beginning until the end of the turnaround period, which normally lasts several years.
- The fourth category is the turnaround process itself, which contains dimensions of great importance for the outcome: the start-up phase, pace and timing, planning and learning and CEO involvement.

**Change of CEO**

According to our definition of the turnaround process, the starting point of the case study is characterized by an unacceptably low performance of the firm, which has led to growing mistrust directed towards the incumbent CEO. If the CEO has a long and strong record in the firm there may be some delay and resistance to the change process and reorientation. If no improvement is observed or expected the first step in the process is released—the appointment of a new CEO. In one of our five case studies (Ericsson in the middle of the 1980s) the incumbent CEO was able to defend his position in a period of severe crisis, turned the firm around, and came back to an even stronger position than before the crisis. However, this seems to be an exception.

Lesson 1: If the Board—after having experienced a serious performance gap—wants a radical turnaround reorientation, it should replace the incumbent CEO with an externally recruited CEO, preferably with executive experience of strategic and structural changes of a similar nature (mental blueprints).

Lesson 2: The Board should be willing to give the newly appointed CEO its full support—a 'carte blanche' for the CEO—and at the same time present challenging goals and demands for reasonably fast improvements.

'It is impossible to save a rich and profitable firm', said one of the most experienced Swedish turnaround consultants. Even if top managers have made severe mistakes and there are obvious crisis signals from the environment and the internal report system, a CEO with a long record of good performance and credibility has a very strong position in relation to the Board. It takes time until the CEO has lost so much confidence with the Board that they start to discuss a replacement. The decision process in itself takes further time, and not until heavy losses are reported should a replacement decision be expected. Also on the evidence of our case studies it seems very hard to get a turnaround process started unless there is a performance crisis.

The dramatic change processes are often induced as a result of a financial crisis combined with a change of the CEO and TMT. A change of the CEO presupposes that the Board has experienced a serious performance gap and as a consequence lost confidence in the incumbent CEO. The analysis of the performance gap could be complicated in periods of deep recession. How much should be assigned to environmental factors and how much should the CEO be held responsible for? In retrospect, with some years' perspective, the analysis may be clear, but in the middle of a crisis and when the main actors are under pressure the Board may feel a high degree of uncertainty and may need some time to reach a decision to replace the CEO. One very crucial and often debated question is whether the new CEO should be recruited internally or externally.

Our own conclusion, which also finds support in the academic literature, is that the probability of choosing an external CEO candidate increases if the Board experiences a very serious situation and also realizes the urgent need for a radical strategic and structural reorientation. On the other hand an internal recruitment may be considered less risky as the Board and the key managers have better knowledge of the internal candidates.

In the ASEA case, the Board appointed Percy Barnevik, then Executive Vice-President at Sandvik, an integrated steel and mechanical engineering firm. It was the most surprising external recruitment in many years both for the ASEA managers and for the Swedish business community. ASEA was considered to be one of the most important and most complex firms in Swedish industry, with an old-fashioned, technocratic culture. Barnevik, an MBA without any formal training in engineering, had a strong track record from Sandvik, but so far he had no experience from any major CEO position. He represented a more profit- and market-oriented style of strategic thinking, which was in sharp contrast to the dominating values amongst the members of the Board and in the technocratic culture of ASEA. However, the situation was considered serious, and traditional answers to solving the problems had been proved wrong. The Board stood up for their new CEO and gave him the mandate to take forceful and also painful action. In the ASEA case, more than in the ABB case, the Board's mandate and support was of great importance for the establishment of a power platform.

On the other hand, when Percy Barnevik was appointed CEO of ABB he was very well known within the industry and also to the international business community. He had an outstanding track record. It has even been proposed that one of the main reasons behind Brown Boveri's decision to merge with ASEA was the desire to get Barnevik as CEO for ABB. The experience from the ASEA turnaround process gave him and his management team the proper credibility, a strong power platform and 'mental blueprints' for the guidance of the new turnaround process. Without this earlier experience it is difficult to see how the (so far in 1992) successful turnaround would have been accomplished.

In one of our four other case studies we observed the consequences of conflicts between the Board and the new, externally recruited CEO about the adequate actions and strategies to be implemented. The result of these conflicts was serious delay in the process of change, which took place in small steps with strong ingredients of a power play between the CEO and the Board. One of the obvious risks is that the initial retrenchment phase (Robbins and Pearce, 1992) turns out to be too slow and fragmentary, which calls for more radical reductions later on. There is also a risk of too slow a pace in the change process.

## The Initial Situation

For an outsider candidate considering an offer to become CEO with a challenge to start a turnaround process in a performance crisis, the most interesting question is whether there are idle assets and viable core competences in the firm. Asset reduction and cost reduction are the main activities in the first phase of a turnaround. Assets released from, e.g., real estate or inventories can be transferred to offensive activities like marketing, introduction of new products or acquisitions in the recovery phase.

A newly appointed CEO often has to work under hard time pressure to start a turnaround process and there can be strong resistance from people who feel that their positions are threatened. A high degree of crisis awareness in the organization can break the resistance. The creation of an atmosphere for change is one of the challenges for a new CEO.

*The company status*

> Lesson 3. Viable core competences and core businesses are important prerequisites for turnaround success.

> Lesson 4. Adequate bridge financing is an important prerequisite for turnaround success.

In order to accomplish a successful turnaround, it is important to identify some existing businesses and core competences for future expansion. Nelson (1981) makes important distinctions between low, moderate and severe adversities, and states that moderate adversity offers the best chance for a successful strategic change process. If the adversity is low, no radical change activities will be undertaken. On the other hand, if adversity is too severe, the resources will not be adequate for a successful turnaround.

Like in the ASEA and ABB cases, management should be able to identify and uncover viable businesses and core competences to build future expansion upon as well as adequate financing to take the firm through the turnaround process. Our conclusions also find support in other studies of key success factors in turnaround management (cf. Bibeault, 1982).

The viable core businesses and core competences are sometimes hidden or mismanaged. One reason could be that top management has focused on diversification into unrelated business. Both in firms with slack resources and in firms with stagnating core businesses, managers can find reasons to diversify into unrelated businesses for risk distribution or growth, respectively. New businesses are more attractive for top managers to work with, and the core businesses may be forgotten or mismanaged in periods of diversification. Another reason for a firm's running into a crisis could be that the core businesses have lost their competitive power because of poor operating efficiency.

Whether there are mainly external or internal reasons for the crisis situation, a turnaround process is resource-demanding both financially and in terms of management capacity. For the new CEO it is important to find and get access to the financial resources by activating idle or hidden assets for the change process. In established firms with a long record of high performance there are normally enough funds and potential for cost cutting and asset reduction to 'buy' a reasonable time period for a turnaround process. In very serious situations the cash flow could be the most critical variable for survival.

At ASEA the main reasons for the crisis situation in 1980 were a stagnation in the core business due to a macroeconomic recession, considerable overcapacity in the industry and inadequate organizational structure, including a costly and inefficient central staff. However, ASEA was a rich firm in terms of financial assets and core competences. There were enough resources for Percy Barnevik to implement a series of rapid and initially costly restructuring programmes.

A new top management team has to be composed and presented as soon as possible after the promotion of a new CEO. For an externally recruited new CEO it is a matter of balancing internally recruited members of the top management team, who represent continuity and experience, against externally recruited managers who are not influenced by the firm's culture, do not have to defend previous action and are not initially bounded by the political network. A new CEO can also have a need to bring in some of his or her earlier colleagues if there is a lack of top management competence.

Barnevik was careful not to have externally recruited members of the top management team. He interviewed more than 100 ASEA managers and representatives of the unions before he started his change programme and picked the members of the new top management team amongst the senior ASEA managers. This was one way to show respect for ASEA's core competences and to get acceptance from the technocrats.

Also at Ericsson, another of our case studies, there were excellent core competences and enough financial resources when the firm ran into a performance crisis after a hazardous diversification into the office automation business, called Ericsson Information Systems (EIS). There were serious delays before the retrenchment phase was started, but as soon as the decision to get out from EIS was taken, the process was rapid. Even before the pull-out from EIS was completed, the expansion of the cellular (mobile) systems was started. The basis was Ericsson's core business, electronic exchange systems called AXE. Heavy investments were made, both in new technology and marketing, and Ericsson became one of the world's leading suppliers of cellular systems.

*The climate for change*

Lesson 5. An important prerequisite for a successful turnaround is the initial crisis consciousness and the climate for change within the organization.

With its roots in the initial situation we can identify the third important prerequisite for turnaround success as the crisis consciousness and climate for change within the organization. One of the main explanations of why companies run into situations of crisis is their inability to accomplish adequate change, inasmuch as earlier success had led to inflexible standard operating procedures and strong counterproductive corporate values (cf. Starbuck et al, 1978; Tushman and Romanelli, 1985). As Miller and Friesen (1980) suggest, there is a momentum in the current strategic and organizational direction which causes the firm to go 'too far' in the established direction. Therefore radical strategic change cannot be accomplished by stepwise, incremental change. In most cases, before major change can take place, a crisis needs to have been experienced.

In the ASEA case the organization experienced a vacuum, waiting for a new CEO to be appointed and bring about change. There was an awareness in the organization, at least amongst the managers, of the need for change, even if there were different opinions on what the content of the reorientation should be. There was also a widespread awareness of the fact that the outcome of earlier attempts at strategic change were disappointing. The technocratic hard core of ASEA had resisted several 'attacks' of radical change.

## The Turnaround Reorientation

The third category in the analysis of turnaround success is the turnaround reorientation, a holistic concept covering both strategy, structure and culture.

> Lesson 6. Intellectually the turnaround reorientation is the most demanding part of the turnaround process. It requires a 'helicopter view' and the capacity to draw consistent conclusions from large amounts of information.

During the structuring phase, CEO/TMT initiate a series of changes, which require a holistic view and therefore could not have easily been initiated from the lower levels within the organization. Initially, power is centralized at the top management level. Solution of short-term, emergency problems, development of strategic visions, determination of business portfolio priorities, reorganizations, introduction of new control systems, and appointment of managers are primarily decided upon and controlled by top management.

Contractive and structuring activities are initially in focus and decisions of a contractive nature are typically made and also to a large extent implemented by CEO/TMT. The ASEA turnaround was a mix of corporate and divisional portfolio balancing, with the focus moving from the corporate to the divisional level. Right from the beginning, most formal planning activities (e.g. analysis of environment, competitors and internal strengths and weaknesses) was done at the divisional level, but with an intensive strategic dialogue with the top management level.

In the expansion and consolidation phases power is decentralized, and SBU managers take the initiative and responsibility regarding major parts of the strategic planning.

*Strategic change*

Lesson 7. Core business and core competence strategies are presenting the best opportunities for turnaround success.

In the face of a turnaround situation the CEO is under time pressure to start the action programme in order to show improvement of performance to the target level and sustainable growth as soon as possible. Overwhelming evidence has been provided both by academics and practitioners that a phase of retrenchment is necessary to cure the patient before the expansion can start (cf. Robbins and Pearce, 1992).

A part of the retrenchment phase is to make priorities and reduce the number of businesses in order to prepare for the expansion phase with a smaller number of existing core businesses. Alternatives like acquisitions of other established businesses or greenfield investments in new businesses are too risky in this stage of the process. The conclusion is that core business strategies are the most attractive business portfolio alternatives for a successful turnaround.

In the middle of a crisis situation it is hard to analyse the reasons behind it in order to find the most vulnerable businesses. Especially in integrated firms with a functional organizational structure, the breakdown of economic data is a complicated procedure and therefore the information on the product level is seldom a reliable or even accessible base for strategic decisions. The first step in the analysis is therefore a special study of strategies, competition and profitability per product. The outcome of such a study may include surprises for the managers and hopefully a basis for a selective combination of brake and throttle strategies.

In the ASEA turnaround the generic corporate strategy was not changed in the sense that it was not questioned that ASEA should remain one of the leading all-round suppliers of heavy electrical equipment. The emphasis on international growth was presented from the beginning in order to raise volumes to the extent that rapidly increasing R&D costs could be absorbed. The major change in strategy took place on the product group level where priorities were dramatically changed on the basis of detailed analysis of product strategies and profitability. As the business portfolio was in general the same after the turnaround, we have classified the strategy as fine-tuning on the corporate level (cf. Bibeault, 1982; Hambrick and Schecter, 1983). Within this strategy some mature businesses were drastically reduced whilst others were expanded from the beginning. The goal for each of the businesses that was given priority was to remain or become world-class (No. 1 or 2) in terms of market shares and technology. ASEA could not realistically have the ambition to become the overall leader in the industry. The resources for such a goal were not sufficient and many markets were still protectionistic. In many niches, however, ASEA formulated goals for reaching internationally leading positions.

From our cases we can also draw the conclusion that the basis of a successful corporate turnaround is that each SBU can develop its own viable competitive strategy. Each business must primarily be surviving on its own qualifications and no 'new' synergies can be discounted in the early stages of the retrenchment phase. Synergy arguments should not be used as excuses for neglecting the implementation of retrenchment programmes for weak businesses. This is to a great extent true, even in integrated corporations such as ASEA and ABB. This conclusion does not imply a rejection of synergy effects, but should be interpreted as a warning signal.

Lesson 8. The handling of synergies between related SBUs is a critical management issue, especially within integrated companies based upon common core competences.

Lesson 9. Business portfolio strategy should also respond to demands from the stock exchange markets, which during the 1980s did not favour conglomerates.

The cultivating of synergies in a divisionalized and decentralized organization is an important top management issue. Especially in technically integrated firms there is a delicate balance between the encouraging of the manager's own initiatives and disciplined internal (top-down) coordination and cooperation. There is an obvious risk that technically integrated firms with a strong common core competence will go too far in the breakdown of the firm to independent SBUs with their own strategies. Integrated firms often perceive a multi-level competition on the business family (corporate) level as an all-round supplier, for instance in the systems or contraction engineering business and on the single product market (cf. Prahalad and Hamel, 1990).

ASEA and ABB are examples of such firms, where the competitive situation is complex and the ability to coordinate major systems and contraction engineering projects between several contributing SBUs is of decisive importance for the position in the industry. Both in ASEA and in ABB the CEO, Percy Barnevik, has chosen an international matrix in order to efficiently coordinate the systems' strategies.

Our findings from the ASEA and ABB cases and other cases like Swedish Match indicate that the CEO is anxious to present internal synergies in order to build a corporate image which has to do with more than financial relations to the SBUs. Such an ambition has been very important in allaying the suspicion towards conglomerates on the part of investor relations and the stock exchange. The ASEA and ABB managements have been very active in communicating the 'stick to the knitting' message and, unlike most competitors, warning of the dangers of diversifying into resource-absorbing and risky businesses even if the profit prospects are attractive. The CEO who initiated the Swedish Match turnaround worked hard to make internal synergies visible and wipe off the conglomerate label from the corporate image. In this case, however, the message was never accepted by the capital market, and the major reason was that the performance improvement was too slow. Obviously synergies have no value for the investors until they are proved to have a positive impact on the key figures.

*Structural change*

> Lesson 10. Divisionalization and decentralization are important instruments to vitalize the organization and increase the profit- and market-orientation.
>
> Lesson 11. Critical points in the restructuring are the definition of the SBUs and to follow-up with adequate control and report systems.
>
> Lesson 12. Other critical points in the decentralization are the appointment of SBU managers and the strategic dialogue between the two top management levels.

The reason behind a firm's crisis problems is in most cases a combination of external, macroeconomic and competitive factors and internal lack of efficiency. Many of the firms we have studied were in the initial stage characterized by a basically functional structure leading to top-heavy decision-making and bureaucracy. This was true of ASEA when the turnaround process started. There was an indisputable potential for improvements of the internal efficiency. The major problem was how to overcome the resistance and bring about changes.

For most firms with related businesses a transformation from a U-form (functional) to an M-form (multidivisional) type of organization presents a great potential for efficiency improvements (cf. Hoskisson, 1987). Ouchi (1979, 1984) also advocates the advantages of the M-form organization with the argument that it is superior when it comes to taking into consideration what is best for both the different businesses and the corporate entity. The M-form offers the broadest spectrum of control mechanisms: market, bureaucratic and clan control. By combining market control with both bureaucratic and clan control, management can reach the highest standards of professionalism in terms of strategy formulation and implementation.

In the case of Swedish Match there was already before the turnaround situation an M-form organization. The new, externally recruited 'turnaround-CEO' considered the definitions of the different SBUs as inconsistent and unclear in terms of both products and markets. One of the first steps in the turnaround programme was to reorganize in order to make clearer the delimitations of the SBUs and at the same time put together businesses with potential synergies.

However, there are also costs for the breakdown of a functional organization into divisions, especially in technically integrated firms. In principle, each SBU should have a complete set of functions, which implies extra or double costs for overheads. An even more serious consequence could be if the creation of internal markets leads to power-consuming internal negotiations and disputes over internal pricing. If there are tendencies towards these variants it is important that CEO/TMT can intervene and formulate the rules of the game to minimize the internal negotiations and disputes.

A critical factor in the introduction of new goal-setting procedures for the M-form organization is that the new SBUs can be delimited clearly enough to establish their own profit-and-loss account and also balance sheet, both designed for the consolidation in the corporate computer-based report system. The divisionalized organization will not work properly until the systems have been integrated. The finding from both the ASEA case and several others prove that there can be serious disturbances on this point.

Another critical factor in the process of decentralization is the appointment of managers who can take the full responsibility for a division or other important profit centre. In the Swedish Match (conglomerate) case there was a combination of a severe crisis and new SBU managers. The CEO and senior managers got involved in declining businesses in order to strengthen the balance sheet, reducing production capacity and divesting. They were very active both in the stage of formulation and in the implementation of strategies. When the emergency action programme was working or completed and the newly appointed SBU managers were operative, top management changed their style and started a process of delegating power and responsibility.

### Cultural change

> Lesson 13. Cultural change in the depth of a large organization is a slow process. The most obvious changes in the fundamental attitudes can be observed in the case of profit centre managers, often in connection with the appointment of many new managers.

In the management literature there is a strong agreement amongst leading scholars and experienced managers that a change in corporate culture is a slow process. In a turnaround process there are normally many dramatic changes to be implemented within a short period and therefore there is an obvious risk that the corporate culture will put the brake to the process and cause serious delays. If there is a widespread crisis awareness in the organization the implementation will be faster, partly because the basic values have been questioned and partly as a consequence of the fact that the acceptance of uncomfortable changes will increase even if the basic value system is not changed.

In our ASEA case we have found that some of the basic values were not changed until several years after the introduction of the turnaround process. Many senior persons at ASEA had great difficulty in accepting the new emphasis on profitability and market orientation which, according to this 'silent majority', would threaten the long-term investment in technology. The fastest change in basic values came in the case of the new group of managers who took over the responsibility for the operations and later also for the strategy of the divisions and profit centres.

## The Turnaround Process

### The start-up phase

> Lesson 14. The new CEO should immediately take the initiative and establish the change process at a high pace. It is important to show 'early improvements' and to skilfully handle the initial emergency situation.

> Lesson 15. The new CEO should give the organization a sense of long-term direction, but at the same time strengthen the crisis consciousness in the organization by stressing the seriousness of the prevailing situation.

The new CEO's position of power is essentially composed of the legitimate power designated by the Board. The position of power held by a new externally recruited CEO is both uncertain and questioned. The best chance for the new CEO to immediately establish other power positions is to demonstrate expert or referent power (French and Raven, 1959). By taking the initiative, the new CEO starts strengthening his or her power platform in the organization (Greiner and Bhambri, 1989), and it is important for the new CEO to fill that 'hole', before any opposition, especially from senior managers, has been established.

One explanation of the low level of visible opposition to Barnevik's turnaround programme was that he took immediate command of the firm by means of a dramatic reorganization and reshuffle of the top management team. This action came like lightning and took most ASEA insiders by surprise. Barnevik's fundamental attitude has always been to maintain a fast pace in the change process without being politically insensitive. In his view, slow changes create passive managers. Thus a fast pace keeps inertia to a minimum. Barnevik stated as a newcomer at ASEA: 'It is more important to act quickly than to end up exactly right.'

In addition to his legitimate base of power and the Board's support (in the ASEA case), Barnevik began to be respected within the organization for his programme: short-term problem solutions which significantly improved operational performance (building up his expert and referent power bases), and long-term visions. Barnevik demonstrated great political skill in getting his retrenchment programme accepted by showing the seriousness of the prevailing situation at the same time as he was formulating positive long-term visions. He deviated from established traditions, for instance vertical integration and guaranteed employment, from the beginning. Barnevik was visible in the organization and his style of management could be characterized as 'hands on'.

Amongst a majority of the senior managers at ASEA there was a great deal of scepticism towards Barnevik's programme for a turnaround. By tradition, however, these managers were loyal towards the firm and its CEO. Loyalty, a feeling of responsibility, a passion for engineering competence, and hard work were fundamental elements of ASEA's corporate culture. There was also a widespread understanding amongst top and middle managers that extra-ordinary measures were necessary to take ASEA out of the crisis. But the 'silent majority' had no idea of what these measures were. Many of them had been waiting for a change of CEO as a starting point for 'putting new life into the firm'. As the first improvements became visible, several of the senior managers changed their opinion, whilst others never accepted the logic of the new strategy and therefore left ASEA.

Early in the turnaround process, Barnevik also presented his vision of ASEA as one of the leading firms in the heavy power equipment industry. In order to make this vision real, ASEA had to grow considerably and change from being a Swedish exporting firm to become a truly multinational, market-oriented corporation with a strong international position. ASEA should also exploit its technical competence more efficiently and thereby improve its profitability. This vision was challenging to the organization. Especially the striving for leadership was widely accepted. However, the means—reorganization, profit-ability- and market-orientation—were questioned.

Lesson 16: The new CEO can make use of the 'Bennborn effect', which involves current members of top management contributing well-articulated ideas towards formulating a new strategic orientation and thereby significantly facilitating its implementation.

Lesson 17: CEO and TMT must establish a productive strategic dialogue with SBU managers and gradually delegate the strategic initiative to the SBU managers.

The prompt action in Barnevik's start-up of the turnaround process would hardly have been possible without the contribution of ideas from a small number of managers who supported his ideas. There was especially one of the vice-presidents, Arne Bennborn, who had formulated plans for a matrix organization which he had presented internally several years earlier without getting any support either from the acting CEO or the Board. We call this phenomenon the 'Bennborn effect': current members of the management group contribute well-articulated ideas towards formulating a new strategic orientation and thereby facilitating its implementation. Barnevik won both time and efficiency in the formulation and implementation of the first change programme thanks to the Bennborn effect.

Amongst the middle managers, there were young persons who quickly accepted the new ideas and became important agents of change. As soon as the new organizational structure was presented, they were appointed in order to reduce uncertainty and to keep the pace in the change process high. Especially in ASEA but also in ABB, the appointment decisions were amongst the most important ones in the early phases of the turnarounds, because the management style is built on a tight dialogue between the TMT and the SBU managers. The dialogue is a part of a learning process which leads to SBU managers gradually taking over the strategic initiative.

*Grand plan and learning*

> Lesson 18: CEO's and TMT's first strategy ('grand plan') must be durable, with gradual adjustments and step-wise implementation.

By definition a corporate turnaround is started in a critical situation which means high financial and time pressure. Normally successful turnarounds should be completed within a time-period of 4–5 years (cf. Schendel et al, 1976; Hambrick and Schecter, 1983). This leaves room for very few strategic mistakes, labelled 'strategic loops' by the CEO of Swedish Match. The initial visions or grand plans presented by the top management must be robust when discussed and questioned. At the same time processual planning, learning and quick adaptations to emergent situations are important aspects of a successful turnaround.

In the ASEA case, it is obvious that Barnevik very early had visions and the draft of a grand plan. He had planned for stepwise implementation and, in some cases, he even held back information of the next steps in order to keep the organization focused upon the actual activities. Both the development of the corporate strategy and the organizational structure show important aspects of processual planning and learning.

ASEA's mature businesses were turned around more rapidly than expected and as a result they remained very important in the business portfolio. From the beginning, Barnevik had been prepared to make much more dramatic divestments of mature businesses, but he was convinced that ASEA to a high degree should 'stick to the knitting' and continue to exploit the technical synergies between the core products.

The learning aspect of the restructuring is most clearly demonstrated by the step taken from divisions to legally independent subsidiaries and also the introduction of coordination mechanisms within each company function in order to culture the vast, but scattered, specialist competence within this large corporation.

Our emphasizing of a viable grand plan in turnaround situations does not imply that we look upon strategy development as an entirely rational strategic planning and strategic design process (cf. Mintzberg, 1978; Mintzberg, 1990). Initial visions and grand plans give strategic directions in more or less general terms and fall into the categories umbrella and processual strategies in the classification of Mintzberg and Waters (1985). The strategic direction is gradually modified and adapted but time pressure does not allow for a total strategic reorientation in the middle of a turnaround process.

Formal strategic planning (and economic control) systems were, in all of our cases, used as instruments for delegation of the strategic initiative in M-form organizations. We would like especially to emphasize the importance of strategic planning and strategic plans as 'instruments' for a strategic dialogue (Brandes and Brege, 1992) between top management and SBU management. In our view, formal strategic planning and analysis does not exclude learning (cf. Mintzberg, 1990). Rather, a productive strategic dialogue (often of a dialectic nature) promotes learning and is an important prerequisite for a turnaround success.

## Pace and timing

> Lesson 19: CEO and TMT should maintain a high pace in the implementation of change, but at the same time show a feeling for the timing of important actions and the limits of management capacity.

High pace in the change process is an important attribute of turnaround success, and so is top managment's feeling for the timing of different activities. It is important to create a momentum in the change process. Different kinds of inertia—perceptional, political, resource-based, value-based and market-based inertia—are often easier to overcome at a high pace. At the same time the pace can sometimes be too high and create too much confusion and bad implementation. The pace has to be sensibly adapted to the situation. For example, Barnevik showed his political skills when he, after negotiations with the labour unions, delayed by a year the transformation of divisions in legally independent subsidiaries.

Compared to our other cases ASEA experienced a turnaround at a high pace. Swedish Match, on the other hand, had severe problems handling different kinds of inertia:

- Inadequate financial resources to implement the retrenchment phase (to absorb write-off losses, etc.).
- Shortage of competent SBU managers to take over the strategic initiative from top management.
- Time delays in changing the resource base to fit a strategy change from

standardization and large-scale strategic thinking to customer-oriented strategies.

- Time delays in changing positions in the market networks.
- Time delays in divestment activities, due to a business cycle recession and a shortage of credible buyers.
- Strategic mistakes ('strategic loops') that called for a new structuring of the corporation.

*CEO involvement*

Lesson 20: CEO and TMT can never abdicate.

The successful 'double turnaround' of ASEA and ABB brings up the question of the importance of CEO and top management involvement in turnaround processes. How important are they? In the mass media, especially in the business press, myths are cultivated about the powerful actions of the CEO during a turnaround process; he or she is proclaimed a hero/heroine after successfully bringing the company out of a serious crisis, achieving a so-called turnaround. In the same manner, the CEO bears the sole responsibility if the firm fails. Swedish examples of company heroes are Jan Carlzon, Scandinavian Airlines Systems (SAS), and Percy Barnevik, ASEA and ASEA Brown Boveri (ABB). This trend in the mass media is international.

In the academic world the predominant perspective is different. According to this view, the possibilities for the CEO and top managers to independently choose and implement the strategy are very restricted. Top management is caught between a deterministic environment and an organization characterized by bureaucracy and inertia.

Other researchers, however, maintain that possibilities exist for management's strategic choice, e.g. Chandler (1962), Child (1972) and more recently, in an article dealing with turnarounds, Greiner and Bhambri (1989). Top management's influence is greatest during periods of revolution, i.e. when the firm dramatically changes its strategic orientation (Tushman and Romanelli, 1985).

Our findings from the five case studies (Brandes and Brege, 1990, 1993), support the view in favour of a strong and deeply involved CEO and TMT. A skilful top management intervention is a necessary but not sufficient condition for a successful turnaround. We would especially emphasize the following aspects of active top management involvement in the turnaround processes:

1.   Top management involvement is most important in the early emergency and structuring phases (i.e. change of strategic direction).
2.   Frequent top management involvement in the implementation of strategic change is often forgotten in the strategic management literature.

3.   In contrast to, e.g., Tushman and Romanelli (1985), we recognize an active top management involvement also in the expansion and consolidation phases of the turnaround. This observation seems valid from a descriptive and a normative perspective. The role of top management in 'normal', evolutionary situations is not only symbolic.

4.   The 'centrifugal forces' and 'momentum of change' (cf. Miller and Friesen, 1980) are strong in large decentralized organizations. Top management has to delegate, but at the same time practise an intense control by means of a productive strategic dialogue. The CEO/TMT can never abdicate.

## REFERENCES

Bibeault, D. B. (1982). *Corporate Turnaround—How Managers Turn Losers into Winners*, McGraw-Hill, New York.

Brandes, O. and Brege, S. (1990). *Market Leadership* (in Swedish), Kristianstad, Liber.

Brandes, O. and Brege, S. (1992). Strategic management as a dialectic process. In: Mattson, L-G. and Stymne, B. (eds) *Corporate and Industry Strategies for Europe*, Elsevier Science Publishers B.V.

Brandes, O. and Brege, S. (1993). 'Strategic turnarounds and top management involvement: The case of ASEA/ABB. In: Lorange, P. et al (eds) *Implementing Strategic Processes—Change, Learning and Cooperation*, Basil Blackwell, Oxford, 91–114.

Chandler, A. (1962). *Strategy and Structure: Chapters in the History of American Industrial Enterprise*, The M.I.T. Press, Cambridge.

Child, J. (1972). Organizational structure, environment and performance: The role of strategic choice, *Sociology*, **6**, 2–22.

French Jr., J. and Raven, B. (1959). The bases of social power. In: Cartwright, D. (ed.) *Studies in Social Power*, Ann Arbor, Institute for Social Research, University of Michigan, pp. 150–167.

Greiner, L. E. and Bhambri, A. (1989). New CEO intervention and dynamics of deliberate strategic change, *Strategic Management Journal*, **10**, 67–89.

Hambrick, D. C. and Schecter, S. M. (1983). Turnaround strategies for mature industrial-product business units, *Academy of Management Journal*, **26**, 231–248.

Hofer, C. W. (1980). Turnaround strategies, *The Journal of Business Strategy*, **1**, 19–31.

Hofer, C. W. (1988). Designing turnaround strategies. In: Quinn, J. B. et al (eds) The *Strategy Process—Concepts, Contexts and Cases*, Prentice-Hall, Englewood Cliffs, NJ, 678–686.

Hoskisson, R. E. (1987). Multidivisional structure and performance: The contingency of diversification strategy, *Academy of Management Journal*, **30**(4), 625–644.

Miller, D. and Friesen, P. H. (1980). Momentum and revolution in organizational adaptation, *Academy of Management Journal*, **23**, 591–614.

Mintzberg, H. (1983). *Power In and Around Organizations*, Prentice-Hall, Englewood Cliffs, NJ.

Nelson, P. B. (1981). *Corporations in Crisis: Behavioral Observations for Bankruptcy Policy*, Praeger Publishers, New York.

Ouchi, W. G. (1979). A conceptual framework for the design of organizational control mechanisms, *Management Science*, **25**(9), 833–848.

Ouchi, W. G. (1984). *The M-Form Society: How American Teamwork Can Recapture Competitive Edge*, Addison-Wesley, Reading, MA.

Prahalad, C. K. and Hamel, G. (1990). The core competence of the corporation, *Harvard Business Review*, May–June, 79–91.

Robbins, D. K. and Pearce, J. A. (1992). Turnaround: Retrenchment and recovery, *Strategic Management Journal*, **13**(4), 287–309.

Schendel, D. E., Patton, R. and Riggs, J. (1976). Corporate turnaround strategies: A study of profit decline and recovery, *Journal of General Management*, **3**, 3–11.

Starbuck, W. H., Greve, A. and Hedberg, B. (1978). Responding to crisis, *Journal of Business Administration*, **9**, 111–137.

Tushman, M. L. and Romaneli, E. (1985). Organizational evolution: a metamorphosis model of convergence and reorientation. In: *Research in Organizational Behavior*, Vol. 7, JAI Press, Greenwich, CT, 171–222.

# 10

# XEROX: ENVISIONING A CORPORATE TRANSFORMATION

**Greg Bounds**

*College of Business, University of Tennessee*

**Fred Hewitt**[1]

*Aston Business School, Aston University*

Xerox is a global company engaged in a total corporate transformation. This chapter provides a case history of that transformation. It shows:

- The dramatic results achieved.
- The actions taken to achieve those results.
- How the change in management approach was managed.
- How all employees were mobilized to bring about changes.
- The tools involved, including quality, benchmarking and process improvement.
- Restructuring for continuous change.

## XEROX'S GLOBAL SUCCESS

Bernard Fournier, Managing Director of Rank Xerox Ltd, received the first 'European Quality Award' from King Juan Carlos of Spain in Madrid on 20 October 1992. For Xerox and its affiliates, this was the latest accolade in a

---

[1]Fred Hewitt is the former Vice-President of Central Logistics and Asset Management, Xerox Corporation

*The Implementation Challenge*, Edited by D. E. Hussey
© 1996 John Wiley & Sons Ltd

series stretching over more than a decade. Twelve years earlier, Fuji Xerox had won Japan's premier quality award—the Deming Prize. In 1989 Xerox won the Malcolm Baldridge National Quality Award in the United States (US). Winning the Baldridge Award was particularly remarkable since Xerox had entered all 50,200 employees at the 93 US locations of its Business Products and Systems Group into the competition. Other comparably sized companies tended to enter only one division or focused their quality initiatives on one location.

In the period between the Deming Prize and the European Quality Award, Xerox affiliates also won national quality awards in Australia, Canada, France (twice), Mexico, the Netherlands and the UK. The geographical diversity of this decade-long success story is a clear indication that total quality management has become internalized within Xerox to a level which is evident in few other Western companies. An all-pervasive obsession with quality is generally associated only with Japanese companies, such as Toyota, and is rarely evidenced in the West.

It is probably significant that Fuji Xerox, in Japan, was the first Xerox success on the road to global recognition; and it is also significant that much of Xerox's competition which emerged in the 1970s is Japanese. In the early 1970s, MITI identified office products in general and copiers in particular, alongside automobiles, motorcycles, cameras and televisions, as business areas in which low cost, high-quality products could and should dominate the market. Faced by such fierce competition, Xerox had no choice but to match or beat its Japanese rivals in terms of quality. In any event, Xerox's response has been dramatic.

The headline of the leading article in the *New York Times'* Business Day Section on 3 September 1992 read:

Japan is tough but Xerox prevails.

In this article, an NEC Corporation spokesperson in Japan, referring to the Xerox 5100 duplicator which is manufactured in the US but has captured 90% of the high-speed duplicator market in Japan, is quoted as saying:

The machines are better than anything we can get in Japan. We are not concerned it is an American product. We wanted the best and most efficient machine.

Perhaps this, more than any formal award presentation, indicates how well Xerox has responded to the quality challenge.

So what is it that this corporation has done? What are the characteristics of its approach to total quality management? What is its vision for the future? How have Xerox leaders attempted to transform the company? Answers to these questions can be found in the following description of three general phases of the ongoing transformation at Xerox.

# PHASE 1: IMMEDIATE QUALITY IMPROVEMENT

From its beginning, in the early 1980s, Xerox's quality focus was external and business oriented, relating employees and internal work processes to external customers' requirements. The stimulus came from outside the company in the form of competition. The reaction was also to look outside the company and, thus, Xerox pioneered competitive benchmarking. In 1983 David Kearns, the then CEO of Xerox, gathered his top 25 managers together at Xerox's Leesburg, Virginia Training Center to review benchmarking data which showed Xerox to be way off the competitive mark in measures of quality, cost and delivery. The benchmarking process motivated Xerox leaders to make immediate quality improvement a top corporate priority, starting with the creation of a quality policy.

## The Xerox Quality Policy

Before leaving Leesburg, these 25 leaders defined the Xerox quality policy which has worldwide applicability and is still in effect today. It states:

> Xerox is a Quality Company. Quality is the basic business principle for Xerox. Quality means providing our external and internal customers with innovative products and services that fully satisfy their requirements. Quality improvement is the job of every Xerox employee.

Amongst the most interesting aspects of this policy is the definition statement. The definition of quality as 'meeting the customer requirements' seems less remarkable today than it really was in 1983. At that time quality was still defined in most companies in terms of negatives and inanimate objects (e.g. defects per hundred machines assembled). Xerox's outward looking, positive view of quality as meeting customer requirements was quite different.

Another interesting feature of the quality policy is the accountabilities statement. By making the bold statement that within a quality company, quality improvement is the job of every employee, the mystique and remoteness of 'the quality department' or 'the quality officer' was put aside. Xerox began what was, in effect, a cultural revolution within the company. Xerox had already pioneered employee involvement programmes, and these were now married to the total quality initiative.

## Massive Doses of Training

Building upon these earlier successful experiences, Xerox's 'Leadership Through Quality' initiative was purposely implemented through a management led training cascade approach (Figure 10.1). Starting with David Kearns and his direct reports, each layer of management was trained in quality practices,

## TRAINING CASCADE

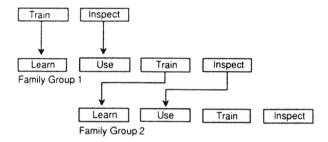

**Figure 10.1**

sent back to their jobs, inspected for conformance to leadership through quality practices and only then certified as proficient practitioners of total quality management. Only after certification were these managers allowed to act as trainers for their own family groups. Total involvement was required, lip service and authorizing others to train one's staff was not acceptable. The managers themselves trained their own staff. When the last trickle of the cascade was complete, Xerox had provided all of its employees with at least 28 hours of training in problem solving and quality improvement techniques (at an estimated cost of more than four million labour hours and $125 million).

The cascade training technique provided employees with a common language and approach to continuous improvement. Every employee was educated and skilled in the problem-solving process and quality improvement process shown in Figures 10.2 and 10.3. This education and multi-level shared

## PROBLEM SOLVING PROCESS

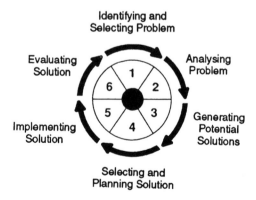

**Figure 10.2**

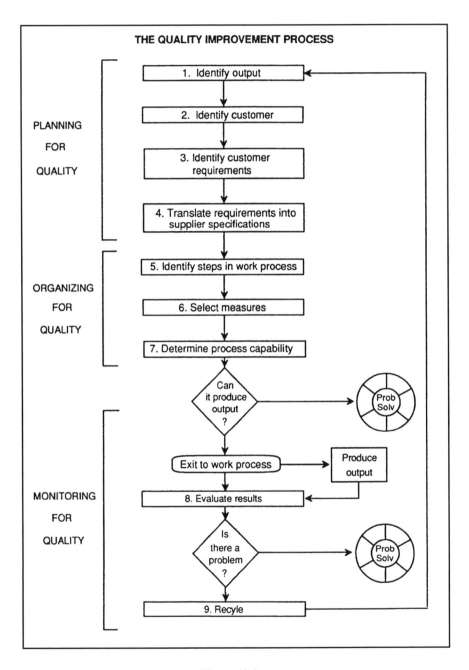

**Figure 10.3**

experience provided the foundation for all of Xerox's subsequent efforts to transform its corporate culture.

## Team Xerox

'Leadership through quality' was not the only major cultural change taking place within Xerox in the 1980s. The company had designated itself as 'The Document Company'. It had pledged to help its customers to reach breakthrough levels of productivity within their work practices through dramatically more effective ways of harnessing 'the power of the document', and to do this required careful team work.

Armed with the new quality tools, techniques and a process, salaried and hourly workers were grouped into teams vested with authority over daily work decisions and asked to make continuous improvements in their work activities. Some 75% of employees participated in one or more of the 7000 quality improvement teams. These teams reduced Xerox costs by millions of dollars and made the phrase 'Team Xerox' more than an empty slogan. They reduced scrap, tightened production schedules, and devised other efficiency and quality-enhancing measures in all functions. As a natural next stage, Xerox extended the concept of 'Team Xerox' beyond its own organizational boundaries to incorporate suppliers and customers into the teams. Xerox gave suppliers training and support in such areas as statistical process control and ensured that suppliers' production control processes were 'process qualified'. Within 3 years, this approach reduced by 73% the number of defective parts reaching the Xerox production line.

## The Role of Benchmarking

Xerox has been involved in benchmarking since the late 1970s. In fact modern benchmarking can be said to have begun with a 1979 Xerox trip to Japan to study manufacturing performance and practice. It is no surprise, therefore, that the Xerox teams seeking continuous improvement used benchmarking, combined with extensive customer preference surveys to direct their performance improvement activities. The company assessed its results in over 200 areas of product, service and business performance identified as key determinants of customer satisfaction. Targets were set at performance levels achieved by world leaders, regardless of industry, and in achieving these benchmark targets 'Team Xerox' also achieved the company's phase 1 goal of immediate quality improvement. It also identified residual shortcomings and thereby defined the requirements for further improvement.

**Cross-functional Ineffectiveness—A Phase 1 Deficiency**

Although they had established a good foundation for continuous improvement in most functions. Xerox managers realized that in these early efforts they had failed to achieve the degree of cross-functional teamwork that would be required to maintain world class status against ever increasing competition. Traditional organization structures hindered cross-functional cooperation and, therefore, impeded the consistent adoption of the cultural changes required for sustained competitiveness. Xerox's hybrid structure was defined by geography, function and product type. Its products were sold and serviced through geographically delineated organizations—Rank Xerox (Europe); America's Operation (Canada and Latin America); Fuji Xerox (Asia/Pacific); and US Operations (USA). Xerox was also functionally divided between marketing on the one hand and product development and manufacturing on the other.

Overall this structure was complex, confusing, fragmented and costly, and it reduced Xerox's responsiveness to customer needs. One particular negative result of this functional fragmentation was that the learn-use-train cascade of leadership through quality had filtered down the organization in a reductionist manner. Having been trained by their immediate supervisors, employees tended to use the training to address only their own narrowly focused functional or departmental concerns. The quality process was rarely applied across functions. Although part of the process was to identify internal 'customer/supplier' relationships, this rarely led to joint customer-supplier improvement initiatives, since bonus schemes, resource allocation processes and information were all still functionally aligned. The exception, however, appeared to be related to a particular type of problem analysis. Where managers had defined work in terms of processes, they were not only more likely to undertake successful improvement initiatives, but these were much more likely to be cross-functional. On the basis of these observations, the next steps in the corporate transformation process became clear. Phase 2 should build upon total quality management, but with a particular focus on process improvement, emphasizing cross-functional processes as an area of particular opportunity.

## PHASE 2: RE-ENGINEERING BUSINESS PROCESSES

**Reorienting Training**

In phase 2 Xerox modified in some respects its approach to training. Tools and techniques were now related to their applicability to specific work processes and market-driven goals. Employees were trained in multifunctional groups and skills were taught on an 'as needed' basis just in time for application to identified process improvement initiatives. The team approach was modified, it was not abandoned. The challenge was to work cross-functionally as a team. The aim was to take a total multi-functional business process and to demonstrate how to optimally use information technology and best practices to streamline and improve the whole process. Xerox focused on what it called 'high impact' teams, cross-functional teams responsible for defined basic business processes which have outputs that significantly impact business results.[2] Ed Leroux, then Director of Training and Education, illustrated the cross-functional nature of these high impact teams:

> For example, previously we defined distribution as simply the transfer of the product from the assembly line to the warehouse. But now we recognize that the distribution process touches everything from the point of supplier deliveries, through where the product gets produced, to the trunk of the service representative making repairs at the customer's site. Now distribution has a much more cross-functional, process orientation. And the process teams are composed of cross-functional representatives from throughout the distribution process, like manufacturing, warehousing, and customer services.

### Planned Learning Experiences

Xerox began to provide these high-impact teams with 'planned learning experiences', rather than just training and educational courses. Under this approach the level of knowledge and skill of the specific team is taken into account, and the learning experience adjusted to their needs. Tools and techniques were provided as needed, just in time to be applied to a process. The team was required to produce a 'readiness checklist', identifying the knowledge and skill level of the team members in respect of relevant tools and techniques, and also describing the documented business processes to be addressed.

### Documented Processes

A document process in this context is defined in terms of activities, outputs and purposes. To understand the purpose of the process, team members must understand the relationship of the process to the company's customer-driven goals and objectives. For workers and managers within the process, this understanding provides answers to questions like: What is the organization trying to accomplish? What does this process contribute? What is my role in that contribution? To ensure the process activities contribute effectively to corporate goals and objectives, team members must also understand the root causes of variation in process outputs. In order to understand the root causes of these variations, usually through the application of statistical process

---

[2]These process teams are high in strategic importance and not necessarily high in the hierarchy

control techniques, the team members must first map activity sequences, decision points, inputs and outputs, usually in the form of flowcharts and time lines.

Carefully constructed documentation thus provides the basis for the identification of potential process improvements and also defines the boundary conditions for potential empowerment of the employees within the process. Within this approach empowerment is not the 'manager getting out of the worker's way'. Having properly framed the improvement initiative in terms of documented processes, empowerment need no longer be seen as the manager delegating authority to the point of having nothing to do. Instead, the manager continually refocuses the team's contribution in terms of the company's objectives, and specifically communicates the scope of employee authority in relation to activities and output. The manager provides workers with a business process context for their team initiatives, and then coaches and supports process re-engineering. Coaches are assigned to assist the process team not only with readiness, but also with continuous learning and applications. Xerox recruits coaches who already have full-time jobs, typically line managers and not just staff professionals. Although the coaches are trained and certified, they are usually already well grounded in improvement techniques.

## Comprehensive Multi-level Applications

Under the revised approach Xerox employees set out to improve business processes throughout the organization along multiple fronts. Broad cross-functional processes which are strategically important and greatly impact business success commanded the attention of senior executives, and those of more limited scope were managed by managers with more restricted responsibility. Individuals at every level of the organization were empowered to improve their work processes and activities. Some of the more detailed improvement work may be integrated with the work of higher level process teams, whilst other improvement work is self-directed and not integrated with higher level activities. In fact, Xerox recognizes a need to continuously improve existing processes, at all levels, whilst also working on new processes which might obsolete the old ones. It might seem to be a waste of time to have workers and supervisors labouring to improve their work processes only to have them subsequently eliminated through re-engineering. However, Xerox does not regard any improvement as waste. Xerox prefers to have all employees engaged in improvement all the time, even at the most atomic (or grass roots) levels of the organization, partly because managers cannot always anticipate which activities will be kept and which eliminated and partly because experience shows that employees who have participated in successful small change initiatives are more likely to be open to radical change than those who have no change experience at all.

### Directions of Process Improvement: Error Reduction, Cycle Time Reduction and Customer Satisfaction Improvements

To guide these improvements throughout the organization, Xerox has set forth three fundamental directions for change: error reduction; cycle time reduction; and customer satisfaction improvement. These directions for change ensure that, although improvement efforts are sometimes fragmented and dispersed, they will always be good for the company and its customers.

Similar to Motorola's Six Sigma campaign, Xerox promotes $10 \times$ error reduction, so that whatever the rate of errors happens to be, it should be improved tenfold. Error reduction is stressed more at the atomic levels of the organization, particularly in areas of direct contact with customers.

Cycle time reduction can be sought at all levels of the organization, but is particularly important at a macro-process level, where cycle time reduction through process re-engineering may totally eliminate activities at more atomic levels.

Error reduction and cycle time improvement should in themselves improve customer satisfaction. Xerox leaders, nevertheless, felt it important as part of the phase 2 initiative to explicitly articulate that the purpose of improvements to the company's processes remains, above all else, to provide increased satisfaction to its customers. There should be no doubt that business process re-engineering is compatible with, and indeed built upon, the company's original Xerox quality policy; it may be a way of cutting costs, but it is not a way of cutting value to customers.

### Xerox Business Architecture

Although the relationship between business process re-engineering and leadership through quality was at first tenuous, the two initiatives soon became intertwined and synergistic. It became evident that the key to empowerment and performance improvement was a radical simplification of business processes. Specifically, taking a cross-functional view of ways of doing business in support of satisfying customer requirements could lead to breakthrough levels of performance improvement. It was recognized that this approach could yield a quantum simultaneous improvement in quality, customer satisfaction and business results.

One example of this process-focused approach can be seen in Xerox's supply chain integration efforts. The matrix in Figure 10.4 represents a depiction developed by Xerox executives of the key business processes or cross-functional flows that serve customers. Prominent amongst these was the

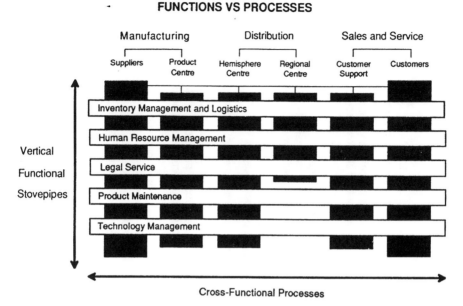

**Figure 10.4**

process by which Xerox manages its trading assets and ensures that customers' orders are fulfilled in a way which always meets their requirements, without the company incurring competitive disadvantage in terms of logistics cost or inventory carrying cost. In fact three business processes received priority attention, namely customer engagement, product design and engineering (soon renamed as time to market) and inventory management and logistics. By studying the last named in detail, it is possible to illustrate Xerox's overall approach at this stage to total quality-driven process re-engineering.

**Inventory Management and Logistics**

Each of the key business processes is assigned a process owner (or sponsor), a clearly defined set of missions and objectives, and resource in the form of a high-impact team responsible for accomplishing the mission. The responsibilities of a process sponsor are listed in Figure 10.5. The position of process sponsor is not usually full time, but a collateral activity of a manager who also holds a full-time corporate or line position. For example, Dr Fred Hewitt became the sponsor of inventory management and logistics (IM&L), the process essentially responsible for 'getting the right things, to the right place, at the right time'. At the time of his appointment, he was Director of Distribution

## BUSINESS PROCESS SPONSORSHIP

| Responsibilities | Execution/Implementation Approach |
|---|---|
| • Provide strategic direction to business process area owners and process improvement projects | • Establish business process area goals, desired state and critical success factors |
| • Initiate BAA and process improvement projects to achieve goals and desired state | • Determine projects required, commit resources and assign responsibility for process improvement projects |
| • Provide quality assurance to ensure that process improvement projects meet strategic and business architecture requirements | • Acts as primary customer for process improvement projects outputs <br> • Conduct periodic inspections of process improvement projects |
| • Demonstrate role model commitment and support for business process management | • Represent business process area (direction, resources, cross-functional and cross-organizational issues, etc.) in senior team management process |
| • Manage cross-process and cross-organizational/functional boundaries/seams to ensure process integration and effectiveness | • Resolve and/or escalate cross-organizational, cross-process issues |

Figure 10.5

and Technical Services for Rank Xerox in Europe, and a pioneer in developing multinational systems for optimizing inventory levels among European operating units.

The IM&L team's mission was to (1) develop IM&L strategies and processes, (2) ensure their implementation through procedures and systems across Xerox worldwide and (3) share with the operating units the responsibility for achieving ongoing improvements in customer satisfaction, logistics costs and asset utilization.

## The Multinational Inventory Optimization Council (MIOC)

As the IM&L process sponsor Hewitt was primarily responsible for orchestrating the involvement of other key managers and executives through their participation in IM&L process councils and sub-groups. The multinational inventory optimization council (MIOC) was the top-level council of the IM&L business process. The MIOC executive team was composed of handpicked senior managers who not only displayed the right sort of mind set, but also were significant stakeholders in the change efforts that would follow. These senior level directors and vice-presidents from all different parts of Xerox corporation (from engineering, manufacturing, sales, service, from Europe, North America, Latin America and the Far East) were charged to look for cross-functional, cross-unit opportunities for radical process improvement.

## The Integrated Supply Chain Process Principles and Vision

The MIOC executive team developed the following integrated supply chain process principles:

- Customer satisfaction is key
  —100% customer satisfaction at the lowest cost and levels of inventory is the objective of the IM&L process.
  —Customers will be provided with an integrated approach to all IM&L activities.
- Demand-driven supply chain
  —Customer orders will drive actions in all echelons of the supply chain.
  —Manufacturing flexibility is essential.
  —Build/customize to order, deliver to customer in 1 week are key targets.
- Time to customer is a competitive advantage
  —Removing time from the physical supply chain requires Xerox to remove time from the information pipeline.
  —Information pipeline effectiveness is critical for quickly empowered responses.

- Common product language
  —Customer requirements must be easily and unambiguously translated into items to be delivered, the components necessary to build these items and the raw materials necessary to assemble the components.
- Complexity managed through high-performance work systems
  —Complexity in the product array will be transparent to our customers and managed by our employees through high-performance work systems.
- Recycling is a key feature of the supply chain
  —to both fully utilize all assets and meet environmental concerns, Xerox will recover and recycle whenever possible.

Overall the vision was seen as creating

An integrated Supply Chain which never fails to meet customer requirements.

Meeting only three times a year, MIOC addressed issues ranging from the mundane to the esoteric, directly or through a number of sub-councils. MIOC essentially served as an advisory council to then president Paul Allaire and the top five senior executive vice-presidents, to give feedback on the changes needed to realize the vision of a world-class inventory management and logistics process.

### Central Logistics and Asset Management

The MIOC executive council significantly enhanced Xerox's vision of what an ideal logistics and asset management business process should look like, but a further initiative was deemed necessary if the vision was to become reality. In the autumn of 1988 Fred Hewitt was appointed vice-president of a new group, central logistics and asset management (CLAM), to provide full-time coordination of the implementation of the changes required in each business to realize the IM&L process vision. Over the next 3 years he built an organization of change agents who worked as full-time business architects to re-engineer and transform Xerox's supply chain processes worldwide. Inventory management and logistics is a core process in itself, but CLAM as early change agents also facilitated work in other areas, particularly those that were highly integrated with the IM&L agenda. The vehicle for this coordination was a business process board composed of process sponsors from all areas actively involved in change initiatives.

As with all processes re-engineering initiatives at Xerox, the CLAM team was responsible not only for solutions definition but also for working with line organizations to ensure that the improved processes became institutionalized within those organizations. Such institutionalization clearly requires creative behavioural modification, as well as technical implementation, as can be seen from one of the first IM&L process innovations introduced across Xerox, the revised production planning process.

**Revised Production Planning Process (P3)**

Xerox developed P3 prototypes with new product showcases before applying it broadly throughout the corporation. P3 moved the manufacturing and warehousing planning away from a negotiated quarterly forecasting process. In the past, manufacturing and marketing organizations had established manufacturing production schedules with fixed lead times, based upon a demand forecast suggested by the marketing groups. The gamesmanship that ensued usually resulted in suboptimal results for the objectives of the integrated supply chain, with either surplus inventory or poor service levels being the outcome.

With P3, however, warehouses are nothing more than a central staging area which holds only replenishment stock. Inventory levels and associated production schedules are determined on a factual basis, not on forecasts or opinions. Instead of shipping out to a forecast, manufacturing ships products in reaction to a defined event, which may be an end customer order or the generation of an internal replenishment order. Production planning becomes nothing more than replenishment control, with minimum/maximum inventory levels determined statistically and empirically based on factors such as time in the pipeline, likely need of safety stock, supplier lead times and forecasting error.

Institutionalization of these changes in the supply chain has required the establishment of a significantly different mentality throughout all functions of Xerox. P3 teams make data-driven production decisions on the production floor, and are empowered to shut down production and send workers home or off to training, without vice-presidential signatures. P3 teams communicate with warehousing managers and work within the empirically determined limits for inventory levels. For some product types, warehouse inventory is now non-existent. Through the removal of barriers across the supply chain, Xerox has been able significantly to improve the quality of its delivery process. Customer satisfaction levels concerning Xerox's ability to 'deliver as promised' have reached an all time high, despite the fact that business results have also dramatically improved in terms of reduced supply chain costs and reduced inventories. Empowered employees, using simplified, fact-driven business processes, are well on their way to effecting the Xerox vision of

a supply chain process which never fails to meet customer requirements.

P3 and other process re-engineering initiatives orhcestrated by CLAM within the IM&L process illustrate the progress which Xerox made in phase 2 of its change agenda implementation strategy. To the functionally oriented gradual continuous improvement process of phase 1 had been added a cross-functional process-oriented set of change initiatives capable of achieving step-function breakthroughs in productivity. Both approaches shared a common total quality based commitment to customer satisfaction. Each approach complements the other. But even so the question remains as to whether they represent a sufficiently radical approach to ensure ongoing success in the ever-changing and increasingly more competitive world of the 1990s and beyond. Senior Xerox managers chartered to look forward to 'Xerox 2000' apparently think not.

## PHASE 3: RESTRUCTURING FOR CONTINUOUS CHANGE

To take Xerox to a new level of effectiveness and make sure that its structure reinforces the strategy and the culture that its leaders have been trying to develop, Xerox has recently (1992) structured its organization. Chairman and CEO Paul Allaire described the purpose in the introduction of the communique used to announce the restructuring in February 1992:

> I have said on a number of occasions that we will need to change Xerox more in the next five years than we have in the past ten. The shape of that change is becoming clearer to us as the result of the work that we've been doing since 1989 when I announced our 'change agenda'. In 1990, the senior management of the company participated in a set of activities called the Xerox 2000 strategic planning process. As that strategic work was reaching its conclusions, I initiated the second effort, using the quality process, to understand how we could run the company more effectively to achieve the Xerox 2000 vision.
>
> As a result of our work over the past 15 months on the nature and shape of this new Xerox, we have decided to move forward. During 1992, we will be implementing a major change of the governance, structure, process, and leadership of our company. Since this change is a direct outgrowth of the Xerox 2000 strategic work, we should think about this as a second phase of Xerox 2000, where we will be 'putting it together'. We will be working together to create an enterprise that builds on the improvements we've achieved in the past five years to ensure growth and competitive success in the 1990s.
>
> The changes required are significant. But there are things that absolutely will not change! First are the Xerox corporate values. They are bedrock of Xerox. They go back to Joe Wilson—they are what make Xerox special. The second is quality as our basic principle. Leadership Through Quality enabled us to survive in the '80s. We've used the quality process to design these changes and will now use it to implement them.

### Xerox's New Structure

When Xerox restructured in 1992, it established a number of global business divisions (Figure 10.6). According to Xerox, a business division is a set of activities, people and assets that approximate a complete 'end to end' business capable of managing its own income statement and balance sheet. Each division has effective control over the complete value-added chain, including

**XEROX 2000 STRUCTURE**

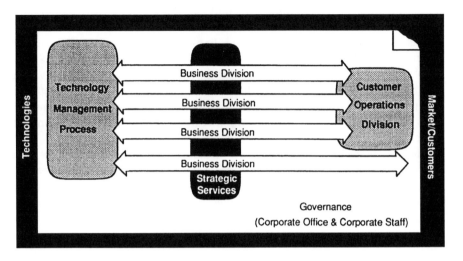

**Figure 10.6**

business planning, product planning, development, manufacturing, distribution, marketing, sales, and customer service and support, although some of these activities may be subcontracted to agents. Each division has a clear set of product and service offerings, a set of primary markets towards which those offerings are targeted and an identifiable set of competitors. Xerox in fact created the following nine business divisions:

- Personal document products
- Office document systems
- Office document products
- X-soft
- Advanced office document services
- Document production systems
- Printing systems
- Xerox engineering systems
- Xerox business services

Within the new structure there are also two functionally specialized entities that serve all business divisions, the technology management process council and the customer operations divisions. These entities help to make sure that Xerox forms an effective linkage between the most advanced technologies available and the customer needs in the marketplace across all business areas.

The technology management process council has responsibility for research and development of technology that sustains the core technological competencies for the corporation. Customer operations divisions are assigned to specific geographies. Their function is to maintain and improve the customer interface on behalf of the business divisions and make sure that Xerox, as a whole company, is easy to do business with. The customer operations divisions are responsible for support of all activities which relate to the customer, including service, administration, integration of major customer relationships, sales support, and providing local administration of the business division sales force.

The two other elements of the new structure are the strategic services and governance (corporate office and corporate staff). The strategic services exist to support the business divisions, particularly in the areas of manufacturing, logistics, supplies (materials) and strategic relationships. These services ensure that Xerox does not throw away the strategic advantages that stem from the size and scope of the Xerox corporation as a whole, even as it breaks into small, more autonomous and more responsive units. CLAM is now a part of the 'integrated supply chain' group within strategic services. Governance consists of a redesigned corporate office and a refocused corporate staff who face the challenge of 'putting it all together' on a strategic level.

## Envisioning the Future

Leadership and communications are recognized as two of the keys required for transforming an organization's culture towards the emerging paradigm. Structural change is not a panacea. It must accompany technological change, business process change, strategic change and, perhaps most important of all, cultural change. Xerox has, over the years, been led by a number of unashamedly visionary individuals. In a personal message to the students, in the textbook entitled *Beyond Total Quality Management* (Bounds et al, 1994), currently Chairman and CEO Paul Allaire describes the vision that he believes will lead Xerox into the future.

> We've embarked on a bold new journey. We are putting in place the *hardware* (the new organization) and the *software* (new ways of managing and working) to enable us to seize the opportunities identified by the Xerox 2000 work. But more needs to be done. All of the work we have done in the past few years has set the stage for realizing a vision for a new Xerox.
>
> What is the Xerox that I envision? I see an enterprise that has very special and unique qualities—an organization that is looked to when people want to figure out what will be effective management in the next century much as they do today when they want to understand total quality management. I see a company that values and celebrates the diversity of its employee body and creates an environment where each individual feels motivated to apply his or her creative energies to the work at hand. I also see a company made up of teams and

communities of people who have the capacity to manage their own piece of the business, who have the freedom to use their own judgement and creativity, and who share in the risks and the rewards. Finally, I see a company that is a learning organization—a company in which learning is pervasive and second-nature, a company in which learning becomes the norm, not the exception. The company I envision will enable and depend on continuous learning throughout the organization—a company in which failures are seen as opportunities, where successes are studied with an eye to improvement, where new ideas are nurtured and implemented, where learning is defined as doing things differently. We're off to a very good start! We are already one of the most diverse work groups in the world. Our work on quality has given us a leg up on empowering our work force and working together effectively as teams. Our presidential reviews and training infrastructure are important ingredients of a learning organization. We are on track to achieve the new Xerox—and it is the right track. So, much of the 'it' is already in place or being put into place. The critical ingredient now is 'putting it together'. To me, that means management. I have become more and more convinced that managing the 'it'—putting it together—is the last big frontier of competitive advantage and the most powerful lever to productivity growth.

*Editorial note: part of the Paul Allaire speech*

To the outside observer the Xerox quality policy, leadership through quality, team Xerox, Xerox business architecture, business process re-engineering and, most recently, restructuring for Xerox 2000 may appear to form a logical continuum. Certainly each successive initiative has been based upon the successes and the failures of prior experiences. In reality, however, the logical nature of the progression is at least in part a matter of post-rationalization on the basis of hindsight. The Xerox story is, in fact, all the more impressive because the participants in that story agree that the only true continuum was a refusal to ever accept the status quo. Envisioning and enacting a corporate transformation requires the acceptance that the race has no end—the change agenda will never be completed. Change is the permanent state in which corporations now exist, and unless they transform themselves not into a new 'steady state' but rather into a 'state of continuous change' they must ultimately fail to meet their objectives. Perhaps this is the challenge for those wishing to envision and enact the ultimate corporate transformation.

## REFERENCE

Allaire, P. (1994). In: Bounds, G., York, L., Adams, M. and Ranney, G. *Beyond Total Quality Management*, pp. 775–777, McGraw-Hill, New York.

# 11

# SEARCHING FOR THE SPIRIT OF ENTERPRISE[1]

**Larry C. Farrell**

*The Farrell Co., Staunton, Virginia*

## BIG TROUBLE AT BIG BUSINESS

*The advantages of smaller size are becoming very great.* (Peter Drucker, 1992.)

Why didn't Peter Drucker tell us this back in 1950? Instead, he and every other management guru this century, kept telling us in no uncertain terms that *bigger is better*. We all bought in and like most important lessons in life, we're learning the hard way it just isn't so. There is plenty of big trouble at big business. But for anyone who cared to look, it isn't exactly news. Of the hundred largest US companies in 1900, only 16 are still in business. Hardly a historical victory for size! The *Fortune 500*'s growth rate has been declining for three decades, and has actually turned negative in the 1990s. But this is not just an American problem. It's worldwide. The 1993 *Fortune Global 500* report, titled 'Another Year Of Pain', shows continued flat revenues, declining employment and one-quarter of the world's largest companies losing money! Big companies everywhere are sagging under their own mass and weight. Japanese giants, for the first time, are planning large-scale lay offs. Many large European companies have simply given up on growth and have embraced

---

[1]This article was prepared by the author from his book *Searching for the Spirit of Enterprise*. Dutton, New York, 1993. This is already being translated into Chinese, Korean, Spanish and Portuguese

*The Implementation Challenge*, Edited by D. E. Hussey
© 1996 John Wiley & Sons Ltd

downsizing with a passion. Most of us grew up believing big business was the world's engine of prosperity. Something has gone very wrong.

### The Life Cycle of all Organizations—From Riches to Rags

Companies, like everything else in our world, must contend with their own life cycle. There's creation followed by growth. Growth peaks and decline sets in, leading ultimately to death. And of course there's always the possibility of *untimely death* along the way. Beating this cycle is tough indeed.

All companies begin with an abundance of the entrepreneurial spirit. This spirit fuels the start-up and drives the company into a phase of high growth. Everyone is fixated on a few fundamental notions such as getting customers because that's the only way to get paid. High growth gets you size. And the passage of time gets you new leaders. The new leaders are almost always professional managers. These subtle shifts in size and leadership produce a new set of objectives. Planning, streamlining and controlling the enterprise become the new order. Managing this and that become more important than making this and selling that. The highest paid jobs become managing other managers. Meetings, reports and bureaucracy erupt on every front. And slowly but surely, lost in the shuffle are the simple, entrepreneurial thrusts that got you going in the first place. Too much managing against too little entrepreneuring sets in motion the painful cycle of decline. Heavy-duty consultants are called in to tell you what's wrong and more MBAs are hired to implement their solutions. None of it helps and the decline picks up momentum. You're headed for mere survival—and ultimate demise. A classic example of throwing out the baby with the bathwater.

### From Those Wonderful Folks at Harvard and McKinsey

How did big business get into this mess? We have no one to blame but ourselves—and the strange worldwide network of management gurus from Harvard,

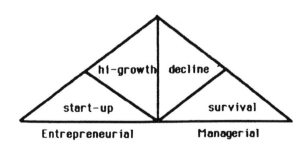

**Figure 11.1**

McKinsey and a thousand other places that all feed on the carcass of big business. For most of the 20th century, the professors and consultants of management have offered up theory after theory. Most of them have been colossal and expensive failures. Look at the track record. What happened to all the theories about economy of scale, learning curve theory and strategic planning? What has become of the almighty promise of conglomerates, matrix management and sensitivity training? These and a hundred other ideas have faded into history.

Yes, something has gone very wrong indeed. And what can we do about it? Here's a hint. America churns out 75 000 MBAs a year. Germany and Japan, the two countries who have been beating her socks off for the past two decades, don't even have business schools! Might it be time to look elsewhere for our management lessons? Wouldn't the lessons of Lever, Honda and Disney be closer to the mark than the next hot theory from the consultants or the business schools?

## THE BASICS OF ENTERPRISE

*The conduct of successful business merely consists in doing things in a very simple way, doing them regularly and never neglecting to do them.* (William Hesketh Lever.)

What are those *things* we must do simply, regularly and never forget to do? You won't find them on the managerial side of the cycle. They're not the things that business schools teach or management consultants preach. If you want to find the bedrock fundamentals of enterprise, those simple things practised obsessively, you've got to look at the entrepreneurial phase of business. Here you will find the lessons of the world's greatest enterprisers, from Lever to Matsushita to Disney to Walton. When you think about it, if you're searching for the spirit of enterprise, why would you look anywhere else?

### Sense of Mission

*Our duty as industrialists, therefore, is to provide conveniences for the public, and to enrich and make happier all those who use them. A decrease in profit . . . or a loss of revenue is proof that we have not fulfilled our obligations to society.* (Konosuke Matsushita.)

High-minded? You bet! The fact is entrepreneurs believe they are doing something important in the world. They believe they're creating value for customers, employees and of course themselves. I call it having a 'sense of mission' about their work. Such high purpose, however, gets quickly translated into two very practical questions: *What* to do (essentially what products for what customers) and *how* to go about doing it. To legendary entrepreneurs like Matsushita, Lever and Watson, these simple words are the two most important questions in business. In modern management lingo, the entrepreneurial 'What' and 'How' is a no-frills version of corporate strategy and corporate culture. Unfortunately, in many big companies, strategy and culture live in separate universes—one the domain of number-crunching planners, the other the province of touchy-feely culture gurus. In too many big companies, neither have much to do with the real running of the business. In stark contrast, the entrepreneur lives and dies on his answers to what and how—and they're inextricably connected.

'"Strategy" isn't a week in Bermuda with the consultants. It's a matter of survival.' What products you're going to make and in what markets you're going to sell them is the whole ball game. And when you get right down to it, it doesn't matter if you do strategy on the back of a napkin, or use £10 or 500 page planning books. The part you absolutely have to get right is: what products and what markets! On the other hand, the purpose of creating a company culture is not to make more wall plaques or hold more meetings to bounce around soft, side issues of the business. The only purpose is to get everyone focused on those few values that will give you the competitive advantage to make the business strategy come true. When the values directly support the product/market strategy, watch out! It's the most powerful way known to energize a group of individuals to achieve a common purpose.

Consider a company like 3M where growth from new products is the strategy—and innovation has been the central value since six Minnesota miners ended up owning a worthless gravel pit and invented sandpaper. Today with $12 billion in sales and 58,000 products, this value permeates the entire company. Inventing products *is* the culture. The result? 3M has the highest ratio of new product revenue (30% plus!) of any large company in the world. Would 3M achieve this remarkable strategic result without a powerful and pervasive culture of innovative action? Never, in a 100 years!

### Customer/Product Vision

*The inclination of my life has been to do things and make things which will give pleasure to people. . . . (Walt Disney.)*

Walt Disney wasn't talking about managing a big studio, or executive stock options. He was talking about the two most fundamental ideas in enterprise— customer and product. And he said the most important thing in the world to him was making products that make customers happy. The really important lesson of Disney and all great entrepreneurs is that at heart they are craftsmen. They have a single, integrated vision of customers and products. They need both to survive. They are in fact, obsessed with making products that customers will buy. But along came the modern functional organization, in its all-out quest for efficiency, and in one fell swoop the craftsman was killed. The functional separation of customer and product is the single most devastating blow to the entrepreneurial spirit ever concocted by management science.

This is not a theoretical problem. Losing the entrepreneur's integrated vision of customer and product can cost you dearly. The classic example is Xerox, which has lost billions over the years by inventing products in California that marketing, 3,000 miles away in Connecticut, simply never got around to selling. The first personal computer! The first fax machine! The list goes on and on. Today companies all over the world are trying to put their humpty-dumpty organizations back together. They could have saved themselves a lot of trouble by watching Mr Toyoda at Toyota. In 1947, on his only trip to America, he became fascinated with the supermarkets' daily delivery of milk from the cow to the customer. He saw this as the ultimate customer-driven organization. He organized horizontally, called it kanban and the rest is history. And of course there is still the Disney Company, telling employees from accounting to wardrobe that they have both products to offer and customers to serve; that their attitude inside the company: 'ultimately affects the quality of service every Magic Kingdom guest receives—a real domino effect!'

To regain customer/product vision, you can start by tossing out those convoluted five-page job descriptions and replace them with three simple questions: Who are my customers? What are my products? And what must I do to satisfy my customers? The message is *everyone* has a small business to run. This sounds simple but the number of employees who can't answer these basic questions can be shocking. And a final thought—it's not a 1-year programme. It has to be a lifetime obsession, as it has been for Charles Forte. From one sweet shop on Oxford Street to the 800 hotels in the Trusthouse Forte empire, he's been absolutely consistent on product quality and customer service—and he's been at it for 65 years. It may sound monotonous but it has one redeeming virtue; if you do it long enough and hard enough, you get very, very good at it.

## High-speed Innovation

*We Japanese are obsessed with survival.* (Akio Morita.)

High-speed innovation is the entrepreneur's ultimate weapon—and it's virtually free. Entrepreneurial Davids like nothing better than competing against muscle-bound Goliaths. So where does high-speed innovation come from? For starters you can be sure it's not a genetic trait. And the current fads of setting up innovation departments or hiring consultants to teach creativity miss the point by a mile. It's a natural, human response we all possess, and the bottom line is: 'anyone can be innovative and move with the speed of light if their life depends on it!' We all know that more gets done in a day of crisis than a month of complacency. The trick then is how to keep this sense of urgency alive in the business—so that innovation becomes a necessity, and everyone has the freedom to act, and act quickly.

Whilst the rest of the world were convincing themselves the Japanese weren't innovators, Akio Morita was crawling around on his hands and knees in a bombed out building in Tokyo, cutting long strips of newsprint and coating it with ferrous oxide to make recording tape. Like everyone else in post-war Japan, the young founder of Sony was 'obsessed with survival'. With no jobs, money or raw materials, 'creating something that someone might buy was an absolute necessity to putting rice on the table'. This goes to the heart of the matter, proving once again that necessity is the mother of invention. It also helps explain why a too big, too comfortable bureaucracy is the last place you'll find high-speed innovation. But you don't have to wait for disaster to strike to get your innovative juices flowing. Start today! A daily dose of urgency and an occasional injection of crisis is guaranteed to conquer anyone's complacency.

Just moving quickly could be the greatest innovation of all for big business. But what it takes is the freedom to act, not exactly an abundant resource in procedure-driven companies. Take the race against time to dominate the world's newest super-industry, Bio-tech. An industry promising more change in medicine in the next 10 years than the last 100—and a huge $60 billion market. Actually the race is over and the entrepreneurs have won hands down. Whilst the giant pharmaceuticals researched it to death through layers of management, 400 scientist-turned-entrepreneur start-ups have exploded on the scene since 1980. As Ed Penhoet, Ph.D. and founder of industry star Chiron, says: 'Everyone's smart in the field, but smart doesn't make it. Bio-tech is a horse race. Getting to the finish line first is what counts.'

Could high-speed innovation be your company's ultimate weapon? Why not? All it takes is feeling the necessity to do it better—and the freedom to do it faster.

## Self-inspired Behaviour

*I'm looking for people who love to win. If I run out of those, I want people who hate to lose.* (H. Ross Perot.)

Self-inspired behaviour—perhaps the sharpest difference of all between entrepreneurs and bureaucrats. But what does it actually mean? What are entrepreneurs self-inspired to do? When I think of legends like Perot, or William Lever, or Soichiro Honda, a couple of images always come to mind. Firstly, they love what they do—they're highly committed to their work. And secondly, they constantly try to get better at what they do—their performance is high. These two ideas, high commitment and high performance, are the backbone of an entrepreneurial approach to work. When you think about it, it's pretty tough to beat people who love what they do and are damn good at doing it.

The much tougher question is how do we create self-inspired employees? Alongside Lever and Honda, no company leader ever did a better job at this than Ross Perot, the quintessential American entrepreneur. Of course, it's also Perot who loves to fire off Texas-sized sound-bites like: 'people who love to win and hate to lose'. This one, however, is based on a very solid idea. It's the idea that drives almost all human behaviour. Since the beginning of time, people have tended to behave in their own self-interest: they do things that bring them positive consequences and they avoid doing things that bring negative consequences. What this really means at work is that everybody wants an answer to the eternal question: 'what's in it for me if I do, and what happens to me if I don't?'

Entrepreneurs are mightily self-inspired to win and not lose because they face the consequences, positive or negative, of their behaviour every day. This almost never happens in a bureaucracy. In some companies, nothing much good happens to people even when they and the company perform well. In other companies, everyone gets a pat on the back and an annual merit increase even if the enterprise is headed for the trash heap. The most common situation, however, is the complete absence of either positives or negatives. Managers and workers just float in perpetual limbo, oblivious to the fortunes or misfortunes of the company and their part in it all. 'If you boil it down to one thing, the single biggest difference between entrepreneurial and bureaucratic behaviour is answering the "what's in it for me" question.' Entrepreneurs get their answers powerfully and frequently. Companies must do the same if they're really looking for extreme performance and commitment from workers. You're never going to revive the enterprise if you can't revive the enterprisers.

## TRANSFORMING BUREAUCRACY TO ENTERPRISE

Of course, the operative question is: can we do it and if we do will it work? The answer to both has to be a resounding yes! The alternative of letting the basics of enterprise get buried deeper and deeper under ever-increasing size and bureaucracy can't be the answer. For the first time in history, the entire global economic pie is up for grabs. There's an explosion of new markets, new products and new competitors. A sea-change of winners and losers is taking place now. The evidence is everywhere. Size and weight will no longer get you into the winner's circle. Fast-moving, customer-driven entrepreneurship will. For business people everywhere, it's time to learn some very old lessons—very fast!

### Dismantling the Twentieth-century Corporation and Starting Over

Transforming today's bureaucracy into tomorrow's enterprise doesn't start with adding something new. No new strategies, techniques, departments or committees are needed. These can't be the solution. They're already a big part of the problem. They're just more of the excess baggage you've been carrying around for years that's got to be unloaded. So the first drill is to start tossing stuff overboard: dismantling the mass and weight you've carefully added over the years. If you feel the load lightening, you're well on your way to starting over with the old-time basics of enterprise. Here's all you have to do. There are a thousand things companies try to transform their bucreaucracy to enterprise. But it's most often the blind leading the blind and few of their attempts actually work. The five suggestions here offer more hope. They come from the masters themselves and they directly attack the deep-down differences of entrepreneurial and managerial behaviour. You may find more elegant or exciting things to try, but skip over these at your peril. You'll never regain the spirit of enterprise if you can't get these right.

### Keep it Small

*Growing big by staying small.* (Johnson & Johnson motto.)

For companies suffocating under their own weight, Peter Drucker's revelation (smaller is better after all) is a dollar late and a penny short. GM, IBM and thousands of other companies made their strategic decisions on size a half century ago. And since that time they've lock-bolted into place a numbing bureaucracy and rusting functional structure designed to help them grow ever bigger. What are they supposed to do now? Unfortunately, their only option is to take apart and tear down the monstrosities they've built—those 'engines of prosperity' that have run out of steam. We're talking about nothing less than dismantling the modern corporation! A few companies like J&J never listened to the experts. Their 83,000 employees are divided into 166 separate, highly autonomous companies. That's an average of 495 employees per company. 'Growing big by staying small' surely beats growing small by staying big!

### Keep it Personal

*If you had to reduce it all down to one thing, it's how to make it personal. So it's their soul that's involved and it's a very personal thing.* (Edward E. Penhoet, Ph.D.)

Penhoet says it best: 'Personal meaning to every worker—I think that is the critical thing. If they see themselves as one grain of sand in the mound or one ant carrying things back and forth, and if they drop out it doesn't make any difference, well then, collectively the whole organization will slow down. So to some degree every individual has to feel the personal heat of the competition—that they are personally involved.'

Why is such straight talk so rare in people management circles? Why do reward and punishment hang in perpetual limbo in so many large companies?

Personal consequences have got to be felt, pure and simple. We can argue forever if the consequences should be financial or a friendly pat on the back. But the bottom line is, as Penhoet states, keeping it personal is *the* critical thing.

## Keep it Honest

*Companies should begin to focus on a new bottom line: making moral decisions.* (Anita Roddick.)

Keeping it honest starts at the top. Plato said no member of a group should receive more than five times the average reward or the group will lose cohesion. That's a far cry from CEO pay in America which has gone from 34 times the average employee's salary to 150 times in the last 15 years! In fact, the chiefs of America's biggest companies have a 'pay-for-performance' plan that most workers would die for. It goes like this:

| Company earnings growth | CEO pay growth |
|:---:|:---:|
| +10% | +28% |
| (20)% | +8% |
| (30)% | +6% |
| (71)% | 0% |

You don't have to become another Anita Roddick, constantly carrying on about the environment, the jobless, and the orphans in Romania. But on the other hand, top executives had better keep it honest within their own company—if they expect cohesion and performance from their people.

## Keep it Simple

*I want to touch a better piston, not watch another concept presentation.* (Soichiro Honda.)

Soichiro Honda, son of a village blacksmith, deeply distrusted sophisticated management concepts, labelling them 'window dressing and no substance'. That was good advice. Consider the case of General Electric, long called the Harvard of Corporate America. GE was going downhill fast awash in management theories when along came Jack Welch, a back-to-basics minded CEO. He explicitly rejected the dubious title and raised GE's market value from $12 billion to $65 billion in 12 years—creating one of the very few big company success stories in the world today. Keeping it simple doesn't have the cachet of modern management theory, but it has one redeeming value—it delivers growth and prosperity! When you flatten the walls, reduce the levels, turn off the photocopiers and fire the consultants, you'll be ready to . . .

### Start Over With the Basics

*The inclination of my life—has been to do things and make things which will give pleasure to people in new and amazing ways. By doing that I please and satisfy myself.* (Walt Disney.)

Sound too simple? Not to Walt Disney. His complete, common-sense description of how he built the world's greatest entertainment company is in fact an exquisite prescription for enterprise. Behind this bit of Disney 'management wisdom' lie the four uncompromising practices that underpin the success of all entrepreneurs and their high-growth companies. Disney described them perfectly: 'Inclination' as *mission*, 'making things and giving pleasure to people' is all about *customer/product vision*, 'new and exciting ways'—a perfect description of *innovation* and finally, 'by doing that I please myself' says I am *self-inspired* by my work. Of course, you can do nothing and hope for the best. But it isn't really much of a choice. The economic facts and our common-sense—in unusual agreement—are delivering the same message. More planning systems, organization studies and management courses won't get you a penny of growth. To get growth you've got to dismantle the bureaucracy and start over—with high purpose, absolute focus on customer and product, a lot of action and self-inspired people. It's called enterprise!

## THE ENTERPRISE OF NATIONS

The spirit of enterprise doesn't live in a vacuum. It's greatly influenced by the sweeps of history—and the larger political and cultural forces they bring. For better or worse, all companies are ultimately a reflection of these forces: a collage of historical context, the quality of the political leadership and the creativity and energy of the people. Because enterprising nations produce enterprising companies, our search concludes with a look at the national environment. History has given us two memorable lessons about the enterprise of nations and their companies.

Firstly, the great 20th century experiment of mass producing the spirit of enterprise was a giant flop—for both countries and companies. From the Kremlin in Red Square to the General Motors Building on Michigan Avenue, top heavy, bureaucratic control is bad for 'business'. A younger Mikhail Gorbachev, as Minister of Agriculture, discovered that the 4% of Soviet farmland under independent, family cultivation, produced a whopping 30% of the country's food. About the same time, GM Chairman Bob Stempel, who was running a company with a bigger GNP than most countries, discovered he had the highest paid workers and the lowest employee morale of any car company in the world. In both the Kremlin and the General Motors Building, something had gone very wrong. Neither big government nor big business could deliver the enterprise of the people.

Secondly, the history of prosperity shows a continual coming and going of winners and losers. The 19th century belonged to the Europeans, spearheaded by the Victorian Liberals of Great Britain. The 20th century winner is clearly North America, with the USA emerging as the richest nation in the history of the world. The 21st century is up for grabs, but the smart money and all the trends are on the side of Asia, led by Japan and over a billion hard-working Chinese. Countries, like companies, are victims of their own hard-to-change life cycles. The point to ponder is what really causes the rise and fall of a people's prosperity? 'And is there anything we can do to change the course of history?'

Of course there is! The underlying forces that propel growth and decline in business are very much at work in the rise and fall of economic states: pursuing a worthy mission, producing goods and services a little better than your neighbour, being a bit innovative and inspiring yourself to do a fair day's work. These are the behaviours that produce prosperity in companies—and nations too. If they're alive in the national leadership and in the people, you're on your way. If they go, decline and fall can't be far behind. The great national challenge of our time is to stop managing our decline—and start again creating our future prosperity. Think about it, but not too long. The enterprise of your nation and the well-being of your children, hang in the balance.

# 12

# MANAGING CHANGE: PERSPECTIVES FROM SUN TZU'S *ART OF WAR*

**Chow Hou Wee**

*Faculty of Business Administration, National University of Singapore*

Professor Wee offers some of the lessons that can be learned from this 2 300-year-old Chinese master of strategy, which has shaped thinking in many Japanese and South Korean boardrooms and is now widely read by managers in China. The article examines the business value of Sun Tzu's thinking in relation to:

• Managing change
• Creating an adaptable organization
• The role of strategy in the change process

The lessons of Sun Tzu, who may well have been the foremost military strategist of all time, are of universal value.

In recent years, military jargons, clichés and analogies have found their ways into the writings of renowned journalists, executives and scholars. For example, Enricho and Kornbluth (1987) described how Pepsi won the 'Cola Wars' against Coke. Saporito (1992) documented that price wars would never end for companies in the airline, automobile, computer, food, retailing and steel industries because of over investments in the past. This had forced many companies in these industries to chase market share at all costs. Labich (1992a, 1992b) used the term 'Sky Wars' to describe the battle for market share amongst the three leading aircraft manufacturers, namely, Airbus, Boeing and McDonnell Douglas. This was followed by Zellner (1992) who reported how

*The Implementation Challenge*, Edited by D. E. Hussey
© 1996 John Wiley & Sons Ltd

the American airlines were killing each other through price wars, and Labich (1992b) who documented how deregulation in the airline industry had led many of Europe's airlines to war. More recently, Schlender (1993a) commented how the American manufacturers of personal computers had begun to attack the Japanese market with new spiffy machines, innovative software and sharply lower prices.

Various studies relating the application of military strategies to business practices had been undertaken (e.g. Kotler and Singh, 1981; Stripp, 1985). In a publication by Ries and Trout (1986), they chose to rely on the works of German general Karl von Clausewitz to illustrate the parallels between military concepts and marketing practices. In addition, Kotler et al (1985), Lazer et al (1985) and Ohmae (1982) and many others had often described the Japanese economic conquest of the world very much like a well-orchestrated military campaign. In a more recent article, Sullivan (1992) cited the works of Abegglen and Stalk (1985) in describing Theory F (for fear) as one of the factors for the success of Japan.

Few writers, however, had given recognition and acknowledgement to the oldest known military treatise in the world, Sun Tzu's *Art of War* and its relevance to strategic thinking and business applications. Written in China centuries before the birth of Christ, it is said to contain the foundations on which all modern military strategies are based. It is proposed that the achievement of Sun Tzu's *Art of War* transcends the military context and offers valuable insights for the management of modern businesses.

There are other reasons for focusing on Sun Tzu's works. With the opening of China, there is an increased interest to know their thoughts, especially in the area of strategic management and practices. This is necessary if one wishes to do business with them. Here, it is significant to note that while the Chinese have turned to the Western world for much help in the area of training and consulting, they have also begun to actively research their own classics so as to relate their applications to management. Sun Tzu's *Art of War* has emerged as a favourite, and today, there are already many publications in China that attempt to relate this classic to strategic thinking and business practices (e.g. Li et al, 1984; National Economic Commission, 1985). Such efforts are in addition to many similar publications that exist today in Hong Kong, Taiwan, Japan and South Korea. In fact, Sun Tzu is a highly regarded guru amongst many corporate strategists in these countries. If one subscribes to the belief that the 21st century belongs to the Asia-Pacific region, it is important to note that its key players—Japan, Taiwan, South Korea, Hong Kong and Singapore—have many cultural similarities that could be traced to their roots in China. Together with China, they can form a significant economic force that few countries can ignore. Without doubt, there is a need for practitioners and researchers in the Western world to begin understanding the philosophy and thinking of the oriental mind set. Sun Tzu's *Art of War* may provide a useful start in this learning process.

A detailed exposition on how Sun Tzu's works can be applied to business practices can be found in Wee (1989, 1990) and Wee et al (1991). The purpose of this chapter is to highlight some of the salient concepts from the works of Sun Tzu that can be applied to managing change. The importance of managing change has been receiving increasing attention from many quarters (Quinn, 1978). For example, the 13 December 1993 issue of *Fortune International* carried a series of cover stories on this subject, including those by Tichy (1993), Dumaine (1993) and Sherman (1993a, 1993b) that touched on a wide range of issues like the need for changing values, organizational structures and new ways of doing business.

## MANAGING CHANGE IN WAR

Without doubt, any military campaign is fraught with changes once the war progresses. It is thus no surprise that the general would attempt to take all possible steps to ensure that he can cope with the likely changes. These are done proactively prior to the *commencement* of battle. Amongst various proactive measures advocated by Sun Tzu, two are worth mentioning. The first is that of detailed planning:

> ... With careful and detailed planning, one can win; with careless and less detailed planning, one cannot win. How much more certain is defeat if one does not plan at all! From the way planning is done beforehand, we can predict victory or defeat.

By detailed planning, Sun Tzu meant:

> Know your enemy, know yourself, and your victory will not be threatened. Know the terrain, know the weather, and your victory will be complete.

In addition, it also involves the requirement for contingency planning. This principle was well articulated by Sun Tzu when he discussed the role of direct and indirect forces and manoeuvres:

> That the army is able to sustain the attacks of the enemy without suffering defeats is due to operations of the indirect and direct forces and manoeuvres.

The second principle is the use of intelligence:

> The reason why the enlightened ruler and the wise general are able to conquer the enemy whenever they lead the army and can achieve victories that surpass those of others is because of foreknowledge (intelligence).

In fact, Sun Tzu expounded on the importance of using human intelligence, and advocated espionage activities (see Wee et al, 1991, pp. 237–244). Of course, business espionage should be condemned and frowned upon

(Beltramini, 1986; Pooley, 1982; Waller, 1992). However, to pretend that business espionage does not exist would be an exercise in futility and naivety. If anything, industrial espionage is rife and commonly practised in the business world, especially in this post-Cold War era (Nelan, 1993).

Besides espionage, it is important to point out that there are many 'above the board' methods of gathering market and competitive information that could be used for the development of business strategies—for example, surveys on competitors and the various industries, market studies, and trade and fact-finding missions (Eells and Nehemkis, 1984). In today's business environment—where competition is rife, consumer tastes are fast changing, and information technology becoming more widespread—the need to rely on intelligence for effective decision-making and dealing with changes has become more eminent (Gordon, 1982; Attanasio, 1988; Bergeron and Raymond, 1992).

## ADAPTABILITY IN OPERATIONS

Despite detailed planning through the use of intelligence, the whole military campaign will be subjected to change once the first battle is fought. This is because war conditions are very dynamic, and it is near impossible to predict the exact outcome of every military movement. What is more important is to be able to cope with the changes as they come along, and revise the military strategies accordingly. This is true even with modern technology. Take the example of the Gulf War. Despite the accuracy of the American missiles, targets were missed and civilian casualties inflicted. It is thus significant that Sun Tzu advocated the principle of adaptability in manoeuvres once the war begins. There are three related concepts pertaining to adaptability—shaping and flexibility, innovativeness and use of initiative.

### Flexibility and Shaping

It is precisely the need to cope with change that Sun Tzu advocated the principle of *flexibility and shaping* in war:

> The guiding principle in military tactics may be likened to water. Just as flowing water avoids the heights and hastens to the lowlands, an army should avoid strengths and strike weaknesses.
> Just as water shapes itself according to the ground, an army should manage its victory in accordance with the situation of the enemy. Just as water has no constant shape, so in warfare there are no fixed rules and regulations.

Thus, the wise general is someone who is able to apply the principle of flexibility so as to take advantage of the changing circumstances in war. Note that one of the most remarkable statements is that there are no fixed rules and regulations when it comes to execution of plans. The general must change his strategies like the way water conforms to the changing terrain. In other words, he has the ultimate authority to decide what he deems most appropriate, given the situation that confronts him.

In the same way, companies must learn to be flexible in order to cope with the changing environment and competitive situations. Here, it is interesting to note that Japanese products are known to be shaped according to the demands of the markets that they are selling to, even though the market size may be small. For example, whilst the United States (US) ignored the markets in Southeast Asia in the 1960s and 1970s, the Japanese courted this part of the world enthusiastically with products that were designed specifically for them. Despite their huge succcesses today, the Japanese have continued to be flexible in their product offerings to newer markets in the Asia-Pacific region. For example, when China needed cars after they opened up aggressively in the 1980s, the Japanese were prepared to do 'backward engineering' in order to sell the Chinese cheap, big and efficient cars. In contrast, the Western companies were reluctant to do so. The results of such flexible policies are very telling by the size of Japanese market shares in these countries. In fact, Kotler et al (1985, p. 254) remarked that flexibility has been the visible trademark of the Japanese and they have not engraved their strategies in stone.

Today, as the top US and European companies begin to close the quality gap against Japanese products in recent years, Japanese manufacturers have shifted to flexible manufacturing systems and strategy as their new competitive weapon. They do this by focusing on more and better product features, flexible factories that can accommodate varying production orders and designs, expanded customer service, innovation and technological superiority (Stewart, 1992b; Taylor III, 1993).

Business situations are always very dynamic as they are affected by various factors—the consumers, the competitors, the government, the general public, the state of technology, the state of the economy and so on. To compete successfully, the company must be adaptive to the changes in its environment, and must not be bound by past practices or traditions. In fact, Bartlett and Ghoshal (1989) argued that the future transnational corporations, amongst other things, must be able to maintain organizational flexibility in order to compete effectively. Their views were supported by Stewart (1992a).

There should not be any fixed rules on how a company should go about developing its overseas markets. If one company cannot do it alone, there is nothing to stop it from joining forces with other companies with similar interests, even if they are direct competitors. Indeed, strategic alliances are becoming an important development in the conduct of business today as they can also provide for flexibility (Sherman, 1992). In fact, Toshiba, the oldest and third largest Japanese electronic giant has made strategic alliances a cornerstone of its corporate strategy (Schlender, 1993b). As of

1993, it had no less than 18 strategic partners in the US, Europe, Canada, and even South Korea. In taking such a flexible approach, Toshiba has been able to enhance both its global position in technology and marketing. Besides Toshiba, many other Japanese companies have created strong partnerships by investing in sagging European rival companies (Rapoport, 1993). In doing so, they have created additional leverages for themselves to compete in the future. Besides the Japanese, the Koreans are pursuing similar flexible strategies in their quest for world market share (Kraar, 1992, 1993).

### Innovativeness

A related concept to the principle of adaptability is that of innovativeness. It is important to point out that whilst shaping and flexibility are more reactive in that they flow according to the situation, innovativeness is more proactive in that it attempts to dictate the situation. According to Sun Tzu:

> Therefore, do not repeat the tactics that won you a victory, but vary them according to the circumstances.

Thus like war, there is a need to constantly search for new and innovative ways of meeting the challenges offered by the ever changing circumstances in business. In addition, the use of new approaches will also prevent the competitor from anticipating one's plans, as one becomes unpredictable through continual innovation. In doing so, it forces the other party to react to the changes created by you. Innovativeness, therefore, means a need to search for new and different ways of doing things, and not to conveniently rely on past strategies. In the words of Sun Tzu:

> He must be able to change his methods and schemes so that no one can know his intentions. He must be able to alter his camp-sites and marching routes so that no one can predict his movements.

It is interesting to note that innovativeness is not lacking amongst Japanese companies. As a nation, the Japanese have demonstrated that innovative behaviour can be planned systematically and proactively. Despite their traditional handicaps such as the seniority system (which tends to muffle and muzzle debate and free expression) and general lack of individual creativity, they have never ceased to amaze the world with their wide array of innovative products through concerted and well-organized teamwork. In fact, they systematically make conscious efforts to manage change. This, in effect, is very well illustrated by the way Japanese companies manage planned obsolescence for products like cars, hi-fi equipment, television, etc. They constantly bring out improved models, modified designs, new styles, additional features and a host of other new product- related attributes to phase out existing ones. In fact, for many products like cars, televisions, home electronics and cameras, their product obsolescence cycles are typically half that of comparable products made by Western companies.

## Use of Initiative

Whilst innovativeness is a proactive, deliberate and systematic approach to managing change,
   the use of initiative requires both the proactive and reactive dimensions. Initiative requires the individual to be very responsive to changes to situations, as well as able to take pre-emptive action. Thus, resourcefulness at the point of decision-making is essential. In addition, the exercise of initiative is often instantaneous and an intuitive act of the individual who is faced with the decision. In fact, Sun Tzu even went as far as saying:

> There are situations when the orders of the ruler need not be obeyed.

Moreover, Sun Tzu gave an example of a situation when orders could be disobeyed and initiative used:

> If the situation is one of victory, the general must fight even though the ruler may have issued orders not to engage. If the situation is one of defeat, the general must not fight even though the ruler may have issued orders to do so.

In the same way, in the management of change, initiative is much needed. The chief executive officer (CEO) or any senior manager for that matter, must respond to the challenges presented by the change, and not shy away from making a decision. At times, the decision to be made may depart from corporate guidelines and plans, but if it is to the benefit of the company, the senior manager must be capable of exercising his initiative to take the bold stand.

   In essence, a company must encourage the flow of innovative ideas and the exercise of initiative on all fronts—from the conception of product/service ideas to the actual implementation of marketing strategies. Pascale (1990) even argued for innovative ways of managing conflicts in order to stay ahead of competition, whilst Naisbitt and Aburdene (1985) advocated innovative human resource management and organization as the future corporate challenge. No matter what it is, it is important that at anytime when opportunities arise as a result of the changing environment or other factors, the company must be capable of capitalizing on them. It must consciously manage change, just like many Japanese companies do (Mroczkowski and Hanaoka, 1989). At times, it may also entail changes to plans that are already made.

   To some extent, innovativeness and use of initiative are very much related to creativity. In recent years, creativity has been actively pursued by organizations and their corporate executives as a means to cope and manage change. For example, de Bono (1971) propounded on lateral thinking for management, Ackoff (1978) wrote his famous book on the art of problem solving, Miller (1986) argued for the need to foster innovation at the point of work and recently Yu (1990) proposed an integrated theory of habitual domains as the basis for forming winning strategies.

## THE ROLE OF STRATEGY IN THE CHANGE PROCESS

The need to be adaptive in order to cope with the changing war conditions gives rise to the importance of understanding the relationships between strategy, structure and behaviour. In the words of Sun Tzu:

> To control a large force in combat is similar to that of a small force. It is a matter of formations and signals.

He went on further to say:

> Order and disorder depends on organization

Implicit in these sayings is that structure actually breeds behaviour, regardless of the size of the army. As such, the way a general organizes his army would affect the behaviour of his troops in battle. In the same way, the way a company is organized and structured will also determine the behaviour of the employees. For example, if a company wants to become international, it must be structured in such a way so as to reward those employees with international experience. Otherwise, no one would want to work abroad.

What then determines structure? In war, it is always *strategy*. In other words, the strategy must be the genesis of any organizational design and structure. Undeniably, with proper feedback, one's strategy could be modified. However, the starting point for any planning exercise in war has to be strategy. For example, in the 1991 war against Iraq, the US-led forces decided on the strategy before embarking on how to organize for combat. In fact, General Norman Schwarzkopf was himself a product of the strategy.

There is a definitive requirement as to why structure and organization must follow the crystallization of the strategy in war. Firstly, there is a need for *flexibility*. This is because battle conditions are quite fluid, and the general on the ground must be given the maximum flexibility to organize and restructure his troops and formations depending on the battle situations. Secondly, as battle conditions change, the general must change his strategy accordingly. In other words, he has to constantly reorganize according to his strategy. Although he begins with a battle plan, that plan can never be cast in stone. He must constantly reorganize his troops for battles as he changes his plan (strategy) to meet the dynamic conditions of war. In sum, he has to be very proactive and seize on any available opportunity to win. This was true of ancient wars, and is still applicable today.

Interestingly, there is no lack of support in the business literature for the relationship between strategy and structure. For example, Chandler (1962) concluded that once a corporate strategy is in place, its structure will follow. More recently Bartlett and Ghoshal (1989, p.20) argued that organizational structure should fit the strategic requirement of the business and the firm's dominant strategic capability. Similar views were expressed by Lorange and Vancil (1976), Henderson (1979), Lorange (1980, 1982), Enderwick (1989) and Ohmae (1989). Unfortunately, there are other scholars who counterargue that it is often the other way around—that is, it is often the structure that drives the strategy (e.g. Pascale, 1990, p.100). This lack of consensus on how strategy affects structure or vice versa has affected to some extent the way many companies manage themselves for competition. In fact, even Japanese companies are discovering that their bureaucratic structures are now affecting their competitiveness (Schlender, 1993a). They have begun to dismantle bureaucratic structures, and instead organize their companies around their new strategies and the changing environment as advocated by many writers like Dumaine (1991), Katzenbach and Smith (1993), and Kirkpatrick (1993).

## ROLE OF LEADERSHIP IN WINNING HEARTS AND BUILDING TEAMWORK

Underlying the use of military concepts and strategies is an important fundamental principle—the need to focus on the heart, and not the mind of management. This is because war is basically 'irrational' and involves substantial and drastic change in the behaviour of the soldiers. It is one thing to train under simulated conditions and against an 'artificial' enemy. It is a totally different experience to be actually involved in the direct destruction and killing of human lives. In essence, it can be very traumatic and emotional. As such, the management of the troops in preparation for war as well as during combat becomes an important skill that no shrewd general can ignore.

To begin with, the general cannot rely on material benefits to motivate his troops. Instead, he has to appeal to their sense of national pride and loyalty. He appeals to their emotions and feelings, and uses the moral cause as justification for aggression. For this reason, the general even goes down to his troops and if needed drinks from the same coffee mug and eats from the same mess tin with his soldiers. In doing so, he wins their hearts which is very important for building up comradeship and team spirit—ingredients so essential for winning wars. Indeed, no shrewd general would think of motivating his soldiers in combat with extra pay or bonus!

The need to focus on the heart brings to mind clearly the importance of leadership and teamwork in the management of change. It is no surprise that Sun Tzu defined the moral influence of the ruler in war as follows:

> . . . that which enables the people to be in perfect accord and harmony with the ruler, for which they are willing to accompany him to life and death without the fear of dangers.

On the general's leadership and teamwork, he said:

> When the general regards his men as infants, they will be willing to follow him through thick and thin. When he treats them like his beloved sons, they will be willing to support him unto death.

Note that the ultimate test of teamwork and leadership is the willingness of the soldiers to sacrifice self-interest to the extent of willingness to put down their lives for a higher level goal. The essence of teamwork can be seen by the following:

> When the general is weak and lacks discipline, when training and instructions are not clear, when the duties of officers and men are not distinct, and when the formations are slovenly, the result is utter disorganization.

Winning the hearts does not mean bending backwards to the whims and fancies of the soldiers. In fact, Sun Tzu offered the following advice:

> If a general pampers his troops but is unable to use them; if he loves them excessively but cannot exercise his commands; if his troops are disorderly but he cannot discipline them; then they are like a bunch of spoilt brats, and are useless.

It is no wonder that Sun Tzu mentioned that the general must possess qualities of wisdom, sincerity, benevolence, courage and strictness. These qualities are necessary as he has to lead by example. For this reason, the military general is one who must survive the tests of the rank and file and the vagaries of each battle. He is never parachuted into the army. Instead, he has to earn every rank through blood, sweat and tears. It is no surprise that when he reaches the top, he has already won the respect of his soldiers. Under such a circumstance, it becomes easier for him to make as well as demand changes according to his judgement. This is because he has already earned the trust and confidence of his soldiers.

Whilst it is very easy for anyone to comprehend the need to focus on the heart in the management of an army for war, it is harder to translate that into management of business. If anything, many Western companies tend to develop policies that appeal to the mind rather than the heart. Managing the heart is more an art rather than a science. For example, there is a need to take a long-term perspective and the employee's contributions have to be viewed over his life time. To appeal to the heart, there is a need for strong social interactions, and the CEO has to adopt a much more personal and people-centred approach. When the heart can be won over, the employees are likely to be highly loyal and less likely to be lured away by higher perks offered by the competitors. In other words, they will find satisfaction in working for the organization as they tend to rely more on psychic rewards. The heart approach facilitates the cultivation of group values, which in turn, favours the development of team building and teamwork—ingredients so essential for the management of change.

In general, Japanese and many Asian companies tend to focus more on managing the hearts of their employees. In contrast, Western companies, largely owing to their cultural influences, tend to focus more on managing the minds of the employees. They do this largely by higher salaries and perks. If special expertise is needed, they will not hesitate to 'head hunt' for it, and this includes hiring the CEO. For example, IBM hired a new CEO in 1993 as it was felt that there was no senior executive within the existing organization capable of doing the job. Interestingly, despite the seemingly elaborate 'head hunting' exercise, the computer industry did not appear to give the new IBM CEO much respect (Dobrzynski, 1993). In a nutshell, the Western approach tends to treat management more as a science, and adopts a much more 'clinical' approach in the way the organization is handled.

In business practice, the heart and mind are not mutually exclusive approaches. Rather, my arguments are that the Japanese and Asian companies tend to pay more attention to the heart whilst the Western companies tend to be more mind-driven. There is nothing wrong with being more mind-driven so long as a healthy balance can be maintained. For example, if teamwork is necessary to achieve success, then there is a need to inject more heart into the organization. This is where I find much of the recent literature on team building and teamwork lacking. Whilst much of this literature tends to expound on the importance and contributions of teamwork and team building, they tend to treat the subject in a rather 'clinical' manner (e.g. Dyer, 1987; Johansen et al, 1991; Katzenbach and Smith, 1993). Little attention is given to building up social bonds within the team—that is, focusing on building up the heart which is so essential to facilitate the management of change.

Ironically, when one traces back into history, it was Mayo's (1933) classic Hawthorne experiment that clearly demonstrated the emergence of the team idea in an organized work setting—one that operated with the heart. In that well-documented Hawthorne experiment, the group maintained high productivity over a 5-year period largely because of psychic rewards resulting from a strong team spirit. The leader of that group managed by the heart, not the mind! In the process, he was able to create changes in the group behaviour that initially even confounded Mayo and his researchers. Mayo's works were very much supported by McGregor (1960) when he wrote *The Human Side of Enterprise* and Likert (1961) the author of *New Patterns of Management*.

Perhaps, it is timely for Western executives to revisit some of these classic works to rediscover the need for the heart in management.

## CONCLUSION

The analogy between war and business is a fruitful exercise, but it is too often taken for granted. Of course, there are limits to the analogy between war and business in that the former is an extreme situation, demanding exceptional responses and a suspension of normal life. War, after all, involves killing and being killed, and often allows for various forms of behaviour, espionage and control of the media for instance. These activities are unlikely to be tolerated in peacetime. Even allowing for the notion of a 'just war' one may feel that a war mentality is not necessary or desirable for a successful business life. Yet, it is equally difficult to deny that many military concepts can be applied meaningfully in business. In particular, they help to develop a mentality amongst corporate executives to win business wars. Thus, Sun Tzu's *Art of War*, a treatise highly regarded by many Asian corporate strategists, may provide some inspirations in this direction.

## REFERENCES

Abegglen, James C. and Stalk Jr, G. (1985). *Kaisha: The Japanese Corporation*, Basic Books, New York.

Ackoff, Russell L. (1978). *The Art of Problem Solving*, John Wiley, New York.

Attanasio, D. B. (1988). The multiple benefits of competitor intelligence, *The Journal of Business Strategy*, May/June, pp. 16–19.

Bartlett, Christopher A. and Ghoshal, Sumantra (1989). *Managing Across Borders: The Transnational Solution*, Harvard Business School Press, Boston, Massachusetts.

Beltramini, R. F. (1986). Ethics and the use of competitive information acquisition strategies, *Journal of Business Ethics*, **5**, pp. 307–311.

Bergeron, F. and Raymond, L. (1992). Planning of information systems to gain a competitive advantage, *Journal of Small Business Management,* January, pp. 21–26.

Chandler, Alfred D. Jr. (1962). *Strategy As Structure*, MIT Press, Cambridge, Massachusetts.

de Bono, Edward (1971). *Lateral Thinking for Management*, McGraw-Hill, United Kingdom.

Dobrzynski, Judith H. (1993). Rethinking IBM, *Business Week*, 4 October, pp. 44–55.

Dumaine, Brian (1991). The bureaucracy busters, *Fortune International*, **123**(13), 17 June, pp. 26–34.

Dumaine, Brian (1993). Payoff from the new management, *Fortune International*, **128**(15), 13 December, pp. 49–52.

Dyer, William G. (1987). *Team Building: Issues and Alternatives*, Addison-Wesley, Reading, Massachusetts.

Eells, Richard and Nehemkis, Peter (1984). *Corporate Intelligence and Espionage*, Macmillan Publishing Co., New York.

Enderwick, Peter (1989). Multinational corporate restructuring and international competitiveness, *California Management Review*, Fall, pp. 44–58.

Enricho, Roger and Kornbluth, Jesse (1987). The other guy blinked: how Pepsi won the cola wars, *World Executive Digest*, April, pp. 44–48.

Gordon, I. H. (1982). Competitive intelligence—a key to marketplace survival, *Industrial Marketing*, **67**(11), November, pp. 69–75.

Griffith, Samuel B. (1982). *Sun Tzu: The Art of War*, 11th edn, Oxford University Press, Oxford.

Henderson, Bruce (1979). *Henderson on Corporate Strategy*. Abt Books, Cambridge, Massachusetts.

Johansen, Robert, Martin, Alexia, Mittman, Robert, Saffo, Paul, Sibbet, David and Benson, Suzyn (1991). *Leading Business Teams*, Addison-Wesley, Reading, Massachusetts.

Katzenbach, Jon R. and Smith, Douglas, K. (1993). *The Wisdom of Teams: Creating the High-Performance Organization*, Harvard Business School Press, Boston, Massachusetts.

Kirkpatrick, David (1993). Could AT & T rule the world? *Fortune International*, **127**(10), 17 May, pp. 18–27.

Kotler, Philip, Fahey, Liam and Jatusripitak, S. (1985). *The New Competition*, Prentice-Hall, Englewood Cliffs, New Jersey.

Kotler, Philip and Singh, Ravi (1981). Marketing warfare in the 1980's, *Journal of Business Strategy*, Winter, pp. 30–41.

Kotter, John P. and Schlesinger, Leonard A. (1979). Choosing strategies for change, *Harvard Business Review*, **57**(2), March–April, pp. 106–114.

Kraar, Louis (1992). Korea's tigers keep roaring, *Fortune International*, **125**(9), 4 May, pp. 24–28.

Kraar, Louis (1993). How Samsung grows so fast, *Fortune International*, **127**(9), 3 May, pp. 16–21.

Labich, Kenneth (1992a). Airbus takes off, *Fortune International*, **125**(11), 1 June, pp. 22–28.

Labich, Kenneth (1992b). Europe's sky wars, *Fortune International*, **126**(10), 2 November, pp. 24–31.

Lazer, William, Murata, Shoji and Kosaka, Hiroshi (1985). Japanese marketing: towards a better understanding, *Journal of Marketing*, **49**(2), pp. 69–81.

Li, Shi Jun, Xian Ju, Yang and Jia Rei, Tang (1984). *Sun Tzu's Art of War and Business Management* (translated), Kwangsi Peoples Press, China.

Likert, Rensis (1961). *New Patterns of Management*, McGraw-Hill, New York.

Lorange, Peter (1980). *Corporate Planning: An Executive Viewpoint*, Prentice-Hall, Englewood Cliffs, New Jersey.

Lorange, Peter (1982). *Implementation of Strategic Planning*, Prentice-Hall, Englewood Cliffs, New Jersey.

Lorange, Peter and Vancil, Richard F. (1976). How to design a strategic planning system, *Harvard Business Review*, **54**(5), September–October, pp. 75–81.

Mayo, Elton (1933). The human problems of an industrial civilization, Division of Research, Graduate School of Business Administration, Harvard University, Boston.

McGregor, Douglas (1960). *The Human Side of Enterprise*, McGraw-Hill, New York.

Miller, William C. (1986). *The Creative Edge: Fostering Innovation Where You Work*, Addison-Wesley, USA.

Mroczkowski, Tomasz and Hanaoka, Masao (1989). Continuity and change in Japanese management, *Human Resources*, Winter, pp. 39–52.

Naisbitt, John and Aburdene, Patricia (1985). *Re-inventing the Corporation*, Warner Books, Inc., New York.

National Economic Commission (1985). *Classical Chinese Thoughts and Modern Management* (translated), Economic Management Research Institute, Yunnan People's Publishing, China.

Nelan, Bruce W. (1993). A new world for spies, *Time*, 5 July, pp. 28–31.

Ohmae, K. (1982). *The Mind of the Strategist: The Art of Japanese Business*, McGraw-Hill, New York.

Ohmae, K. (1989). Planting for a global harvest, *Harvard Business Review*, 67(4), July–August, pp. 136–145.

Pascale, Richard Tanner (1990). *Managing On The Edge: How the Smartest Companies Use Conflict to Stay Ahead*, Simon and Schuster, New York.

Pooley, James (1982). T*rade Secrets: How to Protect Your Ideas and Assets*, Berkeley, California: Osborne, McGraw-Hill, USA.

Quinn, James Brian (1978). Strategic change: logical incrementalism, *Sloan Management Review*, **20**(1), Fall, pp. 7–21.

Rapoport, Carla (1993). Japan to the rescue, *Fortune International*, **128**(9), 18 October, pp. 30–34.

Ries, Al and Trout, Jack (1986). *Marketing Warfare*, McGraw-Hill Book Company, USA.

Saporito, Bill (1992). Why the price wars never end, *Fortune International*, **125**(6), 23 March, pp. 20–25.

Schlender, Brenton R. (1993a). PC wars in Japan, *Fortune International*, **127**(14), 12 July, pp. 14–18.

Schlender, Brenton R. (1993b). How Toshiba makes alliances work, *Fortune International*, **128**(8), 4 October, pp. 42–47.

Sherman, Stratford (1992). Are strategic alliances working? *Fortune International*, 21 September, pp. 33–34.

Sherman, Stratford (1993a). Are you as good as the best in the world? *Fortune International*, **128**(15), pp. 47–48.

Sherman, Stratford (1993b). How will we live in tumult? *Fortune International*, 128(15), pp. 59–61.

Stewart, Thomas A. (1992a). The search for the organization of tomorrow, *Fortune International*, 18 May, pp. 53–58.

Stewart, Thomas A. (1992b). Brace for Japan's hot new strategy, *Fortune International*, 21 September, pp. 24–32.

Stripp, William G. (1985). Sun Tzu, Musashi and Mahan: the integration of Chinese, Japanese and American strategic thought in international business, *Proceedings of the Inaugural Meeting of the Southeast Asia Region Academy of International Business*, pp. 109–118, The Chinese University of Hong Kong, Hong Kong.

Sullivan, Jeremiah J. (1992). Japanese management philosophies: from the vacuous to the brilliant, *California Management Review*, 34(2) Winter, pp. 66–87.

Taylor III, Alex (1993). Here comes Japan's carmakers—Again, *Fortune International*, **128**(15), pp. 63–67.

Tichy, Noel M. (1993). Revolutionize your company, *Fortune International*, **128**(15), pp. 54–56.

Waller, Douglas (1992). The open barn door: U.S. firms face a wave of foreign espionage, *Newsweek*, 4 May.

Wee, C. H. (1989). Planning for war and business: lessons from Sun Tzu, *Pointer*, Jan–Mar, pp. 3–20.

Wee, C. H. (1990). Battlegrounds and business situation: lessons from Sun Tzu, *Singapore Business Review*, **1**(1), pp. 24–43.
Wee, C. H., Lee, K. S. and Hidajat, B. W. (1991). Sun Tzu: War and Management, Addison-Wesley Publishing Company, Reading, M.A.
Yu, Po L. (1990). *Forming Winning Strategies: An Integrated Theory of Habitual Domains*, Springer-Verlag, Berlin.
Zellner, Wendy (1992). The airlines are killing each other again, *International Business Week*, 8 June, p. 30.

# 13

# THE FOUR FUNCTIONS OF ORGANIZATIONS—WHERE DOES THE INDIVIDUAL FIT IN?

**Ralph Lewis**

*Senior Consultant, Mosaic Management Consulting Group Ltd*

**Jon Lawton**

*Management Development Controller, Laurentian Life*

Organizational change is gathering pace: mergers, restructuring, leaner and meaner organizations, delayering, global issues and strategic alliances are all established facts of organizational life implemented in the name of effectiveness! In the midst of all this complexity and change, where does the individual manager stand? Does his or her role demand pushing for change, supporting the organizational vision, even if it means reducing manpower and increasing workloads? So many mission statements and business strategies are couched purely in marketing terms and appear to have nothing to do with the internal aspects of organizations. 'Profit for profit's sake' is not very motivating to a workforce.

Those within an organization often do not receive clear statements of values. Some personnel departments have given up their fight, as they see it, to 'humanize' their organization and have retreated into either apathy or guerrilla warfare. Others have whole-heartedly embraced 'efficiency' and speak in terms of organizational strategies that have no reference to people but to 'resources'—these can sometimes be human! This is a somewhat cynical

*The Implementation Challenge*, Edited by D. E. Hussey
© 1996 John Wiley & Sons Ltd

view—personnel are often caught between different pressures, which they have to try to balance.

To understand these sometimes conflicting positions, it is necessary to go back to basics: to look at the values, purposes and structures of organizations as a whole and then to see where managers can choose to balance their efforts.

All organizations, industrial or social, of whatever shape, size or form, have to carry out four functions to be successful. These are defined by sociologists as:

- Performing goal-orientated tasks.
- Managing the environment.
- Keeping people in the organization working together.
- Establishing common ways of dealing with outsiders.

Any organization (that is, a group of people with a common purpose) has to attain minimum standards in each area, otherwise the organization will cease to exist. This applies as much to Unilever, Ford, the NHS, the IPM and British society as it does to the family or social clubs. The four functions can be placed on a matrix with the dimensions shown in Figure 13.1.

If we examine the four functions in Figure 13.1 below in terms of these quadrants, different organizations can be classified according to the quadrant

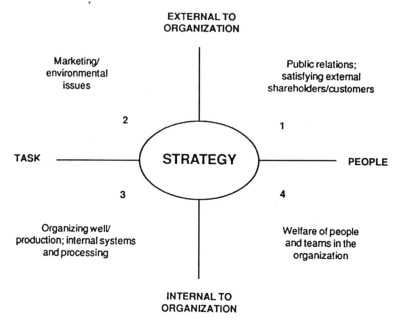

**Figure 13.1**   Organizational Functions

or function that they regard as their main area of concern or purpose. This classification has similarities with other organizational culture models, although with less negative connotations.

## QUADRANT 1 ORGANIZATIONS: CLIENT CENTRED

| | |
|---|---|
| *Purpose:* | To serve clients |
| *Criterion for effectiveness:* | Client satisfaction |
| *Values:* | Service |
| *Structure:* | Loose and flexible to respond to clients |
| *Examples:* | National Health Service (NHS), education |

Examples of quadrant 1 organizations are the NHS, universities and the Government. The NHS exists for the benefit of its clients, the patients; it does not exist to make large profits, or for the welfare of the British Medical Association or other employees (nurses, etc.). Nor does it exist to compete for larger shares of revenue in the total economy. However, there is a need for a minimum standard in each of these areas, based around patient care.

The present political battle over the NHS is, thus, a conflict between those who think that making the NHS more cost-effective will enhance its ability to deliver to the patient and those who think that it will detract. It is impossible to say which view is right at the moment. However, if education is considered, the same arguments advanced for local school budgeting appear to be proving the latter point of view. Recent examples of more experienced, and hence more costly, teachers being made redundant to keep school costs down is a case where the prime purpose is being sacrificed.

## QUADRANT 2 ORGANIZATIONS: MARKETING

| | |
|---|---|
| *Purpose:* | To compete and grow in the market |
| *Criterion for effectiveness:* | Market share |
| *Values:* | Growth, competitiveness, achievement |
| *Structure:* | Market orientated, complex |
| *Examples:* | Unilever, Xerox |

The second quadrant is that of marketing organizations such as Unilever or Xerox. Their major *raison d'être* is to compete in the market place in terms of delivering goods to the appropriate markets. Products are seen as a means of attaining the ultimate goal—market share and growth are important. The Unilever Annual Report, for example, has many pictures of smiling customers using Unilever products. In these organizations, the internal structures are there to respond to the market; cost is important but it must not override the prospect of growth.

## QUADRANT 3 ORGANIZATIONS: PRODUCTION CENTRED

| | |
|---|---|
| *Purpose:* | To manufacture products |
| *Criteria for effectiveness:* | Efficiency, quality, ROA |
| *Values:* | Stability, competency |
| *Structure:* | Well-organized, tight structures, hierarchical |
| *Examples:* | Rover, ICI, manufacturing |

If industrial and commercial organizations are examined, their prime purposes lie on the task side. In manufacturing industry, the focus lies on goal-orientated tasks performed efficiently. The automobile industry needs to concentrate on making cars, or other means of transport, efficiently and well, with emphasis on task specialization, economies of scale and use of assets. Again, there is a need for minimum standards to be set in other areas—there is no point making cars that noone wants to buy, or treating workers so badly that they all leave, or breaking legal and societial rules (as De Lorean found out).

## QUADRANT 4 ORGANIZATIONS: WELFARE

| | |
|---|---|
| *Purpose:* | Welfare of members |
| *Criterion for effectiveness:* | Members' evaluation of satisfaction |
| *Values:* | Caring, support, interpersonal |
| *Structure:* | Varies but is based on the needs of individuals |
| *Examples:* | The family, social clubs |

It must be remembered that the criteria used for judging the effectiveness of an organization make sense only in terms of its prime purpose, and that the criteria used for different quadrants are very different from each other. For example, the family is an organization whose prime purpose is the welfare of the people in it—the family members. Its effectiveness can be judged only by this criterion—in other words, by asking people whether the family is providing them with what they want. It would be nonsense to look at cost effectiveness measures, which unfortunately is what some economists would do. However, the family does need to carry out certain tasks, such as cooking, ironing and cleaning; does need to manage its environment and its market, and to sell its services to that market; and does need to manage relationships with friends, neighbours and relatives (usually the focus of conflict every Christmas). If any of these areas are neglected, the family will be no more—through lack of clothes to wear, lack of money to support its members, or trouble with the neighbours and the police.

Organizations that seem to flourish balance all these quadrants, whilst accepting the predominance of one quadrant. Body Shop is such an example: built on the strong values of its founders, it exists in the marketing quadrant. However, it follows community and social policies (not to mention environmental policies that lead to high standards in quadrants 1 and 4) and also keeps a tight control of finance (quadrant 3). Other examples include IBM and Marks & Spencer. These examples reinforce the need for both 'tight' or hard criteria in certain areas (quadrants 2 and 3) and 'loose' or people criteria in quadrants 1 and 4. Good general managers link all quadrants and allocate appropriate priorities to each area, balancing the needs of the clients or stakeholders.

It is therefore incumbent on any managing director to understand that to talk purely of profits without specifying what he or she is measuring (marketing or production), or who these data are required for (shareholders or employees) indicates a certain business immaturity and naivety.

This is where individual managers can come into their own. By understanding what type of organization they are working in, and the values, purposes and structures that flow from this, they can orientate their own function towards an appropriate role for the business, whilst ensuring that minimum standards are maintained in their departments.

Human resource professionals, for example, need to be both functional experts and all-round business managers if they are to take their place in managing a business. The mistakes that can lead them to lose influence are twofold:

1. ignoring the overall business needs and remaining entrenched in quadrant 4, their functional competency. This leads to a retreat from business reality as described earlier.
2. ignoring their functional area and embracing the marketing, client or production quadrant at the exclusion of their own leads to an activity totally at the whims of its customers.

Of course, it is difficult for personnel specialists to play this broader business role if they have acquired little, if any, business knowledge as part of their professional training.

The 'ideal' way is to see the proper role of the personnel quadrant within the overall business context, which sometimes means wearing two hats at once—the specialist and the generalist. This is, however, what production or marketing specialists also have to do. If when making their decisions they either always emphasize their specialty or always ignore it, they lose their effectiveness.

So everyone in an organization needs to be clear about the following:

1.  What is the overall purpose/mission of the organization? In which quadrant does it fall?
2.  What is the strategy of the organization? What are the minimum standards in the other quadrants?
3.  What is the actual orientation of the organization in terms of the quadrants? How does this need to be changed to meet 1 and 2 given above?

One successful experience of using the quadrants has been in Laurentian Life, an insurance company based in Gloucester. Laurentian Life was formed in 1986 as the result of a merger and, as often happens in these situations, the integration of two cultures under a new commercial charter proved to be more difficult than was anticipated.

In essence, the quadrant model provided a framework and language that allowed the expression of individual perceptions and values, whilst at the same time extending management's constructs about culture. Strong personal convictions were seen in context and the company became sensitized to a broader range of cultural ingredients. Through using the model with managers at all levels of the organization, 'culture' moved from being a theoretical intangible to an issue that could be addressed in terms of practical action. Issues about culture became agenda items and other agenda items were subjected to a review of their cultural implications.

The company moved from finding a way to quantify and express its culture to the more difficult task of integrating expressed values with both corporate and individual behaviour.

Of course, no model provides answers, merely a way of thinking or a means of extending the parameters to the way that we think. At Laurentian Life, the model did both. There was one further aspect, however, that was not anticipated but which merits note. The debate on culture started with managers talking about what the organization needed to do but somehow shifted to managers talking about their own responsibilities and scope for affecting and sustaining culture.

Using the quadrants with employees from the company's headquarters, Laurentian Life found that most of its employees thought the company was clearly orientated towards its administrative systems and efficiency of information processing. This is obviously positive given the organization's stated purpose, the nature of life assurance products and the function of its headquarters in relation to its distribution channels. Against this background, however, employees thought that there was not enough emphasis on the internal—people and marketing—quadrants.

In the people quadrant, personnel, in conjunction with the senior management team, were able to take a series of initiatives in response to a more detailed investigation of the issues that underpin the people quadrant. Internal communication, personal development, training and career management, structures, rewards systems, pay scales, working conditions and employee health have all since come under the microscope in an effort to achieve a quadrant profile commensurate with commercial success.

In the marketing quadrant, the situation was different: the senior team had already consciously made the decision to move the company to a position where it was increasingly 'market driven' and had already implemented a series of strategies to this effect. Using the model, however, highlighted a gap between decisions taken at the top and the perceptions of these further down the structure.

In the short term, considerable effort was made to communicate the company's position to its employees; in the medium term, it introduced a performance management system, which now allows a controlled and much quicker response, in terms of realigning individual effort and understanding with changes in strategy.

In another high-technology company, the emphasis was on the client quadrant—to keep existing clients happy at all costs. However, the loose organization structure and low level of management discipline caused employees to feel that there was a lack of strategic direction in the company, leaving people confused about their purpose, roles and responsibilities. A new personnel director was able to introduce policies and procedures (quadrant 4) that gave employees a sense of clarity and stability, while business training was introduced to rebalance the company's focus towards a more disciplined marketing effort (quadrant 2).

It is also important to realize that every individual will have a preference, stemming from his or her values for a particular emphasis on a quadrant. You can find quadrant 4 individuals who are most concerned with people inside the organization (sometimes in personnel but not always), or quadrant 2 people who put their emphasis on the market, growth and competitiveness. These values can usually be easily identified after a few minutes' discussion.

An organization will only really be successful if its managers understand both their own specialty and the organizational context in which they operate. It is a difficult balancing act but a worthwhile one.

# 14

# CREATING COMMITMENT TO CHANGE: FROM A CLOSED TO OPEN COMMUNICATION STYLE

**Raymond Caldwell**

*Lecturer in Management, Birkbeck College, University of London*

- This chapter defines the fit between the strategies of involvement and commitment and employee communication styles.
- Four employee communication styles are identified and described in detail.
- The author argues that the organization may have to adopt more than one style to achieve its aims.

There has been an enormous upsurge of interest in new and more direct forms of employee communication over the last decade. This has been sustained partly by a strategic shift towards more open, less hierarchical ways of managing organizations and people. 'Delayering'—the removal of management tiers; eliminating job grades and distinctions; increasing teamwork; instilling new values; or sustaining a commitment to quality are all familiar, if a somewhat confusing, myriad of change initiatives that have to be explained to employees. Why is a flatter, less status bound organization founded on teamwork essential to our competitive success? Answering this question requires managers to become more effective communicators and organizations much more professional at managing their internal communications.

Explaining change has become a management necessity. But there are other, equally important reasons why employee communications have grown in

*The Implementation Challenge*, Edited by D. E. Hussey
© 1996 John Wiley & Sons Ltd

significance. Effective communication is one of the most direct forms of 'employee involvement'. Moreover, it is through involvement that the fundamental requirement of a truly competitive organization can be sustained—a more committed workforce (Walton, 1985).

> More involvement means greater commitment. (Lawler, 1992.)

This is the key proposition that has transformed employee communication into a strategic human resource issue for senior management. Informing employees, listening to their concerns, offering feedback, are all direct forms of employee involvement designed to engender greater commitment to the mission, values and performance standards of an organization. Without this dialogue it is difficult to foster a commitment to new behaviours and attitudes. It is no surprise then that many employee involvement initiatives are often synonymous with communication-led strategies for changing behaviour.

This chapter seeks to define the fit between strategies of involvement and commitment and employee communication styles. It does so by mapping out four possible employee communication styles along two key dimensions: the degree of employee involvement and the degree of employee commitment (Figure 14.1). The nature of the link between involvement and commitment is discussed and the characteristics of each communication style are described.

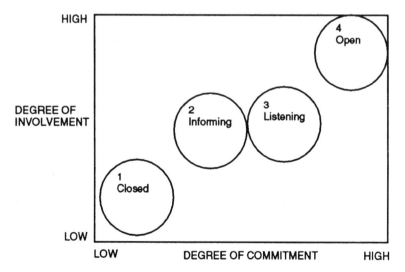

**Figure 14.1**    Four Styles of Employee Communication

# EMPLOYEE INVOLVEMENT

Involvement covers a wide range of mainly *voluntary, employer-led* initiatives designed to harness employee cooperation and build common interests with management. They may range from providing employees with information of concern to them to formal mechanisms of financial participation (e.g. share ownership and profit sharing arrangements). The main focus of interest here is in delineating the move towards more *direct* forms of employee involvement: the face-to-face, two-way flow of communication between managers and their subordinates (see Box). Communication is at the centre of most employee involvement approaches, from the top-down, one-way flow of information to employees to the genuine dialogue that underlies most teamwork initiates on quality, customer care and performance improvement (Herrick, 1990). Rarely, however, are these communication-led forms of involvement designed to change the pattern of authority between managers and their subordinates: ultimately employees have no formal rights to share in decision-making. In this respect one must draw a clear distinction between traditional participative ideals of 'industrial democracy' the principal aim of which is the sharing of decision-maing power and employee involvement that describes

> those practices which are initiated principally by management, and are designed to increase employee information about and commitment to the organisation. (Marchington, 1992, p. 24.)

On the basis of this distinction involvement might be dismissed as 'pseudo-participation' or a purely symbolic gesture. But this would be to seriously underestimate the significance of employee involvement in blurring traditional patterns of authority, redefining work relations and questioning some of the outmoded assumptions of management control.

---

### THREE FORMS OF EMPLOYEE INVOLVEMENT (EI)

Marchington (1992) distinguishes three forms of EI:

- Direct EI is concerned with the two-way flow of communication, ideas and information between managers and their subordinates;
- Indirect EI centres on employee involvement in decision-making via their elected representatives;
- Financial EI relates to employees as economic stakeholder (e.g. through share ownership) in the success or failure of the organization.

# EMPLOYEE COMMITMENT

Always to some extent a positive virtue in itself, 'employee commitment' has become a major priority for many organizations as they respond to intensified competitive pressures. The success of Japanese companies in linking their long-term competitive performance to a committed workforce and its associated virtues of teamwork and consensus-based decision-making have also helped inspire the emphasis on commitment. Increasingly employees are being asked to affirm their commitment to the overall mission, long-term goals and performance standards of their organization, as well as their willingness to change. The assumption is that when employees are highly committed they are more likely to identify with the goals of their organization, and actively seek to achieve them. Committed employees will usually have good attendance records, lower turnover rates and will adhere to company policy (Blau and Boal, 1987). Of course, commitment levels are likely to vary from the top to the bottom of an organization and in relation to length of service, career success and the issues where it is sought. Successful senior managers may be expected to demonstrate high commitment levels and to become a source of motivational inspiration for others, whilst more junior employees may only be required to conform to the behavioural competencies of their job.

Figure 14.1 assumes that there is a positive link between involvement and commitment. A good deal of research evidence would tend to support this link in at least two respects: (1) involvement, both mental and emotional in work activities tends to improve job satisfaction and can increase performance (Miller and Monge, 1986; Leana et al, 1990); and (2) involvement through group discussion and the sharing of responsibility can create commitment to shared goals and lessen resistance to change (Coch and French, 1948; Lewin, 1947; Schein and Bennis, 1965; Randall, 1990). For many experienced managers these benefits are self-evident; they underpin one of the key principles of good management practice: getting things done through motivating others. Nevertheless, the links between involvement and commitment can be overdrawn. Some employees may simply not have the ability or desire to become involved (Blau and Boal, 1987). Commitment may not produce an increase in employee performance or ensure that performance is sustained. In addition, the links between performance and satisfaction and satisfaction and commitment are often 'very flimsy' (Rollinson, 1993). But despite these reservations managers and consultants have been happy to proselytize and practise the virtues of involvement and commitment as an article of faith (Peters, 1989). Like true believers in the prescriptive power of a good idea, they have been content to let the success or failure of practice determine the validity of the linkage between involvement and commitment.

# FOUR COMMUNICATION STYLES

By combining the dimensions of involvement and commitment along two axes it is possible to map out four employee communication styles. They can be characterized as follows:

1. Closed style: We give the orders you follow them.
2. Informing style: We want you to be aware of the issues that affect you.
3. Listening style: We will listen to your views before we decide.
4. Open style: We want you to help us solve our problems together.

Figure 14.2 summarizes some of the key features of each style.

## Closed Style

This style of communication characterizes a traditional hierarchical organization with a high degree of centralized, downward communication. Communication flows follow established formal channels and fixed reporting relationships, invariably underpinned by written rules and procedures. The main modes of ongoing communication are formal meetings, internal memos and other forms of impersonal, paper-based communication.

Naturally, an autocratic culture of conformity and compliance tends to be associated with this formal style of communication. Managers issue orders and instructions and employees are expected to carry them out. There is no two-way communication, both because management tends to be remote and uncommunicative and because employees are treated as a passive audience that is not asked or expected to provide feedback. Nor is there any expectation about employee commitment beyond the effective execution of narrowly defined job tasks and responsibilities. In effect, there are virtually no opportunities for employees to exercise initiative or discretion. Ultimately the overriding goal of this communication style is to command and control the workforce.

## Informing Style

The informing style is characterized by the top-down, one-way flow of information from employer to employee. Whilst esssentially voluntary, it is often reinforced by legislation requiring employers to keep employees informed about specific issues of concern to them (e.g. pay and conditions, pensions and benefits, health and safety). Information is widely circulated using a variety of media: newsletters, notice boards, videos, employee reports. In this respect communication flows often break loose from more formal hierarchical channels. But despite this widening of communication it tends to be managed as a top-down, information-driven activity. Management is invariably communicating to raise awareness of specific issues or to sell a particular

| COMMUNICATION STYLES | CLOSED | INFORMING | LISTENING | OPEN |
|---|---|---|---|---|
| | AUTOCRATIC | PATERNALISTIC | CONSULTATIVE | PARTICIPATIVE |
| ORIENTATION TOWARDS EMPLOYEES | Manager makes decision | Manager presents decision as in best interest of employees | Manager seeks input before making decision | **Manager facilitates decision-making by employees** |
| COMMUNICATION TOOLS, MEDIA, APPROACHES | • written rules<br>• instructions<br>• formal meetings | • newsletters<br>• notice boards<br>• employee reports<br>• one-way briefing sessions | • focus groups<br>• employee surveys<br>• informal discussion<br>• two-way briefing sessions | • self-managed teams<br>• joint problem-solving groups |
| COMMUNICATION GOALS | Command and control | **Disseminate information<br>Sell decisions<br>Raise awareness** | Test and validate decisions | Build autonomy and commitment |

COMMUNICATION PATTERN

One-way, mainly downward flow, low-feedback ← → Two-way, greater upward flow, high-feedback

**Figure 14.2**   Communication Styles: Summary

idea. Rarely are employees' views sought, and whilst there may be some direct feedback it is usually controlled and one-off—there is no ongoing dialogue. Even during formal, face-to-face presentations to employees, where managers may be seeking to sell new proposals on working practices, two-way discussion may be limited to a narrow range of issues where employees are allowed to express their views. In this respect the informing style is usually part of a top-down communication strategy, which management uses to convey selected information or push through changes it has already decided upon.

## Listening Style

The listening style assumes a model of two-way communication: ideas are invited from employees and their views on certain issues are sought. A variety of tools and techniques are used to achieve this, including employee opinion surveys, focus groups, suggestion schemes and informal team meetings. Each of these approaches indicates a genuine willingess of management to listen: both as a way of identifying specific areas of business improvement and as a way of gauging employees' attitudes. Employee opinion surveys, for example, are often useful in testing new ideas, monitoring employee attitudes and identifying potential areas of resistance to change. When used as a tool to support organizational change, opinion surveys usually seek the views of all employees, so that a sense of involvement and ownership is created at the feedback stage. Suggestion schemes provide a formal mechanism for employees to voluntarily communicate their ideas for business improvements. They are a somewhat marginal form of involvement, but have a record of producing some very dramatic improvements in quality, productivity and cost control. These tools of communication and involvement can improve the climate of employee relations by making it clear to employees that their views are sought. In addition, the listening style often underpins a model of management leadership based on the principle of 'engaged listening'. Increasingly managers are being asked to spend less time exercising their instrumental skills of directing and controlling people and more time listening to employees. Listening is involved as a way of helping managers keep in touch with people; of not prejudging issues and overcoming the distortions of formal information flows.

Although the listening style approaches a model of two-way communication, it is by no means an open dialogue. The flow of communication is structured and controlled in predetermined ways. Suggestion schemes are usually a formal mechanism for sifting and evaluating ideas, which can be restricted to specific areas of improvement and not others. Opinion surveys can be very selective in choosing a sample frame, interpreting results and providing feedback—often with disastrous consequences for employee relations. For example, surveying a small sample of employees can undermine a sense of ownership for the results, whilst surveying a larger group of employees, but providing limited feedback, can raise expectations that are not met. These dangers reflect the intrinsic limitations of the listening style. Managers may be listening and taking note, but they may not have truly entered into the obligations of a genuine dialogue which requires them to provide feedback and to mutually agree actions. Ultimately the listening manager can revert to a closed style:

> Yes I hear what you are saying, but my decision is final.

### Open Style

The open style is based on *direct*, face-to-face communication in which employees are active participants, encouraged to ask questions, offer feedback and assume ownership for actions agreed within a framework of open dialogue. In its most advanced forms managers will enter into a dialogue with employees as facilitators who do not prejudge or impose a definition of the problem, but let employees arrive at their own agreed conclusions and actions. This communication style is often associated with the most extensive forms of employee involvement such as quality circles and self-managed teams, which seek to harness employees' contributions, encourage changes in behaviour and build commitment to new performance standards.

The open style is the direct opposite of the closed style, with its rigid, top-down flow of communication. It is characteristic of flatter, leaner and more team-oriented organizations where employee initiative is encouraged as a vital way of responding to external change. Generally decision-making power is widely dispersed and there are uninhibited flows of communication up, down and across these organizations, which are facilitated by informal networks and the levelling power of information technology. The formal apparatus of bureaucratic communication, memos, written regulations, files and all forms of unnecessary paperwork are discouraged in order to free-up individual initiative and encourage more informal face-to-face communication. Team-based-groupings are often the central hubs of new informal patterns of communication, which create shared standards of performance and help to counteract top-down directives and sanctions. In sum, the open style is designed to facilitate the creation of more flexible organizations which empower employees to exercise greater initiative.

## CONCLUSION

The characteristics of the four styles have been sharply drawn, some more so than others. The closed style (1) and the open style (4) are poles apart, whilst the informing style (2) and listening style (3) are in such close proximity that they may shade into each other (see Figure 14.1). The reality of course is that any organization may have characteristics of one or more styles. The two axes of involvement and commitment simply provide a continuum along which a whole range of communication styles can be plotted, including hybrids. For example, an organization may find it appropriate to use the influencing style in building employee commitment to a quality programme or new team-building initiatives, whilst retaining a rigid control style in the area of strategic decision-making and financial management. In this respect different styles of communication can be interspersed in an organization, depending on the hierarchical level, the subject matter discussed and who is going to influence or make the decision. Moreover, an organization may be in transition from one style of communication to another, so it is unlikely to conform to the static characteristics of a single style.

The four styles are a one-sided simplification of reality. Nevertheless, they provide a useful starting point for defining the fit between strategies of involvement and commitment and styles of employee communication. If greater involvement and commitment are sought as part of a quality programme, then an organization may move towards the open style. This will mean a greater emphasis on direct, face-to-face communication with employees as a way of influencing changes in attitudes or behaviour and encouraging joint problem solving. Alternatively the listening style may be useful in gauging employees' receptiveness or resistance to change. Ultimately, however, each organization must decide which communication style is most appropriate and how to achieve it.

## REFERENCES

Blau, G. J. and Boal, K. B. (1987). Conceptualizing how job involvement and organisational commitment affect turnover and absenteeism, *Academy of Management Review*, April, pp. 288–300.
Coch, L. and French, J. R. P. (1948). Overcoming resistance to change, *Human Relations* 1, no. 4, pp. 512–532.
Herrick, N. (1990). *Joint Management and Employee Participation*, Jossey-Bass Publishers, San Francisco.
Lawler, E. E. (1992) *The Ultimate Advantage: Creating the High-Involvement Organisation*, Jossey-Bass Publishers, San Francisco.
Leana, C. R., Locke, E. A. and Schweiger, D. M. (1990). Fact and fiction in analysing research on participative decision making: a critique of Cotton, Vollrath, Froggatt, Lengnick-Hall and Jennings, *Academy of Management Review*, January, pp. 137–146.
Lewin, K. (1947). Frontiers in group dynamics, *Human Relations*, 1, pp. 5–41.
Marchington, M. (1992). *Managing the Team: A Guide to Successful Employee Involvement*, Blackwell.
Miller, K. I. and Monge, P. R. (1986). Participation, satisfaction and productivity: a meta-analytical review, *Academy of Management Review*, December, pp. 727–753.
Peters, T. (1989). *Thriving on Chaos*, Pan Books.

Randall, D. M. (1990). The consequences of organisational commitment: methodological investigation. *Journal of Organisational Behaviour*, September, pp. 361–378.

Rollinson, D. (1993). *Understanding Employee Relations: A Behavioural Approach*, Addison Wesley.

Schein, E. H. and Bennis, W. G. (1965). *Personal and Organisational Change through Group Dynamics*, Wiley, New York.

Walton, R. (1985). From control to commitment in the workplace, *Harvard Business Review*, **63**, No. 2, pp. 77–85.

# 15

# MANAGEMENT TRAINING: A KEY TOOL FOR STRATEGY IMPLEMENTATION

**D. E. Hussey**

*David Hussey and Associates*

- The research evidence is that many organizations have not fully understood the value of using management training for strategic ends.
- Six situations are defined where training aids implementation.
- Each is supported by examples of successful training initiatives by organizations which have seen the potential of training as a tool of implementation.
- Training initiatives of this type usually need a different approach than more traditional training for personal development. Advice is given on this approach.

## MANAGEMENT TRAINING FOR STRATEGIC PURPOSES

The idea of using management development and training to achieve organizational aims, as well as developing individuals, has been known for a long time by a minority of companies. However, the research and observations about this approach is of recent origin. Lusterman (1985) found that there had been a significant increase in management training in the USA, and that in numerous cases programmes were being used in the implementation of new strategies. Putting bottom line objectives on to training programmes was

*The Implementation Challenge*, Edited by D. E. Hussey
© 1996 John Wiley & Sons Ltd

becoming the norm rather than the exception. Bolt (1985) provided case examples from Motorola, Federated Department Stores, Xerox and General Foods, showing how implementation had become the focus of training programmes with measurable changes in corporate performance as the desired result. Hussey (1985) drew attention to case examples of companies that used training in this way, and contrasted them with research findings which showed that most British companies had no idea that training could be used for such a purpose. Ascher (1983) had found that only one-third of respondents believed that there should be a direct link between corporate objectives and training actions, and that many of these were interpreting the question in a somewhat abstract way, assuming that if training is good for the individual it must also contribute to corporate objectives.

The number of UK companies using training in a proactive way at this time was very small. However, more recent research amongst a similar sample by Tovey (1991) showed more top management involvement, and a more thoughtful approach to management development. Slightly more than half the sample linked the management development and training activities to corporate objectives and strategy. This still left 46% who felt that the links were inadequate, despite the fact that the sample was drawn from the larger UK companies which might be expected to be amongst the leaders in training thinking.

Mason (1993) surveyed organizations which were in the middle of the *Times Top 500* (or their equivalents from the industries excluded from this listing). His findings were broadly similar to Tovey's, in that there had been a considerable movement from the position of the 1980s. However, a somewhat lower percentage of organizations had established a link between training and strategy. Both the Tovey and Mason figures should be taken as indicative, as the samples may not be typical of the universe.

The introductions to the first two books on this theme were both dated January 1987, but the different publishing schedules meant that Nilsson (1987) appeared before Hussey (1988). Nilsson's book was largely based on experience in Hewlett-Packard. Hussey's drew from a mix of his experience and the research programme of Harbridge Consulting Group.

Tovey (1991) found in her survey that the management development people in the sample were generally aware of the major trends affecting business, which were seen as forces for change. However, the implications were seen by most only at a superficial level. For example, most organizations sampled had taken some action to 'delayer' and saw this as a strategic issue which had been included in company courses. Few had recognized that an impact of delayering is to change how managers have to manage, so much of the training communicated and explained the reasons for delayering, but gave managers (or those managed) little help in coping with the new situation.

Alexander (1985) researched the problems which American companies found when implementing strategy. About two-thirds of the sample reported that the capabilities of employees were inadequate for the new tasks. When key skills are lacking, they can only be obtained by recruitment or training, or by some form of strategic alliance. The value of using training to fill gaps so that implementation is facilitated is attractive and obvious. This is only one of the roles that training can fulfil in implementation. If Alexander's respondents had been aware in the beginning that there were shortfalls in skills and knowledge, no doubt they would have taken action before this became a problem. Training initiatives can help to develop understanding of a new strategy, and build enthusiasm for and commitment to it. In addition, training can be used to help work out the many detailed tasks that have to be undertaken to convert the strategy into action. Training can thus be a very powerful tool in implementation.

There are at least six different sorts of implementation situation which may be aided by training:

- Implementing a new policy
- Implementing a strategy
- Effecting an organizational change
- Changing the culture of an organization
- Meeting a major environmental change
- Solving specific problems

**Implementing a New Policy**

There is not a great deal of difference in concept between using a training initiative to implement either a policy or a strategy, and in some situations the distinction between the two terms may become blurred. One difference may be the degree of precision with which quantified corporate objectives can be set as the desired outcome of the training.

> One of the world's largest multinationals, always seen as one of the best managed, identified that more attention had to be placed on competitor analysis both at top level and in the development of marketing plans by each operating unit. This was after careful analysis had revealed that much of the company's recent growth was without profit, because of weaknesses in the market place where the competitors were proving more aggressive than the assumptions on which past plans had been based. Many companies would have issued a policy statement, in the form of an edict, that in future strategies should be formulated after more rigorous competitior analysis. Many would have failed to cause any change whatsoever, because:
>
> - most people would be complacent about their own approach, whilst accepting that others needed to do better;

- some would believe the issue was unimportant and only pay lip service to it;
- others would not understand the policy;
- a few might not receive or read the statement.

Aware of these probable outcomes the chief executive of this multinational personally directed a worldwide educational initiative to bring the new thinking to life. He led top managers in a week long introduction to the theme of 'what about competition', and insisted that several hundred senior people should spend two weeks on a strategic planning workshop. He introduced an 8 hour audio-visual presentation to thousands more managers as a basis for discussion of, and commitment to, genuine strategic thinking. Many week long implementation workshops have been held throughout the world, with practical training in competitor analysis which has led to the implementation of more realistic strategies.

Not surprisingly, this policy change has been made to work, and is enthusiastically endorsed by thousands of managers who are now convinced of its practical value. (Hussey 1988).

## Implementation of Strategy

The right training initiatives can bring the understanding and commitment referred to earlier, and can ensure that the right skills are available so that implementation is possible. The four examples given below show what can be done.

Lorenz (1986a,b,c) described how ICL used management training as a major means of implementing its strategy. Some 2,000 managers were put through a programme which was uniquely designed around the company and its industry to improve competitiveness against American and Japanese rivals. The training programme, which cascaded through all levels of management, was held to have

> done at least as much as the company's new range of products and systems to give ICL an unexpected chance of prospering in the threatening shadows of IBM, Digital Equipment, and the Japanese computer giants. (Lorenz 1986a.)

There were several tiers of courses, launched at the same time. All senior managers went through the top level course over an 18-month period. Courses focused on key strategic concepts and industry issues, and were designed after a careful study of the company.

Rose (1989) demonstrated that management training was the key to the success of the strategic changes instituted in the retailers Woolworths in the UK. This lacklustre group underwent a change of ownership and management, which amongst other things resulted in a change of the group name to Kingfisher. The Woolworth store strategy was considerably changed: indeed some critics felt that until this happened it actually had no strategy, which was one of the reasons for its poor performance. However, the new strategy involved much more delegation to local branch management, and at the time the strategy was formulated it was felt that branch management lacked the skills to operate in the way that was now esssential for the success of the strategy. A training programme was developed for branch management, and was held to be a critical step in the implementation of the strategy.

One of my consulting assignments with the British operations of an international insurance company was advice on the design and installation of a process of planning. The training workshops which were developed to launch the process were also used as the first in a series of strategy formulation meetings, when real issues were worked on. As an example, competitor analysis was not taught as an academic concept. Instead, dossiers were prepared on major competitors and used for real analysis by the planning teams who attended the workshops. Each workshop was attended by a team to whom one aspect of the planning task had been delegated. Much more work was done outside of the workshop, before strategic plans were put by each strategic business to top management for agreement. In this case training was used at the formulation phase, integrated with all the other actions the company was taking, and linked to a modest consultancy input. A result was considerable enthusiasm for strategic change, and a completely different understanding of the competitive environment in which the company operated. Many immediate actions were implemented by the SBU managers, as not all of the actions identified were strategic. Even some of the research subsequently undertaken amongst brokers, as a result of a new appreciation of the information needs of the company, brought immediate benefits in an increase in requests for quotations by many brokers who had not realized the firm's involvement in certain types of insurance.

Coast (1995) describes how management training was used to help Otis Elevators implement its joint venture strategies in Central Europe. Here the need was for the top management teams of these businesses to develop business plans and to implement them. He describes in detail the design of the programme, and its redesign during implementation when it was realized that the English language fluency of those attending was much lower than expected. Apart from its desirability, the language problem forced a low reliance on lectures, and a high use of group and project work. The programme was designed as seven modules of three days each, attended by the managing directors and their direct reports of each company in the region. The projects were all actions that the teams themselves planned to use to improve the performance of their companies. The timing of each module was set to coincide with business situations so that the training initiative became an extension of the business. External consultants helped with some aspects of the programme, but 70% were taught by Otis managers. In addition to aiding the implementation of the overall strategy of Otis for the region, it facilitated the strategic development and performance improvement of each of the businesses.

### Effecting an Organizational Change

In both policy and strategy implementation there is the possibility that an individual may feel threatened because of lack of skill or knowledge to meet a new situation, or because his or her psychological contract has been changed. The concept of the psychological contract partly explains why changes are sometimes resisted. Although a person's salary or job title may not have altered, there may be a change in the unwritten expectations that the person has of the job. Perhaps previously certain decisions could be made without head office approval. Now the changes require that they be referred. This may take some of the job satisfaction away. The same thing may happen when authority is delegated to people whose psychological contract had included the comfort of a boss who has made all the real decisions. With an organizational change it is even more likely that 'people' problems will emerge during implementation, and that these will frustrate implementation unless they are addressed. Training offers one way of approaching these problems.

'Delayering', 'downsizing' and 'rightsizing' (I do not believe there is any difference between them) are common responses to strategic pressures, both to reduce cost and to take decision-making closer to the customer. That at least is the theory, and many organizations have implemented it successfully. Some have achieved implementation merely by ripping out layers without changing individual jobs, or training people in the new skills needed. Scase and Goffee (1989) found in their research in the UK that many managers were frustrated by the extra pressures put on them, and felt they were on a treadmill from which few could see an escape and from which they obtained little job satisfaction.

Organizational change often accompanies a new strategy, and both can be frustrated unless implementation is effective. L'Oréal in the UK used a training approach to secure the implementation of a new organizational structure. A new strategy was devised to increase market share for hair care products in the retail market. Because in the past distribution had focused on certain major retail outlets through which L'Oréal already achieved a disproportionate outlet share, it was clear that the new objective could only be achieved if distribution were extended to outlets where at the time L'Oréal were not represented or had a poor outlet share. The sales and merchandizing teams had been organized to meet the previous pattern of sales, and it was apparent to the management that the new strategy would only succeed if these teams were to be restructured to meet the changed distribution strategy. Originally the company thought of implementing the structural change through announcement at sales conferences and supported by normal management action. Although this may have been ultimately successful, the fear was that it would take too long, during which time the success of the new strategy would be in jeopardy.

The changes in structure had an impact on the job of every person in the sales and merchandizing teams. For example, the two teams were being amalgamated, so that every person would handle both tasks in the future. Different types of outlet would be called on, and transfer orders on wholesalers would be taken from many retail chemists. Again this was to be a new activity. The concern was that changes to the psychological contract would be perceived in a hostile way and that the turnover of sales representatives, which was already high, would increase. There was also a fear that many of the people would not have the knowledge or skills to enable them to cope with the new job requirements.

The training initiative took the form of a two-day workshop which was repeated on a regional basis so that all persons affected by the change attended. The new structure was announced in advance, but was not implemented until after the workshop. In the workshop there was immediate agreement with the new market share objective. A case study was provided, based on real market research, which required participants to work out a distribution strategy to attain the agreed objective. It was clear to all that whatever strategy was decided, the target could not be met without changes in the types of outlet through which the company reached the consumer. It was also clear to everyone that a change of distribution policy would require a change of structure. The new organizational structure was explained in the context of this shared understanding. The rest of the workshop provided training in some of the new knowledge that would be needed by participants, and identified the further training that participants themselves felt would be essential for them to become fully effective. This identification was done on the basis of an informed understanding by participants. The training element of the workshop included bringing in different types of retailer so that they could explain their requirements for merchandizing and sales support.

This approach was reviewed by L'Oréal a year later, when the firm claimed that the workshop had enabled them to achieve the market share objectives. An unexpected benefit was a reduction in the turnover of sales representatives, presumably because of the greater feeling of commitment to the firm which had been built up in the workshop and subsequent management actions. It is doubtful whether so much would have been achieved by more traditional approaches to implementation.

## Changing the Culture of an Organization

Culture has been increasingly recognized as a factor in strategic performance, popularized in particular by Peters and Waterman (1982). Many organizations devote a considerable amount of effort, including a great deal of training activity, to maintaining a particular culture. The Peters and Waterman research, and a film based on this, showed how Disney consistently used training to develop a consistent attitude to customers at Disneyworld.

There are also many occasions when a strategic change requires a change in company culture, and again a training initiative may be one of the most powerful tools that can be used. In this case the training programme must go hand in hand with the management process. Goshal et al (1988) described how the change of strategy at Scandinavian Airlines System after 1981 required a cultural revolution. This was led by the president Jan Carlzon and owed much to his personal energy. The needed change was from a bureaucratic organization that referred all decisions upwards, to a customer responsive entity where all reasonable decisions were taken by the person having point of contact with the customer. Management actions to change the process included 'junking' the procedures manuals.

> Education was considered necessary to reap the full benefits of the new organization, and both managers and front line staff were sent to seminars. (Goshal et al 1988.)

Training initiatives could also be used more than they are to aid implementation in acquisition strategy, particularly where full integration takes place, and it is desirable to get both parts of the new organization working together and to a common philosophy.

Globalization strategies are causing many US and European organizations to introduce common training across geographical frontiers, holding the same courses but running them in appropriate languages. One of the reasons may be to build a similar culture across units of the organization which historically had been run as separate companies.

## Meeting a Major Environmental Change

The implementation needed may be to bring awareness of the change, or the working out of detailed tasks in response to a change. Sometimes this sort of approach may also be used to formulate strategic actions.

Sometimes changes in the business environment can only be seen in the broadest of terms, yet the company has to begin to reposition itself to pressures that can only partly be foreseen.

> In the mid 1970s British Petroleum began to think about some of the organisational issues caused by the environment in which it operated. Until 1973 this had followed a predictable path. After the OPEC initiatives of that year the relative stability was succeeded by turbulence. It became clear that the world of the future was going to be very different from the past, and that one of the requirements would be for managers who could cope with changes, many of which could not even be visualised.

At the same time BP was changing as a business, moving in new directions and becoming more diversified. This again overlaid a different pattern of managerial needs, making limited functional experience in one industry alone inadequate for the successful operation of the BP of the future. It was not that BP would overnight become unrecognisable, but that it could start to draw away from many of the experiences and characteristics that had made it successful in the past. In fact the pace of change has been fairly dramatic, and the BP of today had many significant differences with the BP of 1978 when I was first involved. It also has many cultural values and skills which were recognisable in the 'old' BP, and it is these which have played an important part in helping BP adapt to new circumstances.

In thinking about these issues it was realised that modern managers in BP would have to be able to manage in a very different way from their predecessors, and that the pressures on them would intensify as BP underwent future changes. It was not just that the managers of 1977 faced a different situation from managers of 1973, but that the situation would change many times as their careers developed. It was in 1977 that BP began to look seriously at the management educational implications of the diagnosis, and whether an educational initiative could be used as a means of ensuring that the younger managers of the day would be in a position to manage effectively when they became the senior managers of the future. (Hussey, 1988.)

## Solving Specific Problems

Training works in the implementation situations described above. It is not surprising that it also works in some situations as a means of solving problems. For example, one multinational engineering company used a training mechanism as a means of improving profitability at branch level. After careful research, a course was designed which included all the skills needed to improve performance, including planning, financial numeracy, marketing and team-building. A high level of project work was included, and many of the recommendations from the projects were subsequently implemented.

In another example a workshop was run for a unit of British Petroleum, which had been set up to supply high technology products and services for large ships. Ten months after beginning operations, losses had reached £500,000 without a single sale. The workshop resulted in solutions, and incorporated enough educational input to enable the managers to apply them. In a short space of time after the event sales of £1.5 million were achieved, which were accredited by the management of the business to the actions developed in the workshop.

Butler (1992) described how strategic skills were improved at BAT through a workshop initiative which used work teams of managers to solve strategic problems posed by top management. The aim was to develop the skills of those taking part and to solve the problems.

# A STRATEGIC APPROACH TO MANAGEMENT DEVELOPMENT AND TRAINING

The concepts discussed here can be applied in isolation from an overall approach to management development and training which is linked in all its aspects to the vision and strategies of the organization. I believe that there is an overwhelming case for taking the overall strategic or business-driven approach, and have argued this on many occasions (Hussey, 1988, 1993, 1994, Chapter 21, and 1995; Hussey and Lowe, 1990). This argument is beyond the scope of this chapter: detailed models and approaches will be found in the references.

There are three points from an overall concept which are directly relevant to the use of training for stratgy implementation, and these do require discussion. They are approaches to control of training, access to strategic information, and attitudes to training that cascade down the organization.

## Control of Training

In many organizations training is controlled by expenses rather than results. A lesson that not all managers have learnt is that what is spent does not necessarily correlate with value given, so just increasing budgets without consideration of effectiveness is not very clever. However, there is another adverse effect of this method of control. It means that the three main criteria on which the success of those responsible for providing the training are:

Did we come out under the budget?
Did we train a lot of people with the money?
Did they enjoy themselves?

These are not necessarily bad things in themselves, but become bad because of the internal pressure. In most organizations those responsible for providing training would rather economize on expense than spend somewhat more to increase the effectiveness of the training to the organization and the participants. People tend to act in accordance with the way they are measured, and if they are not measured by real value given, they will not take decisions which increase it at the expense of the way they are measured. Many, but not all, the initiatives needed for strategic implementation are more expensive in costs than traditional approaches to skills training: but the traditional approaches are unlikely to give much help to implementation. Therefore budgets for this type of approach must be set sensibly, and attention must be paid to measuring the outcome.

## Access to Strategic Information

A training initiative may be used to communicate a strategy in depth, to build commitment to it, to change attitudes, to unlearn practices that inhibit the strategy, to develop the host of lower level actions that may be required, and to ensure that the appropriate competencies are developed across the organization. None of this will happen if those designing, developing and implementing the programme are not given full access to top management and all the relevant strategic information. This may seem self-evident, and I would not say it, were it not for my certain knowledge that many organizations do not consider those involved in management development and training to be entitled to such access and information.

### Attitudes to Cascaded Training

In some circumstances it may be appropriate to target a business-driven training initiative at a narrow segment of people. More often the real need is for training that cascades from the top down, not necessarily with an identical programme, so that all concerned with the implementation of the strategy, at whatever level, are involved. There are two aspects to this which may require a different policy than the organization has historically applied. Firstly, there must be a willingness from the top for appropriate cascade training to be developed. One of the few areas where UK companies have applied a widespread cascade approach to use training to implement a policy is in total quality management. (Unfortunately too few of those organizations have looked at all aspects of the necessary culture change, and too many have treated TQM as an add-on, working to different 'rules' to the rest of the organization. This has meant that the TQM initiatives have not always been successful.) There are many other circumstances where implementation demands a cascaded approach, but does not get it.

Many organizations do not attempt to force people to attend courses against their will, and thus many training courses are run for those who volunteer, which is not always the same as those who need the training. The nature of implementation initiatives is that there must be much more compulsion to attend. The whole approach may fail if key people are allowed to opt out. This is even more important when the training is helping to change attitudes as well as provide skills: it is just the people whose attitudes are harmful to implementation who, left to themselves, might decide not to attend the programme (or more likely agree to attend, but do not turn up on the day).

## DESIGNING A TRAINING INITIATIVE

A training initiative which is intended to achieve any of the strategic changes described earlier requires skilful design, and in most cases needs to be specially tailored to the requirements of the company. Although this costs more than a standardized training initiative, the value to the company may be immense.

The successful implementation of a strategy, if it is the right strategy, may be worth millions.

The tailored course may be a new concept to some readers. For this reason the three main approaches to the design of in-company training are first contrasted, following which the main steps in designing and developing a tailored course will be discussed.

## The Standard Course

Although this may be delivered to a company audience, it is essentially the same course that the consultant will give to any other client. The client pays for delivery, and does not finance the development of the course. Often, when a course is put together by an in-house trainer, he or she will use various guest lecturers who employ standard material. Even if the course is completely delivered by internal trainers, it could equally well be given to another company, and includes nothing that is unique to the originating company. This is the cheapest type of course, and in the UK is one of the most common ways of approaching in-house training. It is unlikely to have any value in the sort of corporate change or implementation situations discussed here.

## The Slanted Course

Here the provider uses what are basically standard materials, but spends some time trying to make the course more appropriate for the client. The activities undertaken may vary between merely learning the client's buzzwords to a genuine effort to make the course fit. When carefully approached with the overall objective, this approach may sometimes be appropriate for a particular change situation. There are also many implementation situations where the slanted course is not specific enough to bring about the necessary changes. Most UK suppliers who claim to offer tailored courses are in fact offering slanted courses. There is no common agreement on the meaning of words, and some suppliers do not know the difference anyway.

## The Tailored Course

This is a unique course built around the company situation. Concepts are translated into the context of the company, and a high proportion of the teaching material will be written especially for the situation. There are degrees of tailoring, but generally a course which is intended to implement a strategy, organizational change, or a new policy will be highly tailored.

It is possible for a company to design, develop and deliver its own tailored course using internal resources. Few organizations have the ability or objectivity to do this well, although sadly not all who try know this! Usually this sort of course will be better if experienced outsiders are used. The reason for this becomes apparent when the main phases of work needed to develop a tailored course are considered.

### Clarify the objectives of the initiative

Much care should be taken to determine the aims of the initiative and the target population to whom it is directed. Aims should be realistic and should be related to other management actions needed or being applied. For example, it is unrealistic to think that any training initiative can change the culture of an organization, unless actions are also undertaken to alter the many other management practices and organizational policies which contribute to the culture. If the aim of the programme is to identify all these areas, this should be clear in the objectives. Thought at this stage should be given to how the organization will know that it has been successful.

### Research

The length of this phase will be affected by the objectives of the course, the complexity of the organization, and the quality of diagnostic work that has already been undertaken. Whoever undertakes this task must be able to combine consultancy skills with a knowledge of what will work in a training situation. The purpose of this phase is to understand properly the issue around which the course is to be built, the priorities and weightings of the topics, the culture of the organization, and the needs of participants. Thus it may involve a study of company material, interviews with key managers, group discussions with potential participants, and even surveys within the company.

### Design and specification

After the research phase, the course can be specified in detail. This should result in a document for agreement with the sponsors showing the aims of the course, each topic included (with reasons), the teaching method, the materials to be developed, and the objectives for each topic. Agreement at this stage is essential if wasted effort is to be avoided. The key skill at this stage is in course design.

### Development of the course

This is usually the most time consuming phase, since often the situation faced by the company has to be mirrored in the course materials. These materials have to be researched, written, approved and prepared for teaching. In addition to the appropriate functional, and often multifunctional, knowledge, a mixture of consulting, training and writing skills is needed.

*Piloting*

After a full review has been made of the developed course, it is desirable to run the first session of the course as a pilot. When the course is to be repeated many times, this is easy to organize. There are practical difficulties if the course is to be run only a few times in a short period, and a full pilot may not be possible. In these situations it is important to leave an interval between the first and second sessions of the course so that amendments can be made if these prove necessary. In cases where a pilot is possible, it should be followed by a careful review and any necessary modifications to the course.

*Evaluation*

As a rule training in the UK is rarely evaluated, apart from an end of course review which measures happiness more than it measures effectiveness. A course designed to achieve a corporate result is usually easier to evaluate, because in addition to personal learning objectives, there is a planned change of some sort in actions and results. Where there are only a few sessions of a course planned, the costs of evaluation may be more difficult to justify. If the course is intended to cascade through an entire organization, then a break whilst an evaluation is made may be prudent.

A tailored course may be the most effective way of converting the intention to use training for implementation into concrete action. If done well, it carries little risk of failure and can bring enormous benefits. But whether the course is developed and delivered internally or by outsiders, a professional approach is vital for success.

## CONCLUSIONS

Training is a very powerful tool for the implementation of strategies, and could be used much more widely. It is a tool, not an end in itself, and should form part of an implementation programme.

Many more organizations could apply the principles discussed here to ensure that:

- The vision and strategies are communicated clearly and are understood.
- Those involved in implementation are equipped with the necessary knowledge and skills to play their parts in the process.
- Where helpful those participating in the training initiative may help work through and develop action plans to help implement the strategies.
- Commitment to the strategy arises for the understanding given, and the building of the skills to implement.

The examples of successful training initiatives given in this chapter show what can be achieved. All that usually stands in the way is a blockage in the organization which prevents the strategy being related to training activity, lack of knowledge of the special approaches needed to ensure success, unwillingness to spend time or money on training, and a reluctance of senior managers to be involved in any form of training that cascades down the structure. These are poor reasons for not using what in many situations is one of the most effective implementation tools available.

## REFERENCES

Alexander, L. D. (1985). Successfully Implementing Strategic Decisions, *Long Range Planning* **18**(3), June.

Ascher, K. (1983). *Management Training in Large UK Business Organisations*. Harbridge House, London.

Bolt, J. F. (1985). Tailor Executive Development to Strategy, *Harvard Business Review*, November/December.

Butler, J. E. (1992). Learning Skills for Strategic Change, *Journal of Strategic Change*, **1**(1), January/February.

Coast, C. R. (1995). Central Europe—Management Training, *Team Performance Management*, **1**(2).

Goshal, S., Lefèbure, R. B., Jorgensen, J. and Staniforth, D. (1988). *Scandinavian Airlines Systems (SAS) in 1988*. Case Clearing House of Great Britain and Ireland, Cranfield, No. 389-025-1N.

Hussey, D. E. (1985). Implementing Corporate Strategy: Using Management Education and Training, *Long Range Planning*, October.

Hussey, D. E. (1988). *Management Training and Corporate Strategy*. Pergamon, Oxford.

Hussey, D. E. (1990). Effective Management Training and Development. In: Hussey, D. E. (ed.) *International Review of Strategic Management*, Volume 4, Wiley, Chichester.

Hussey, D. E. (1994). *Strategic Management: Theory and Practice*, 3rd edn. Pergamon, Oxford.

Hussey, D. E. (1995). Business Driven Management Development, *Croner's Journal of Professional HRM*, Issue 0, September (promotional prelaunch issue).

Hussey, D. E. and Lowe, P. L. (eds) (1990). *Key Issues in Management Training*. Kogan Page, London.

Lorenz, C. (1986a). ICL: Metamorphosis of a European Laggard, *Financial Times*, 12 May.

Lorenz, C. (1986b). ICL: A Painful Process of Change, *Financial Times*, 14 May.

Lorenz, C. (1986c). ICL: The Power of Saturation Training, *Financial Times*, 16 May.

Lusterman, S. (1985). *Trends in Corporate Education and Training*, Report No. 870, The Conference Board, USA.

Mason, A. (1993). *Management Training and Development in Medium-sized UK Business Organisations*. Harbridge Consulting Group Ltd, London.

Nilsson, W. P. (1987). *Achieving Strategic Goals Through Executive Development*. Addison-Wesley, Reading, Massachusetts.

Peters, T. J. and Waterman, R. H. (1982). *In Search of Excellence*. Harper and Row, New York.

Rose, D. (1989). Woolworth's Drive for Excellence, *Long Range Planning*, **21**(1), February.

Scase, R. and Goffee, R. (1989). *Reluctant Managers: Their Work and Lifestyles*. Unwin Hyman, London.

Tovey, L. (1991). *Management Training and Development in Large UK Business Organisations*. Harbridge Consulting Group Ltd, London.

# 16

# MEETING BUSINESS AND MANAGEMENT TRAINING AND DEVELOPMENT NEEDS THROUGH COMPETENCY ASSESSMENT

**L. E. A. Tovey**

*Consultant,*
*Harbridge Consulting Group Ltd,*

Recent years have seen the development of a plethora of approaches to competency assessment. Whilst many serve a purpose, it is arguably not that of meeting long-term business objectives. In this chapter, I hope to dispel some of the confusion which has arisen and to strengthen the case for a strategic approach to competency assessment. I have begun with a comment on the development of the management training and development market in the UK, which leads into the inception of the concept of competency assessment in the UK. Linked to the comment on the development of the management training and development market is an explanation of why I believe a strategic approach to competency assessment is the only route to take if real business value is to be gained. An outline of the approach is given, explaining how the output can form the basis of an organization's human resource development strategy.

*The Implementation Challenge*, Edited by D. E. Hussey
© 1996 John Wiley & Sons Ltd

## LINKING MANAGEMENT TRAINING AND
## DEVELOPMENT TO CORPORATE STRATEGY

*The Making of British Managers* (Constable and McCormick, 1987) and *The Making of Managers* (Handy, 1987) represented a watershed in the history of management development. These were the first reports on the subject to achieve significant public recognition. The reports highlighted that management training in the UK was elitist, sparingly applied and lacked relevance in the face of increased competition. As such, they heightened the awareness that although 'best practice' in management training and development existed, it was thinly spread.

The above publications have generated considerable discussion and flowing from this there has been a shift in emphasis. There is a growing recognition of the need to redefine management training and development as a strategic issue and therefore that organizations should concentrate on refining the link between management development and business objectives and strategies.

This growing recognition is illustrated by the conclusions of two of Harbridge Consulting Group Ltd's research initiatives. Since 1983 we have undertaken a continuing programme of research into management development in the UK, and in 1983 and 1991 published reports on management training and development in large UK business organizations (Ascher, 1983; Tovey, 1991).

The sample of companies interviewed were drawn from *The Times Top 150*, plus large organizations in the financial and public sector. In the 1991 report, 54% of respondents stated that management training and development strategies were explicitly linked to corporate strategy and objectives. This represented a considerable improvement since the 1983 report when only a third claimed such a linkage. However, in the 1991 report there were still 46% of respondents who saw the link as inadequate. It is a positive sign that these respondents had an awareness of this need. In the 1983 report, 20% felt that training should be based entirely on individual needs.

The greater importance given to management development can also be seen in an increase in the level of involvement and support shown by senior management. For example:

- Some 67% of respondents stated that one or more board members contributed towards formulation of training and development policy.
- Management development issues are being more frequently discussed at board level than was the case 8 years ago.
- Six of the companies interviewed have recently set up executive or steering committees with responsibility to decide on and oversee management development activities.
- In a number of cases the chief executive officer (CEO) played a very active role in management development.

It is not only in the UK that there have been major changes in attitude towards management development but also across the whole of central and Eastern Europe. For example, the first MBA programmes have recently been introduced in Germany. It is noteworthy that the EC Phare programme is supporting the training of managers in many of the former communist countries.

A number of factors, at least in British business, have contributed to the need to link management development more closely to business objectives. Each is briefly explained below in terms of its contribution to this recognition. No judgement is made on the relative magnitude of the contribution and the list should not be viewed as exhaustive.

- Business conditions increasingly make it essential for organizations to give a higher priority to human resource management and development in their strategic thinking. Personnel departments previously had a low status in that there was a tendency for them to be seen as a separate department rather than as part of the business process. Although awareness of this issue is increasing, it is still a problem. The Price Waterhouse Cranfield project on international strategic human resource management (1991), which surveyed a broad sample of personnel directors in 10 countries (5,449 usable responses were obtained) established that in Switzerland, Denmark, Germany, France, Italy and the UK as many as one in seven organizations do not involve the personnel function in the formulation of corporate strategy, even at the consultative stage.

    Furthermore, the report states that in the UK almost three out of 10 organizations, and in Germany nearly four out of 10 organizations are without any kind of personnel strategy. Even where there are personnel strategies the impact may be less than their existence would imply. Often such strategies are not translated into work programmes and deadlines for the personnel function. The report concludes that

    > whatever the explanation, it is clear that it is only a minority of personnel departments across Europe that establish clear policies, translate them into work plans and then evaluate the results. Together with the findings on the lack of influence of HR specialists on corporate strategy, this raises a substantial question mark over the extent of strategic human resource management in Europe.

However, the questioning of the status quo by those organizations at the leading edge of human resource management and development has inspired radical changes in approach. In these organizations there is an emphasis on building human resource functions with greater strategic capabilities and a deeper understanding of business objectives and the actions that need to be taken in order to achieve them.

- The publication of major reports such as those of Constable and McCormick (1987) and Handy (1987) as mentioned above. In addition, other less widely acclaimed research has also made a valuable contribution.
- The pressures of the 1990s and the need to find new and innovative ways in which to respond to and cope with the issues arising from these pressures. Examples are given below:
  — Demographic profiles in many countries which suggest a shortage of school leavers.
  — The increased diversity in the workforce, partly as a solution to expected labour shortages (although the impact of shortages has been delayed by the current recession) but also due to the increased career progression of women and the cultural diversity resulting from globalization and the impact of European harmonization.
  — The enormous change facing most organizations as they meet intensified competition, respond to the need to be more cost effective and at the same time meet enhanced customer demands for service and quality. Almost every aspect of this change has a human dimension.
  — The considerable delayering and downsizing initiatives many companies have chosen or been forced to embark upon render the investment in their remaining people resources more important.

All these factors support the case for drawing management development strategy and the resulting actions much closer to the corporate strategy than is the case in many organizations.

The recognition of the need for a closer link between management development and corporate strategy is further illustrated by a change in the investment pattern of organizations. Hommen and Tijmstra (1990) state that investment in organization design and management development has 'traditionally' been much smaller than in technology and marketing. Companies are redressing the balance as they see the former as part of the competitive strategy. There has been an evolution of new organizational structures and designs to cope with external demands and pressures. Hommen and Tijmstra (1990) state that the trends can be illustrated as follows:

| From: | To: |
|---|---|
| Bureaucratic | Customer orientated |
| Hierarchical | Networking |
| Product orientated | Relationship orientated |
| Power culture | Achievement culture |

In the new design, management development has a more significant role to play. The new structures aim to create an environment where each individual can contribute to his/her full potential.

The factors described indicate a growing awareness of the need to link management development actions more closely to the achievement of corporate strategy. However whilst companies at the forefront of management development are striving to refine this link, they recognize that there is some way to go (in the Harbridge Consulting Group Ltd 1991 report on management training and development, 46% of respondents saw the link as inadequate). This has led to some searching questions being asked about exactly what constitutes good management practice.

The research and discussions surrounding the question of what makes a good manager in the 1990s has resulted in a redefinition of the managerial role. As organizations continue to change and adapt to new circumstances, the evolving strategies and cultures will place new demands on this role. Defining the requirements of the role, and ensuring that managers are equipped to meet them is central to the competency ethos. The idea is a simple one: if an organization's managers are equipped with the right competencies to carry out their jobs effectively, corporate success should not only be improved, but also accelerated. However, as is often the case with a new concept, a plethora of approaches have been developed, some highly effective, others of a more questionable nature.

## SELECTING THE RIGHT APPROACH TO COMPETENCY ASSESSMENT FOR THE ORGANIZATION IN QUESTION

The various approaches to competency assessment can be divided into two main categories: generic and tailored. Although there are a number of benefits to the generic approach (or disadvantages to the tailored approach, strategic or otherwise), which will be explained later, it will frequently be inadequate. Some of the points leading to this conclusion are given below:

- It is unlikely that a generic approach would meet fully the needs of the specific business, as it cannot take account of the critical success factors of the business which relate to its commercial objectives.
- The likelihood except at the lower managerial levels of the organization that competencies should be the same regardless of the industry sector or organization is small. Even within one organization different clusters of competencies, depending on functional and business differences, will often exist.
- A generic approach will unavoidably result in an incomplete picture. The missing information concerns a company's culture. It is often the case that certain dimensions of an organization's culture or climate inhibit the development, or even the very existence, of competencies that the

organization requires and is trying to promote. As Jill Fairbairns (1991) points out

> only by introducing this perspective can a more reliable assessment be obtained of the fit between individual priorities and organisation priorities.

- A great deal of controversy has surrounded the Management Charter Initiative approach, which is generic.[1] There is much evidence to indicate that many organizations have some reservations about the applicability of national competencies to a specific situation. In the January 1992 issue *of Personnel Management*, a study was published stating that 70% of respondents maintained that the MCI had not influenced the way their managers are trained and developed. As the Council for National Academic Awards (CNAA) points out in its *Review of Management Education* (1992), although the sample was self-selected from readers of the magazine, they did represent mainly large- and medium-sized employers. Only 8% said that they definitely did not agree with the MCI in principle, and a further 21% thought it not relevant to their needs. The conclusion of the CNAA was that

> many, therefore may join late if MCI makes a good case for its value to employers.

More recently in the 'Appointments' section of *The Times*, Widget Finn (1993) reports that

> Employers have been slow to adopt the MCI middle-management standards, which form the basis for national vocational qualifications (NVQ) at level 5. The MCI estimates that there has been a 10 per cent take-up from the 500 companies it has contacted.

- According to the MCI, the process of assessment will be placed in the hands of accredited institutions. Inevitably this means taking the process away from management. Yet management development practitioners have been striving for the greater involvement of line managers as it is they who should help to ensure that management development is directly linked to the needs of the business and that the learning process is continued and action taken back in the workplace.

---

[1]The Management Charter Institute was established in 1988 to improve the quality, relevance and accessibility of management education and development. The MCI is a non-profit-making organization, funded by subscriptions from private and public sector organizations and a grant from the Department of Employment. Corporate members pay subscriptions to the MCI which are proportional to the size of their organization. Membership application forms are available from the MCI Centre, Russell Square House, 10–12 Russell Square, London, WC1B 5. Tel: 0171-872 9000

- In today's constantly changing environment competencies need to be updated on a continuous basis. It is easier to do this with organization-specific competencies than with those designed to be generally applicable. By the time the latter have been re-evaluated, they will already be out of date.

In certain circumstances, however, these disadvantages will not apply. The appropriate competency assessment approach or that of 'best-fit' may need to vary to meet the needs of a particular situation. At lower managerial levels of an organization a generic approach becomes more appropriate. This is also the case in traditional, more hierarchical businesses. These points are best illustrated by means of a diagram (see Figure 16.1).

In a relatively stable industry and in structured, hierarchical organizations—where managerial performance can be more easily defined and measured uniformly—a generic approach would probably be more appropriate. On the other hand, where the business environment is changing rapidly and organization structures are more complex and differentiated, a tailored strategic approach is likely to be more applicable. In many instances, a balance between the two approaches may be required to meet the specific needs of the organization and to ensure that sufficient flexibility exists to update competencies as business conditions change.

The idea of 'best fit' can also be applied to organizational level. As Figure 16.1 illustrates, the tailored strategic approach becomes less applicable at lower levels of the organization as the impact of strategy on individual jobs becomes

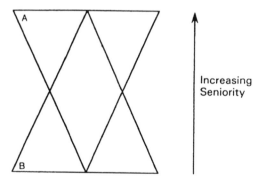

Triangle A: Impact of Strategy on Organization Level

Increasing
Seniority

Triangle B: Appropriateness of Generic Approach
vis à vis Organizational Level

**Figure 16.1**   Organizational Competency Focus

less significant (triangle A). Conversely, a generic approach becomes less appropriate higher in the organization as the impact of strategy on individual jobs increases (triangle B). As organizations in the 1990s move more to flatter structures, and the impact of strategy on jobs and individual behaviour becomes more apparent, the case for a more strategic tailored approach to competency assessment is strengthened.

There are, however, a number of disadvantages associated with the tailored approach strategic or otherwise, for example:

- It can be perceived as costly, time consuming and, as 'reinventing the wheel', although arguably it is more cost effective.
- Some organizations find it easier to secure senior management commitment to a generic approach, as considerably less senior management time will be required for this than for a tailored approach.
- There may be difficulties tying in the competencies identified through a tailored competency assessment with, for example, NVQs and the MCI management standards, should the organization wish to do this.

In my opinion, the advantages of a tailored strategic approach far outweigh the disadvantages. Some of these have already been discussed in relation to the generic approach, such as the linkage to critical success factors of the business, the greater involvement of line managers and the ease of updating. An additional important advantage is that of securing the commitment of all employees across the organization. It requires the involvement and support of senior management as well as the lower organizational levels who share in the development of the competency analysis. There is thus a greater likelihood of gaining commitment to the outcome than with a generic approach. A strategic tailored approach can subsequently be applied to all aspects of a company's human resource development strategy providing data to underpin selection, assessment, development and succession. In business conditions where strategic focus is an imperative, job competencies which reflect the critical success factors of the company become essential. Where this occurs the link between management development and corporate strategy will be strengthened, enhancing both individual and business effectiveness. Where standards are not set in the context of the business needs and do not enshrine the strategic drivers for the organization, effort is likely to be individual rather than business focused.

## THE RIGHT APPROACH TO COMPETENCY ASSESSMENT

If one examines the alternative approaches to competency assessment that organizations adopt there appear to be three main options:

1.   **Strategically driven approach**
     Defining corporate-wide competencies which will be derived from the strategic drivers of the business and which can be cascaded to all management levels and business functions. These core competencies are regarded as critical to business success and all employees must be able to identify with and demonstrate the behaviours involved to function effectively in the organization's structure and culture, and therefore achieve the company's mission.

2.   **Job related approach**
     Taking the individual job as the unit for analysis and focusing on developing a skills profile around the technical, professional, business, and managerial requirements of the job. These competencies will vary by job category, level and function and will guide the employee's efforts towards successful job performance.

3.   **Hybrid approach**
     Combining both of the approaches outlined above.
     Clearly the ideal scenario is to have specific, meaningful job-related competencies which are also related to the strategic needs of the business.

Harbridge Consulting Group Ltd have developed an approach which consists of five main building blocks, the components of which are selected and blended depending on the situation and needs. A brief overview of each stage of the approach is provided below (see Figure 16.2).

**1.   The Strategic Review**

Stage one is concerned with gaining a full understanding of the strategic requirements of the business and entails gaining a clear understanding of the business environment, the corporate mission and the business strategy being pursued. This represents the starting point for defining the strategic areas of competence for the business.

**2.   Strategic Areas of Competence**

It is essential at this stage to clarify and confirm the critical success factors for the business strategy so that areas of strategic competence can be identified. A strategic area of competence is defined as an area in which the organization must be competent if it is to succeed in its mission and which has implications for individual capabilities. For the organization to succeed, it is necessary for it to possess capabilities in each strategic area of competence. Together they are sufficient to achieve the mission. The list must therefore reflect the absolute minimum number of areas in which capabilities are required to accomplish the mission.

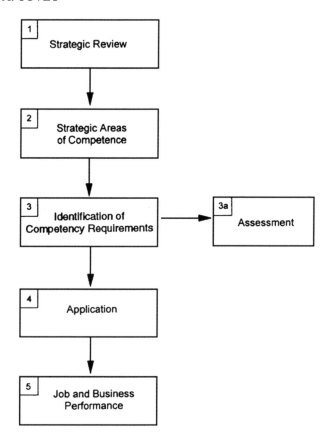

© Harbridge Consulting Group Limited 1992

**Figure 16.2**   A Strategic Approach to Competency Assessment

### 3.   Competency Requirements

Competency requirements refer to the discrete dimensions of behaviour that lie behind success or failure in a particular job or job category. Such dimensions may include knowledge, skills, behaviours and other factors which can be precisely defined and assessed for management development purposes and will be influenced by organizational level and culture.

Competency requirements are derived from three sources:

- *the requirements of the business* as reflected in the strategic areas of competence;

- *the implications for the job itself*, both in terms of business, professional and technical requirements as well as personal and managerial and leadership competencies;
- and from the *organization* in terms of the culture—and therefore the behaviour required—and the level at which the individual operates.

### 3a. Assessing Competency Requirements

By measuring the difference between competency requirements and the extent to which these are possessed by employees (whether by self-assessment, peer/ subordinate assessment, or through assessment centres), the size of the training and development gap can be established and compared to the management's current training and development provision.

### 4. Application

The effectiveness of these activities will depend upon a clear description of critical competencies which must be derived from the strategic requirements of the business. They will be explained in more detail later under 'The Human Resource Development Strategy'. The extent to which this human resource development cycle (see Figure 16.3) is successful eliminates the need for unplanned internal placement and external recruitment.

### 5. Job and Business Performance

For the competency assessment to be successful, that is, impact on job and therefore business performance, it needs to be built around a sound strategic understanding of the company's business. For this reason the Harbridge Consulting Group approach allows for the need to think flexibly around a particular situation and to be able to adopt the most appropriate methodology. The tools available are therefore selected and blended depending on an organization's situation and needs.

## APPLICATION

Having outlined the approach, I would like to discuss in more detail how an organization can use the output, firstly, to orchestrate organizational change and secondly as a basis for management development strategy.

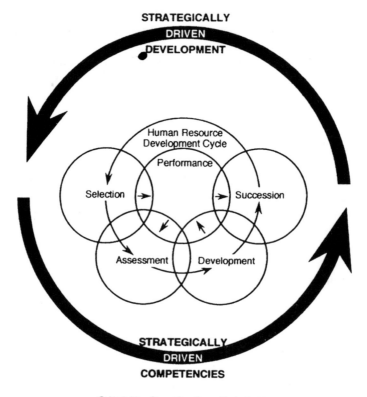

© *Harbridge Consulting Group Limited 1992*

**Figure 16.3**   The Human Resource Development Cycle

## ORCHESTRATING ORGANIZATIONAL CHANGE

Suppose an organization is in the process of redefining its mission and identifying strategic areas of competence which will be both necessary and sufficient to ensure it will achieve that mission. It will subsequently need to ensure that the culture, i.e. the underlying pattern of values, beliefs and assumptions which shape behaviour, supports the identification, acquisition and nurturing of the knowledge, skills and behaviours required for success in the identified strategic areas of competence. Corporate behaviours can be defined which will be related to the strategic drivers of the business and which all employees must be able to demonstrate in order to function effectively in the organization's structure and culture and achieve the company mission.

In reality, the pattern of events will rarely be so clear-cut and well defined, but in today's fast changing and highly technical environment a framework which will shape employee behaviour in line with business requirements needs to be supplied.

Defining these core competencies and promoting them will ensure that every individual can relate to the company mission and strategy and will reinforce and further develop the new evolving culture so that it becomes standard practice.

## THE HUMAN RESOURCE DEVELOPMENT STRATEGY

In today's fast changing and highly technical environment an organization's people represents the primary opportunity for developing a sustainable competitive advantage. If this concept is accepted, it follows that organizations need to strive for competitive superiority in the areas of selection, assessment, development and succession. As shown in Figure 16.3 a competency assessment approach such as this provides the foundation on which an organization can build an effective human resource development strategy.

### Selection

This is the fundamental building block, in that no amount of training and development can substitute for lack of raw talent. Effective selection will depend on a clear definition of critical competencies.

### Assessment

Assessment takes two forms. Firstly, there is assessment of current job performance which is an ongoing responsibility and which culminates in the formal annual appraisal. Secondly, there is an assessment of the employee's potential which guides career direction and planning. It makes sense to assess employees against key competencies which relate to the critical success factors of the business. Standards must be set according to business needs.

### Development

Development of individuals is based on the assessment of their performance and potential. It impacts directly on current job performance as well as preparing them for succession to future positions. Current and future business challenges have been analysed in stages 1 and 2, to determine what knowledge and skills the organization will require. Training and development initiatives should therefore be shaped according to the requirements of the individual *and* the identified criteria for corporate effectiveness.

**Succession**

Succession planning helps to ensure that identified replacements are available to meet the organizational requirements of the business. The extent to which this is successful eliminates the need for unplanned internal placement and external recruitment.

Relating succession planning needs to the strategic drivers of the business will ensure that high-potential individuals are equipped with the right competencies to ensure business success.

Having outlined how the approach can be applied in theory, I felt it would further the reader's understanding to conclude this chapter with a case study.

## COMPANY A: CASE STUDY—AN INTERNATIONAL AUTOMOTIVE COMPANY

In 1989 the automotive industry was starting to experience the worst trading conditions for years. Whilst downsizing and restructuring were inevitable if company A was to remain competitive, labour conditions meant that retention and development of high-calibre people was essential. Managerial training therefore had to change in line with the new business situation, which meant a review of existing management training to ensure focus and relevance.

The following objectives were agreed for the assignment, which took place in 1990:

1. To identify and understand the key external factors impacting on the automotive industry, and company A in paticular, in the 1990s.
2. To establish the most important strategic areas of competence for company A in the 1990s.
3. As a result of (1) and (2), to formulate the training initiatives required to address the key issues in the European sales operations.
4. To determine priority and other competency requirements by country, level and function, in terms of:
   • The organization's need to respond to market conditions.
   • Individual training and development needs.
5. To assess the impact of organizational structure and culture on company A's ability to implement change through management training and development.
6. To assess both the quantity and quality of training currently provided, by source, in order to identify the gap between current provision and future requirements.

The assignment focused on a specific group of company A's employees, namely middle managers and potential managers in vehicle sales, parts and service activities in several European companies. The desired outcome was a comprehensive assessment of training and development needs against a set of strategically defined competency requirements.

The team for this assignment consisted of five consultants.

## The Approach

The first stage of the assignment was a major review of strategic documentation relating to the automotive industry. This was analysed using industry structure analysis and the issues facing the automotive industry identified. A briefing pack was prepared for each consultant to use throughout the assignment which included:

- Company A—company information, including background and history
- Industry trends
  — opportunities and threats
  — other
- Strategies of international automotive companies
- Market data forecasts
- Industry map—European automotive industry
- Company A—strengths and weaknesses
- General information about the automotive industry

In order to gain a deeper understanding of the business issues facing company A in the 1990s from which strategic areas of competence should be identified, 85 face-to-face interviews were conducted with managers and staff at five different organizational levels. These interviews were conducted in Britain, Germany, Spain, and the Netherlands as well as company headquarters. The programme included an interview with each of the managing directors of the four national companies.

To ensure consistency of information an interview guide was developed for use by the consulting team. Interviewees were briefed on the background to the project and the purpose of the interview. A summary of areas included is shown here:

- Background of interviewee (biographical data).
- Strategic and operating issues, including:
  — critical issues facing the automotive industry and prioritization of these
  — the situation in the 1990s
  — current understanding of the issues
  — competitors.
- Strengths and weaknesses of company A.

- Company A's knowledge of and response to market place issues.
- The contribution of training, including
  — quantity and quality of training
  — impediments to training
  — sources of training.
- Individual training and development needs

After the responses had been collated and subjected to content analysis seven strategic areas of competence were identified:

- **Business knowledge and skills**. Areas of expertise and knowledge in core business functions (such as finance, strategic management, marketing) which help provide the company A manager with a balanced commercial perspective.
- **Managing the dealer network**. The organizational, business and 'people' skills needed to develop relationships with, and provide more effective support to, a dealer network with rising expectations and increasing levels of professionalism.
- **Europe and 1992**. A practical appreciation of the impact of 1992 on the organization and the knowledge, skills and understanding needed to perform in the post-1992 era.
- **Human resources management**. The 'people' management and leadership skills needed to create and maintain a highly committed workforce in an organization facing tougher competition and increasing pressures for higher productivity and cost effectiveness.
- **Information technology (IT)**. A clear understanding of how managers can use IT to contribute towards the achievement of business objectives supported by the necessary personal skills, knowledge and confidence to exploit this in current and future positions.
- **Innovation and change**. The capacity to create and implement fresh ideas and new ways of working so that the organization can anticipate and adapt to external changes and competitive developments.
- **Organizational communications**. The effective flow of information up, down and across the organization in order that individuals can relate their efforts to a common goal and have adequate information to perform their jobs.

Given the geographic scope of the assignment, and the large population to be covered, it was decided that a self-assessment questionnaire would be the most effective instrument to use. The questionnaire was subsequently structured around the seven areas of strategic competence listed here. Each area in the questionnaire consisted of a number of clusters with each cluster being subdivided into a series of individual competency requirements, for example:

*Strategic area of competence* : business knowledge and skills
*Cluster* : marketing
*Individual competancy* : understanding of present and future customer requirements
: understanding the strengths and weaknesses of the competition.

Respondents were asked to select the three strategic areas of competence which they considered would be of most importance to company A in the 1990s and to rank them.

In each section of the questionnaire relating to a strategic area of competence respondents were asked to assess:

1.   Their existing level of personal competence in relation to their current position.
2.   The level of personal competence required to perform in their position in the 1990s.

A further section of the questionnaire examined respondents' perceptions of the impact of organizational structure and culture on the way their company operated in Europe. This section covered several areas, including:

● The extent to which the structure of the organization was considered to help or hinder achievement of certain factors.
● The sharing of information across organizational boundaries.
● Actions leading to success and failure in the company.
● The treatment of individuals.
● Leadership attitudes.

The final section of the questionnaire sought views about the quantity and quality of current training provision in the company, both at European and national levels.

The inclusion of a biographical section in the questionnaire enabled a number of different data cuts to be made to allow comparison between countries, functions and levels. As the questionnaire relied on self-assessment, participants were strongly recommended to score the questions after discussion with their boss, colleagues and subordinates.

The questionnaire was completed by those individuals interviewed in the four countries, and by an additional 85 respondents, ensuring that positions and levels in each group were statistically represented to maintain consistency and accuracy of information.

Tracking of returns was coordinated through contact partners in each country. The responses were analysed by means of a tailored computer program, which was used to identify priority and other training needs.

In analysing the responses to the first section of the questionnaire (the ranking of the strategic areas of competence) a weighting system was used. A formula was devised where an area was awarded:

- Four points each time it was rated as the most important.
- Two points each time it was rated as the second most important.
- One point each time it was rated as the third most important.

The scores for each area were totalled to produce an overall weighting and therefore priority ranking. All data were computer analysed by total survey population and also by each of the population samples identified in the biographical data section of the questionnaire. An assessment was then made, using a 5-point scale, of each of the existing levels of competence and the levels of competence needed for the 1990s. The difference between the ratings for existing levels of competence and the ratings for competencies needed for the 1990s for each strategic area of competence was used to gauge the level of training need using the matrix illustrated in Figure 16.4 where: P=Priority training need, where existing level of competence is rated at 1 or 2 (none or very low) and level of competence needed is at 5 (high), or where existing level of competence is rated at 1 and level of competence needed for the 1990s is rated at 4; N=other training need: includes all other responses where existing level of competence is rated lower than the level of competence needed for the 1990s;

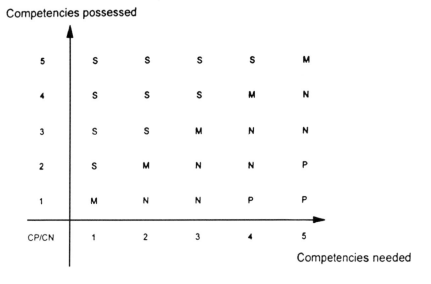

**Figure 16.4**   Identifying the Competency Gap

M = match, where existing level of competence and level of competence needed for the 1990s are rated as being equal; S = surplus, where existing level of competence is rated higher than that needed for the 1990s.

Analysis of the questionnaire results produced a significant number of findings. These provided the client organization with information about:

- Those *strategic areas of competence* perceived as most important to company A in the 1990s.
- Perceived *priority* and secondary *training needs* for the population as a whole and for specific subgroups.
- The impact of *organizational structure and culture* on company A's ability to respond to changing business requirements.
- The extent to which current training provision was meeting existing needs.

The italicized items are expanded on here.

## Strategic areas of competence

Innovation and change and human resources management were identified as the most important strategic areas of competence for company A in the 1990s. These were closely followed by business knowledge and skills.

## Priority training needs

- Relatively high levels of training need were found for both innovation and change and human resource management, with more than 50% of respondents identifying some competence shortfall in many of the individual competency requirements in these clusters. Very little of the training need was, however, identified as 'priority training need'. This is significant, but not surprising given the weighting of the strategic areas of competence.
- Information technology and Europe and 1992 were the areas regarded as the least important. They were, however, the areas for which the greatest training need was identified. On average, 40% of respondents emerged with some training need (competence shortfall) for the information technology cluster, whilst an average of 65% of respondents reported a shortfall in the Europe and 1992 cluster.

Perhaps more importantly, the levels of priority training need were significantly higher for these two clusters than any other.

## Organizational structure and culture

### Structure
- It was considered that the structure of the organization was a considerable hindrance to risk taking and innovative approaches to problem solving.

- A clear majority considered the structure to be a hindrance to market focus and responsiveness to changes in the market-place. About half the respondents also believed that the company structure hindered customer focus and encouraged a reactive attitude towards the market.

There was clear indication that, given the changes in business and market requirements, the structure of the organization was likely to impede its effectiveness and act as a brake on remedial training efforts.

### Culture

- There was a wide discrepancy between what respondents perceived to be actually needed to succeed within company A and what they believed *should* be needed. Openness, teamwork, support for one's subordinates, creativity/flexibility, customer focus, quality and taking the long-term view were the dominant factors which respondents believed should be needed for success but which currently were not. They accepted that working hard, performing well and being loyal to the company were, and indeed should be, needed to succeed. However, they also felt that success within the company depended too much on fitting the 'company mould', supporting one's boss, minimizing mistakes and risk-taking, and getting results at any cost.
- Over 50% of the survey population believed that senior management did little to promote openness, trust and teamwork. The majority, however, felt that they could rely on their immediate boss to support them, and to seek their ideas and opinions. Nearly half the respondents also felt their immediate bosses allowed them to explore and proceed with their own approaches and solutions to problems.
- Some 90% of respondents believed that the organization's culture was one in which managers exercised all power and authority. A total of 48% believed that other levels were permitted to contribute information, but another 42% believed that the prevailing attitude was either that 'managers exercise power as of right' or that 'managers know best'.

The findings concerning the organizational structure and culture were very significant, given that innovation and change and human resource management were rated as the two most important strategic areas of competence to company A in the 1990s.

## CONCLUDING REMARKS

A competency assessment approach such as this provides the foundation on which an organization can build an effective management development strategy. For this to be successful it needs to be built around a sound strategic understanding of the organization's business. As this strategy is implemented, individual line managers have responsibility for applying the development cycle by basing their selection, assessment, development and succession actions on strategically derived competencies which impact on job and therefore business performance. Avoiding unnecessary competency clutter and complexity, and ensuring that the competency requirements remain strategically focused, will help ensure that the competency assessment becomes the shared realm of human resources staff and line management.

## ACKNOWLEDGEMENT

Laura Tovey would like to acknowledge the support of Fred Cannon, Director, Human Resource Practice Area, who originated many of the approaches discussed in this article.

## REFERENCES

Ascher, K. (1983). *Management Training in Large UK Business Organisations*, Harbridge Consulting Group Ltd, London.
Constable, J. and McCormick, R. (1987). *The Making of British Managers*, British Institute of Management, London.
Council for National Academic Awards (1992). *Review of Management Education*, October.
Fairbairns, J. (1991). Plugging the gap in training needs analysis, *Personnel Management*, February.
Finn, W. (1993). Is the top talent measurable? *The Times*, 1 April.
Handy, C. (1987). *The Making of Managers*, National Economic Development Council, HMSO, London.
Hommen, J. and Tijmstra, S. (1990). New challenges for management development, *European Management Journal*, **8**(3).
Personnel Management/Price Waterhouse survey. (1992). Management Charter has had little impact so far, *Personnel Management*, January.
Price Waterhouse (1991). The Price Waterhouse Cranfield Project on International Strategic Human Resource Management, Cranfield.
Tovey, L. (1991). Management Training and Development in Large UK Business Organisations, Harbridge Consulting Group Ltd, London.

# 17

# DEVELOPING COMPETENCIES THAT DRIVE BUSINESS PERFORMANCE

**Fred Cannon**

*Director, Harbridge Consulting Group*

- The need to strengthen the link between business strategy and management development becomes critical in achieving strategic change.
- This chapter shows how to replace managers' 'learning by accident' with 'learning by experience'.
- An argument is given for a strategic approach to competencies.
- Against this background the author provides an explicit case history of how one multinational turned management development into a source of competitive advantage.
- The focal point of the approach is business-driven management development.

Using management development as a competitive weapon has been an emerging theme in recent years. In this connection, a number of writers have focused on the need to strengthen the link between business strategy and management development. In my own firm's research, this need was identified in the mid-1980s (Ascher, 1983) and has been comprehensively described by Hussey (1988). Key articles have appeared arguing that management development is a major strategic tool and should be integrated with business strategy to enhance organizational ability to compete in a complex and changing world (e.g. Margerison, 1991).

As Osbaldeston and Barham (1992) have argued, putting management development at the heart of business strategy enables the organization to build

*The Implementation Challenge*, Edited by D. E. Hussey
© 1996 John Wiley & Sons Ltd

its competence and to create the learning organization essential for future global competition.

My own experience of working with international companies on both consulting and educational assignments suggests that until more recently the rhetoric has got somewhat ahead of the reality. I believe that this situation is now changing and that in response to some hard questions being asked about the contribution of management development, talk is beginning to be translated into action.

These changes are occurring because the business requirements themselves are changing. Increasingly, and rightly, the pressure to take costs out of the business, to become more productive, to achieve returns on a shorter time scale is being transmitted to the world of management development. As a result, chief executives are being forced into an assessment of the people implications of the business strategy and into developing human resource actions that are expected to impact on the bottom line. For those of us who chose to enter human resources rather than 'personnel' this is good news indeed.

Management development has had an easy time. Many line executives in my experience have not been entirely sure what the term means. Neither have they been able to get a straight answer from those who are supposed to know—the practitioners. In the case study described later in this article, bright, articulate people had difficulties in getting to grips with what management development meant to them, what was inside the boundaries of management development and what was not.

The situation is changing. The well articulated conceptual links are being replaced by action on the ground. Firms are beginning to sharpen the link between their business strategies and what they expect their human resource folks to deliver. Furthermore, this has to make sense because it matches the lessons of experience shared by us all.

## THE LESSONS OF EXPERIENCE

We all know the facts. Only a minute part of a manager's time is spent in the classroom.

If we lump together learning from assignments with learning from bosses or others then up to 75%—the bulk of development—takes place on the job. What we also know, although it's probably less well documented, is that much of this learning takes place by chance. Putting it simply, we have let our managers learn by accident.

Our challenge is to replace learning by accident with genuine learning through experience. Moreover to do this in a way which goes with the flow of the business, avoiding too much structure and unnecessary paraphernalia. As the authors (McCall et al, 1988) of a recent study of how successful executives develop on the job expressed it:

> All too often management development is viewed as a bag full of devices; career path planning, human resource planning, mentoring programmes, rotational systems, development plans on the appraisal form, training courses, education centres, early identification programmes . . . it is instead an organisation's conscious effort to provide its managers with opportunities to learn, grow and change, in the hope of producing over the long term a cadre of managers with the skills necessary to function effectively in that organisation.

Replacing learning by accident by learning from experience requires new thinking about management development. In this new agenda of business-driven management development, learning and development occur as part and parcel of normal business life rather than as a 'bolted on' activity. But for this to happen in a way which connects to the business requires coherence, clarity and focus on the critical skills needed by individuals at all levels in the organization. The identification, development and application of competencies that link the business strategy to individual performance and development, and to business performance improvement is what makes management development business driven (Figure 17.1).

## MANAGEMENT COMPETENCIES

At the end of last year, Harbridge House ran a series of seminars around the theme of strategically driven competencies. A number of important points emerged from this experience.

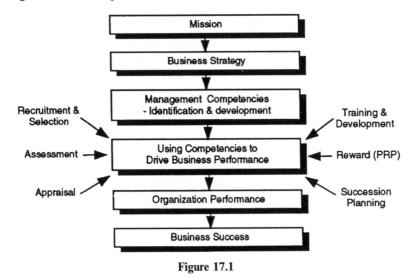

**Figure 17.1**

Firstly, most people felt that management competencies were becoming a minefield. Indeed, a number of organizations were beginning to complain of 'competency clutter'. Whilst the principle seemed good, the complexity that followed put questionable value on the level of effort involved.

Secondly, opinions were split around the generic versus organization specific approaches. My own view, well documented by Tovey (1994), is that both have a place but that in the context of flatter organizations and business-linked management development, the *process* of identifying and developing company specific competencies adds very significant value.

Thirdly, there was a need to distinguish between what one might call job-based competencies from competencies that could be termed strategic or organization-wide. Whilst the line between the two is not surprisingly blurred, there are some important differences in orientation.

Clearly, a job or group of jobs will require a specific set of competencies to optimize performance. These competencies may vary by job category, level or function. When we are addressing such a well-defined population the resulting competencies and behavioural indicators clearly help the process of performance management.

The problem starts when this approach is extended to derive competencies for the management population as a whole. The end result can be too rooted in the present and be so general as to be meaningless for effective performance development. It is my belief that for competencies to drive business performance they must be derived from the people implications of the business strategy and apply across all levels and functions of the business. In short, they should define in crystal clear terms the behaviours required by everyone in the conduct of their jobs. These competencies will drive individual performance and development so as to convert strategic priorities into organizational performance and business success.

Being clear about the critical skills needed for both individual and business success is a simple but important principle. If we are to bet everything on our people—and we should—then putting this principle into practice lies at the heart of developing competencies that drive business performance.

## MAKING IT HAPPEN

Premier Foods Europe is the name I will use in this chapter for an existing multibillion international food company.[1] Created through a number of mergers, the company employs over 30 000 people across all European countries. With a clearly stated mission to become the most successful branded

---

[1]Premier Foods is the pseudonym for an actual operating company

food company the top management team has nailed its colours to the mast with respect to the priority it places on people and their development.

The story starts with a commitment to assess the current state of management development across the various countries, functions and management levels. In recognition of the need for change, characterized by an increasingly competitive business environment, the company commissioned Harbridge House to conduct an audit of its management development process.

The findings from this survey, which generated a 97% response rate, signalled a number of areas for priority attention and was instrumental in gaining top management's attention to improving the role of management development across the company.

To act on these findings, a carefully selected task force, facilitated by Harbridge Consulting Group, was established to develop a strategy for change in the role played by management development in the business. To accomplish this process, the task force used the well tried and tested Beckhard–Harris change model (Beckhard and Harris, 1987) to define the desired future state for management development (the 'vision'), to agree the current reality (using the survey results) and to develop a transition plan to move the company from one to the other on a reasonable time scale.

As a result of this work, a number of important stakes were put in the ground. Firstly, a vision for management development was agreed—itself a challenging but highly rewarding process (Figure 17.2).

Secondly, the critical success factors and management competencies were identified and developed in support of the mission and business strategy. The resulting management competencies (headers only) are illustrated in Figure 17.3.

Thirdly, and with much debate, a set of management development principles was established as 'marker buoys' to guideline managers' actions down the route mapped out to achieve the vision (Figure 17.4 shows the headings only for each of the principles).

---

**The Vision for Management Development**

We believe that outstanding people, more than physical assets, financial resources or brands, make the difference in achieving superior business results.

The continued development of people must therefore be a top priority for all Premier Foods Europe managers.

President and CEO, Premier Foods Europe

---

**Figure 17.2**

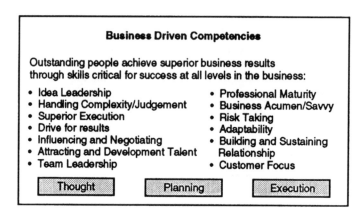

**Figure 17.3**

Whilst the process described here may appear logical and straightforward in retrospect, the reality was different. Managing this reality required gaining consensus from a highly diverse group of talented professionals drawn from several countries and areas of the business. The reasons for success can be boiled down to a small number of factors.

Firstly, the overwhelming evidence produced by the management development survey which generated a compelling argument for change. Secondly, the role of a senior, credible 'champion of champions' whose personal vision and political clout ensured that the momentum was sustained. Thirdly, the personal dedication, conviction and commitment of a small group of influential senior managers who did not let go. The outstanding commitment of all these people was later recognized when the task force members received the coveted Chairman's award.

The principles of change were therefore successfully applied to management development. To make things happen on the ground, however, transition

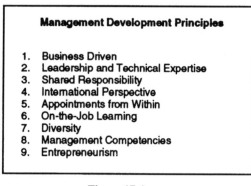

**Figure 17.4**

strategies and plans were required to turn vision into reality. In addressing this issue, the GOLD process was created.

## GOING FOR GOLD IN PREMIER FOODS EUROPE

GOLD was conceived as a process to achieve the vision for management development—for gaining organizational leadership through development. It was a twofold strategy.

Firstly, it was recognized that the vision had to be communicated, that commitment at all levels had to be built. Secondly, that knowledge, skills and behaviours had to be applied reasonably consistently across the company's operations. Thirdly, that whilst both of these were necessary, they were not sufficient. To make things happen on the ground fine ideas needed translating into personal action plans and integrated into the company's performance management approach.

To accomplish this, a 4-day programme, described here, was developed by Harbridge Consulting Group and the task force and implemented throughout the business. In tandem, in the early stages, a core element of the task force was retained to effect the second prong of the strategy: to help address organizational inhibitors or potential blockages to the GOLD process. As successes were scored, so feedback was provided to GOLD participants—by making success feed success progress could be accelerated.

GOLD was conceived as a process, rather than a programme. A process to achieve change in management development through a partnership between line management, human resources and the individual. A process through which management remained the means to enhance business performance rather than become an end in itself. As one task force member put it:

> We are not in the management development business. We are in the business of selling product and delivering profit as a result.

On the ground, that's what 'business-driven management development' meant to those in the business.

## IMPLEMENTING BUSINESS-DRIVEN MANAGEMENT COMPETENCIES

The framework for making business-driven management competencies work is shown in Figure 17.5.

At this point, a summary may be useful. The mission for Premier Foods Europe has been clearly stated. This mission is underpinned by four clear strategic priorities. Each of these priorities has been and continues to be

**Making Business Driven Competencies Work**

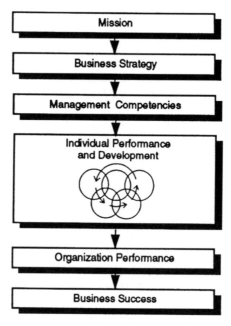

**Figure 17.5**

assessed in terms of the people implications. These implications provide the basis for developing human resource actions. To deliver these strategic priorities focus is required around critical skills at all levels. This focus is provided through 13 management competencies, translated into different behaviours for each level in the business. These competencies drive individual performance and development through the development cycle—the five circles of selection, job performance, assessment, development and succession (Figure 17.6).

Shared responsibility for making the development cycle work in a context where senior management takes responsibility for improving the climate for management development leads to improved performance (measured by seven clearly defined values) and business success (measured by progress towards achieving the mission).

Management development is not a bag full of devices. As the results of the management development survey illustrated, individuals look for a sense of coherence in the management development process. This coherence provides the business focus which makes management development a competitive weapon. The framework shown in Figure 17.5 provides such coherence and is the driving logic behind the GOLD initiative in Premier Foods Europe.

**Management Competences**

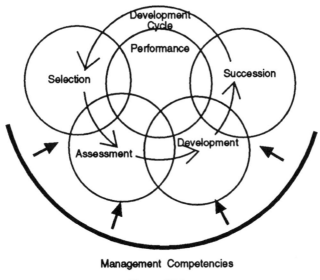

**Management Competencies**

**Figure 17.6**

## GOLD—SOME SPECIFICS

The purpose of GOLD is clear. The programme supports managers of Premier Foods Europe in achieving superior business results through the effective management of people and organization. Specifically, the approach serves to:

- Ensure that line managers understand their central role in the Premier Foods Europe human resource development process and can use the available tools and systems.
- Establish performance-based action plans for personal improvement and for the development of employees on the job.

The issue of senior management commitment has been referred to. This commitment was further evidenced by the participation of the whole executive team in the full 4-day programme. In addition, senior executives allocated slots on the programme including taking part in an open 'dialogue' session in which individuals were encouraged to raise issues of substance directly with their senior managers.

Whilst it is not possible to describe in detail the design and content of the programme some aspects can be highlighted:

- Delivery is top-down. The programme is being cascaded through management levels on a cross-border and cross-functional basis. Typically, a cohort will consist of up to 18 delegates with a mix of five or six nationalities.
- As the English-speaking Euro-managers complete the programme, internal faculty is being trained to deliver the programme in local languages within each of the major countries.
- The programme content reflects the company's belief in developing people primarily on the job; the focus is therefore on the experienced manager.
- The experience helps to demystify the human resources and management development processes. It brings out into the open, for example, the way succession planning is done and where the company stands on such issues as international assignments and external recruitment.
- Delivery is multi-sourced. A combination of internal and external faculty is used with internal presenters being drawn primarily from both human resources and line management.
- Business-based case studies are used to tie the people development to the business strategy. All the case studies are highly customized to the company situation and use real market data.
- The vision and management development principles are presented by a member of the executive team, including the president himself.
- 270° feedback (peers and subordinates) is provided for the 13 management competencies described earlier. This feedback—which is both quantitative and qualitative—is usually shared in small groups and pairs. Boss feedback—the remaining 90° is reserved for the performance appraisal process.
- There is a focus on core skills such as coaching and teamwork. Practical exercises are undertaken around succession planning, performance management and professional development.
- Each participant is expected to develop a personal action plan which becomes part of his/her performance objectives. Both self-development and the development of others feature in these objectives.

So what of the experience to date? With 650 managers trained so far the critical mass has been exceeded. Local language versions of the programme are in place or being developed. The parent company has incorporated GOLD into its core curriculum where it is now being extended internationally, building a common language and shared principles across businesses and continents.

Some qualitative benefits are becoming very evident. Succession planning, as measured by replacement depth, has improved. More importantly, what was previously considered something of a 'black box' is now more fully understood. Managers feel more comfortable handling the process and improvements have been made by, for example, linking the output of succession planning with the career development discussion.

With respect to career development some strong and consistent messages are taking root. Managers are more ready to accept that 'onwards and upwards' is not the only route to success. Professional *self*-development is beginning to replace upward progression as the key principle of career development.

Individuals are more at ease with the people development process. The climate for management development has improved as individuals see how the various pieces fit together and help the business. Focus is replacing fragmentation as management development becomes integrated into the business.

Not only is the link between the business strategy and the human resources strategy better understood but through the process of GOLD the link itself has become sharper as people implications have been more thoroughly worked through and specific actions specified for each area of the business plan.

But above all else managers believe that it is for real. It has passed the point of being regarded as a short-lived fad. They believe that it is for real because they know that senior management believes that it is for real. Increasingly, as the GOLD cadre of senior managers live out their actions, so employees down the line and across the businesses will become committed to the process. As such, a shared culture for management development is evolving across the different cultures of the business.

## SUMMARY

The business environment in the food industry has witnessed significant changes since the 1980s. What is clear, however, is that the intense competition in this global industry is unlikely to wane. To win, grow and sustain profitability will require getting more out of less, achieving high quality and low cost, and responding quickly but carefully.

To get more out of less requires an outstanding commitment to people development. There is no other way. Outstanding people, more than physical assets, financial resources or brands, will help companies outperform their competitors.

Developing and applying competencies that drive business performance has a central role to play in management development that is truly business driven.

## ACKNOWLEDGEMENTS

The author wishes to acknowledge the role and help provided by senior managers in the company concerned. Valerie Waters, currently an independent consultant (Loweswater Learning), also contributed significantly to the development of GOLD and therefore the events discussed in this article.

# REFERENCES

Ascher, K. (1983). *Management Training in Major UK Organizations*, Harbridge Consulting Group Ltd, London.

Beckhard, R. and Harris, R. T. (1987). *Organizational Transitions*, Addison-Wesley.

Hussey, D. E. (1988). *Management Training and Corporate Strategy*, Pergamon Press, Oxford.

Margerison, C. (1991). *Making Management Development Work*, McGraw-Hill.

McCall, M. W. Jr, Lombardo, M. M. and Morrison, A. M. (1988). *The Lessons of Experience*, Lexington Books.

Osbaldeston, M. and Barham, K. (1992). Using management development for competitive advantage, *Long Range Planning*, **25**(6).

Tovey, L. E. A. (1994). Meeting business and management training and development needs through competency assessment, *Journal of Strategic Change*, **3**, pp.71–86.

# ADDRESSES OF CONTRIBUTORS

Some of the authors have changed their affiliations since the articles were first published. The following list provides one contact address for each chapter in this book. This list was correct at the time the book was prepared for publication.

**Mr G. Beaver** *MBA Programme Leader, Nottingham Business School, Nottingham Trent University, Burton Street, Nottingham NG1 4BU*

**Dr S. Brege** *Associate Professor of Industrial Marketing, Linköping Institute of Technology, S-581-83 Linköping, Sweden*

**Dr R. Caldwell** *34 Avalon Road, Fulham, London SW6 2EX*

**Mr F. Cannon** *Harbridge House, Coopers & Lybrand, St Andrews House, St Andrews Street, London EC4 3AY*

**Professor D. Dunphy** *Professor of Management/Executive Director, Centre for Corporate Change, Australian Graduate School of Management, University of NSW, PO Box 1, Kensington, New South Wales, Australia 2033*

**Mr L. Farrell** *The Farrell Company, Beverley House, 324 East Beverley Street, Staunton, Virginia 24401, USA*

**Dr F. Hewitt** *Head, Aston Business School, Aston University, Aston Triangle, Birmingham B4 7ET*

**Mr D. E. Hussey** *David Hussey and Associates, 44 Forestfield, Horsham, Sussex RH13 6DZ*

**Mr R. Lewis** *Ralph Lewis Associates, Kelmscott, Church End, Hampton Green, Minchinhampton, Glos GL6 9AD*

**Mr M. Mainelli** *Z/yen Ltd, Risk/Reward Managers, Garrard House, 31–45 Gresham Street, London EC2V 7DN*

**Professor G. Martin** *Director, Dundee Business School, University of Abertay Dundee, Dudhope Castle, Dundee, Scotland DD3 6HF*

**Professor C. Parker** *The Phoenix Group/Mobilising People, Chemin du Mâcheret 21, 1095 Lutry, Switzerland*

**Professor D. Peyrat-Guillard** *Maître de Conférences, Faculté de Droit, d'Economie et des Sciences Sociales, LARGO, 11 Boulevard Lavoisier, 49045 Angers Cédex 01, France*

**Ms L. Tovey** *Associate, Goldman Sachs International, Peterborough Court, 133 Fleet Street, London EC4A 2BB*

**Professor Chow Hou Wee** *Dean, Faculty of Business Administration, National University of Singapore, 10 Kent Ridge Crescent, Singapore 0511*

# INDEX